Discovering
CAMPHILL

Also by Robin Jackson:

Holistic Special Education:
Camphill Principles and Practice (ed.)

Hermann Gross: Art and Soul

Discovering CAMPHILL

New Perspectives, Research and Developments

Edited by Robin Jackson

Floris Books

Published in collaboration with the Karl König Institute for Art, Science and Social Life: www.karl-koenig-institute.net

First published in 2011 by Floris Books
© 2011 Floris Books
The authors have asserted their right under the Copyright, Designs and Patent Act 1988 to be identified as the authors of this work.

British Library CIP data available
ISBN 978-086315-811-7

Printed in Great Britain
by CPI Antony Rowe

CONTENTS

What would life be like if we didn't have Camphill? What would it be like for so many families, who rely on Camphill and others like it? It would be like switching off the light on a life. Every child and every young adult, whatever their circumstances, is entitled to the fullness of life, to know what their fullness is, to have it revealed to them and to be part of that revelation.

Mary McAleese
President of Ireland
January 2010

Foreword

Discovering Camphill is a fascinating insight into the establishment and development of a unique approach to community living. This book charts the history of Camphill communities, their distinctive methods and vision, their development around the world, and their adaptation and change over the years. It draws on the perspectives of those who live in Camphill communities, and the perspectives of those who study, or work closely with them. From the first community founded in Scotland in 1940 by Karl König and his followers, the movement has spread worldwide with over one hundred communities in more than twenty countries, and this book charts this eventful journey.

Camphill communities have a particular nature which can be difficult to grasp and understand, and Dan McKanan and Nils Christie provide very useful discussions of the communities as social organisations. Dan McKanan explores Camphill in the context of 'intentional community' and argues that Camphill occupies a middle ground, neither sectarian nor secular, and where the aim of providing curative education is in the context of broader life sharing and communal living. Nils Christie asks whether Camphill communities are institutions and, in comparing them to villages, ghettoes and collectives, highlights the distinctiveness of the Camphill approach. On a slightly different tack, Jan Martin Bang provides a fascinating account of the position of Camphill in the evolution of alternative communities in Britain. From the perspective of a historian, Zoe Brennan-Kohn focuses on the past, and tellingly describes how Camphill's roots are grounded in the founders' experience of Nazi-occupied

Europe and the war, and how this has impacted on the development of the communities over time. There are clear echoes of this in Julian Sleigh's account of the development of Camphill in South Africa and Ha Vinh Tho's discussion of the establishment of the Peaceful Bamboo Family in Vietnam.

A crucially distinctive feature of the approach of Camphill, based as it is on Steiner principles and the anthroposophic approach of its founder, Karl König, is the holistic approach to therapeutic intervention. Judith Shapiro identifies five interacting themes: time, nature, spirituality, community and learning, and these themes resonate throughout the contributions to this book. Rhythm and routine are important for children and young people as well as for the structure of communal living, and Judith Shapiro contrasts the nature of time in Camphill communities with that of modern society. Similarly, nature is central to life in Camphill communities and Jan Martin Bang links the Camphill approach to the environmental and sustainability movement that it pre-dates.

Spirituality is core to several of the chapters in this collection and John Swinton and Aileen Falconer set the scene in their chapter based on research into spirituality in three Camphill communities in the UK. The voices of those living and working in Camphill communities shine through, as they explore the meaning of spirituality for themselves as individuals and the spirituality of community. The diversity of this spirituality is also addressed throughout the book.

The approaches to learning in Camphill communities run through many of the contributions but they are highlighted in the links to social pedagogy, a European approach which is becoming increasingly important in the UK. Claire Cameron describes the European context of social pedagogy and emphasises the fact that the Camphill approach was developed in terms of the principles of social pedagogy. Mark Smith also makes the links between the two through his connection to the BA in Curative Education run by Aberdeen University, and this is developed fully by Angelika Monteux and Norma Hart.

Importantly, while this book describes many of the benefits and advantages of the Camphill approach, it also has a sharp, critical perspective. Manuela Costa, for example, argues that the development of 'genesis stories' have a continued impact on the way Camphill sees itself and is seen by others, and this is not necessarily progressive and inclusive. This issue is picked up in Roy Brown's discussion of the quality of life approach, and the need to question the values and approaches of Camphill in relation to issues of inclusion and choice. Chris Walter also raises important issues in his critical reflection on childhood and disabled identity in the context of Camphill. A number of chapters discuss the relationship of Camphill communities to the external world, and the tension around regulations, standards, governance and management. Andrew Plant gives an internal perspective while Steve Baron and Kate Skinner give 'a view from the boundary,' and both these chapters highlight the ways in which Camphill has embraced change, but not without resistance along the way.

It is the balance between a positive, promotional perspective on Camphill and a focused, critical edge which is one of the great strengths of this book. It should be welcomed as a significant contribution to the literature of residential care and therapeutic communities.

Andrew Kendrick
Professor of Residential Child Care
Strathclyde University

Introduction

ROBIN JACKSON

Robin Jackson has worked as a university teacher, school principal and advocacy co-ordinator. He has a particular interest in the early history of Camphill.

> I know you talk a lot in the village, probably with great passion, but outside the community not many people know what goes on inside Camphill and even less is known about what Camphill has meant to those of us who have not been inside.[1]
> (Lakin, 2001: 23)

A brief survey of Camphill literature

The dearth of written material about the Camphill Movement whether in scholarly journal articles or in book form has been commented upon by a number of contributors to this book. This lack of easily accessible literature about Camphill may well have contributed to a common and damaging perception of Camphill communities as 'closed' communities which have little interest in explaining to 'the outside world' the nature of the work they do.

Two possible reasons for this scarcity can be tentatively advanced. Firstly, most of the early Camphill pioneers were German-speaking and may have lacked the confidence to commit themselves to writing in English. Secondly, priority appears to have been accorded to writing for either in-house journals with a limited circulation (e.g., *The Cresset — A Journal of the Camphill Movement*; *Camphill Correspondence*; *Journal of Curative Education and Social Therapy*) or German language publications.

One of the most important — albeit very short — publications about the Camphill Movement was written by Karl König and published in the in-house journal *The Cresset* in 1960. It was then republished in 1981 by Camphill Books with the title, *The Camphill Movement* (König, 1981). The book is significant because it looks at the historical roots of the Camphill Movement — particularly its links with the Moravian Brethren. Too often general discussion about Camphill starts from its founding in 1940 and neglects what went before. Discussion also tends to focus on the life and work of Karl König to the exclusion of significant others — not least his wife Tilla (Maasberg) König, co-founder of the Camphill Movement. Tilla, who came from a Moravian Brethren family background, made a significant contribution to the development of the Camphill Movement.

In his book König explicitly linked the evolution of the Camphill Movement with the history of the Moravian Church. It is worth looking more closely at this link given its critical importance in König's eyes and the fact that it has been in large measure either overlooked or understated in existing literature on Camphill. Although the Moravian Church has never been large, it has had nevertheless a profound effect on the development of Protestantism worldwide (MacCulloch, 2009). The 'Three Stars of the Camphill Movement' identified by König in his book were Jan Amos Comenius (1592–1670), who had been a bishop in the Unitas Fratrum (a forerunner of the Moravian Church), Count Nikolaus Zinzendorf (1700–1760), leader of the Moravian Brethren and the social reformer Robert Owen (1771–1858).

König was committed to the idea of building a Christian community, based on a model similar to that found in the Moravian Church. Like the early Christians, its members would share all things and live a simple life governed by work and prayer. When the Moravians began to expand in Colonial America at the beginning of the eighteenth century, it is known that they adopted a plan whereby each adult person was required to devote his time and labour in exchange for shelter, clothing and sustenance (Hendricks, 2002). Karl Marx was later to proclaim a reworking of this idea: *From each according to his ability, to each according to his needs.* This doctrine has a clear biblical foundation in the New Testament where the lifestyle of the Apostles is portrayed as a communal one (i.e., without individual possessions). It is scarcely surprising that George MacLeod, a leading Scottish theologian, founder of the Iona Community and friend of König, should characterise the evolving Camphill Movement as a form of Christian communism (Ferguson, 2001).

The Camphill Movement also acquired, in large measure through the influence of Tilla König, many of the external elements of Moravian culture: the importance of regular prayer; devotion to the smallest detail in every aspect of one's work; the creation of surroundings which honour the beauty of natural objects; and the need to create an environment where simplicity, quietude, order and discipline are to be found (Jackson, 2008). Perhaps the greatest debt owed by the Movement to the Moravian Church is an appreciation of the meaning of community living, the importance of religious experience in community life, and the spiritual value which is inherent in each community member.

There was no intention or desire on the part of König to develop the Camphill Movement into a sect. In the Movement, Christianity was seen as an indispensable part if its life and work: it worked out of Christianity, not for Christianity. Thus, it was not an organisation for the purpose of disseminating Christian faith. Those who worked in and for the Movement were entirely free to be members of any Christian church, as well as of any group or society, if they so wished. This was the same within the Moravian Church where a member could belong to a Lutheran or any other Protestant denomination. Neither the Moravian Church nor the Camphill Movement engaged in proselytisation.

The Camphill Movement was a community of men and women who tried to live and work in common for a spiritual purpose. Like the Moravian Church, the Movement has sought to explore and challenge many of the burning issues of the day: the meaning, nature and purpose of community living;

accountability; sustainable lifestyles; the elimination of poverty; social justice; personal identity; holistic spirituality; global vision and mission (Anderson, 2006).

Recent research exploring the links between the Camphill Movement and the Moravian Church has indicated that the writings of Comenius may have played a significant part in shaping Camphill philosophy and practice. The purpose of education for Comenius stretched beyond the boundaries of the classroom and encompassed the mind, body and spirit of the individual. Along with Pestalozzi and Froebel, Comenius can be seen as one of the pioneers of the social pedagogical impulse. Like Comenius, the thinking of König was heavily influenced by his personal experience of living in a Europe riven with political, religious and social conflict. Both wanted to see the creation of a more tolerant and open society but both recognised that this could only be achieved through a process of social renewal. The findings of this research have recently been published in the journal, *Educational Review* (Jackson, 2011).

Whilst there are other books about Camphill, most have tended to be written by Camphillers and have been targeted principally but not exclusively at a Camphill audience, for example, *The Builders of Camphill: Lives and Destinies of the Founders* (Bock, 2004) and *The Lives of Camphill: An Anthology of the Pioneers* (Surkamp, 2007). Both these books, which are made up of short biographies of past and present Camphillers, can be viewed as testaments to the personal dedication of individuals seeking the realisation of a communal ideal. Perhaps one of the most compelling books in this particular genre is the photographic essay by Cornelius Pietzner which presents pictures of life and work in Camphill communities in the USA, *Village Life: The Camphill Communities* (Pietzner, 1986).

One book that merits particular attention is the biography of König by Hans Müller-Wiedemann, *Karl König: a Central-European Biography of the Twentieth Century* (1996). I suspect that there are few people, including Camphillers, who have read this weighty tome from cover to cover, which is a pity as it is so richly informative. It is significant that the book was published first in German and only later was translated into English. And then it was an in-house and not commercial publication. More recently a series of volumes have been published by the Karl König Archive: *Karl König: My Task* (Selg, 2008); *Karl König's Path into Anthroposophy* (Selg, 2008) and *Ita Wegman and Karl König: Letters and Documents* (Selg, 2008).

Since Camphill's founding in 1940, there have been a number of commemorative publications celebrating key anniversaries: *A Candle on the Hill: Images of Camphill Life* (Pietzner, 1990); *Shaping the Flame* (2000) and *A Portrait of Camphill: From Founding Seed to Worldwide Movement* (Bang, 2010). Whilst these richly illustrated books are visually very attractive and succeed in conveying a vivid impression of Camphill life, their purpose is essentially celebratory. It is also open to question how many copies of these books have found their way to mainstream book-sellers and thus have been accessible to a wider population than just Camphillers.

Three books which have been aimed, primarily, at a non-Camphill audience are *Community, Normality and Difference* (Baron & Haldane, 1992); *Education for Special Needs: Principles and Practice in Camphill Schools* (Hansmann, 1992) and *Holistic Special Education: Camphill Principles and Practice* (Jackson, 2006). The first book was occasioned by the fiftieth anniversary of the founding of the first Camphill community and was edited by a sociologist and psychiatrist with a long and close association with Camphill communities. It broke new ground by examining a range of challenges that were beginning to confront Camphill communities: the imposition of a narrow definition of 'community care' and the introduction of new regulatory regimes and professional training requirements. The second book, which was written by one of the former Principals of Camphill School Aberdeen, looks at the underlying principles of Rudolf Steiner's approach to education and how the educational curriculum of Waldorf Schools has been adapted for children with special needs. The third book is unusual in that it is made up largely of contributions from co-workers (care staff, teachers, therapists etc.) professionally involved in Camphill School Aberdeen. This book aims to give an insight into Camphill philosophy and practice as they are exemplified in the life and work of Camphill School Aberdeen and to make the case for residential special schools at a time when the purpose, value and future of residential special education was being called into question.

The present book has two principal purposes: firstly, to focus on the findings of research on a number of Camphill communities; and secondly to identify and explore political, social and educational issues and trends that are likely to affect the long-term future of such communities. Where this book departs from earlier books on Camphill is that a significant number of the contributors are non-Camphillers who, by virtue of their detachment, are well placed to make independent and balanced appraisals of the life and work of Camphill communities.

There are two further features of this book which merit highlighting. Firstly, there is its geographical breadth covering Camphill communities in England, Ireland, Norway, Scotland, South Africa, USA and Vietnam. Secondly, there is the very wide range of mainstream disciplines from which the contributors are drawn: clinical psychology, ecology, education, history, social pedagogy, social psychology, social work, sociology and theology. This means that the picture of Camphill which emerges is not unidimensional, partial or parochial. On the basis of the wealth and depth of material presented, readers are free to draw their own conclusions as to the 21st century salience and relevance of the Camphill 'model.'

Conclusion

In the absence of any significant body of literature on Camphill which is based on external and detached appraisal, it is worth noting the observations of Rud Turnbull who has been described by his professional peers as someone who has changed the course of history in mental retardation and is one of the leaders in the field of special education. After reading *Village Life: the Camphill Communities* (Pietzner, 1986), he succinctly identified the quintessential features of Camphill:

... travel through these pages and discover Camphill ...
each person a part of the other, of the earth, and of the
sky — spirits together, many hands, one heart.

Rud Turnbull is a former President of the American
Association on Mental Retardation and is currently Co-Director
of the Beach Centre on Disability at the University of Kansas.
He is also the recipient of national leadership awards from five
disability advocacy organisations in North America including
the Camphill Association of North America.

Two other prominent figures in the reform of public policy
and services for people with developmental disabilities worldwide
were profoundly influenced by Camphill in their thinking and
writing (Lakin, 2001). Burton Blatt, after having written the
book *Christmas in Purgatory* (Blatt & Kaplan, 1966), which
exposed the degrading conditions of people with disabilities
living in state institutions in the USA, made a visit in the late
1970s to Camphill Village Copake. Before his premature death
in 1985 he expressed his wish to retire to Copake as he saw it as
a model form of residential provision.

As a result of a continuous dialogue with Camphill leaders
and friends during the latter part of his long career, Wolf
Wolfensberger modified the principle of normalisation with
which his name has come to be so closely identified. Initially
this principle advocated making available to all people with
disabilities patterns of life and conditions of everyday living
which were as close as possible to the regular circumstances
and ways of life in society. Wolfensberger subsequently revised
this principle because he saw it being interpreted too inflexibly
and narrowly thus failing to take account of what Camphill
communities have traditionally seen as being of pre-eminent
importance — the quality of a person's whole experience of
living.

There is a certain irony in the fact that critics of Camphill
continue to claim that the kind of services Camphill communities
provide run counter to the normalisation principle. What these
critics fail to appreciate is that normalisation should be viewed

as a philosophy and not a technology. It is a system of values and beliefs which should help guide, not dictate thought and action. As Wolfensberger was later to argue this necessitates a sensitive, sensible and pragmatic approach not an inflexible and dogmatic one.

What I found revealing when approaching individuals to contribute a chapter to this book was the prompt and positive response I received. I interpreted that to mean that they, like Turnbull, Blatt and Wolfensberger, have seen something of unique and compelling significance and relevance in what Camphill communities are doing that should be far more widely known. I hope this book succeeds in conveying to the reader in an accessible, informative and insightful manner something of the continuing pioneering spirit of the Camphill Movement. The establishment of the Karl König Institute in 2010 — the seventieth anniversary year of the founding of the first Camphill community — represents an important step forward given its declared commitment to promoting and publishing research on Camphill that will be accessible to as wide an audience as possible.

> It is remarkable when you think that 99.8% of the people with developmental disabilities in the United States have never been part of the Camphill experience and yet the experience of that 0.2% has had such an impact on so many people.[1]
> (Lakin, 2001: 23)

Notes

1. Paper entitled 'Challenge to Camphill from the Perspective of a Public Policy Advocate' given by Charlie Lakin (Director, Research and Training Centre on Community Living, Institute of Community Integration, University of Minnesota) at a Symposium held at Triform Camphill community, Hudson, New York: 3–4 April 2001.

1. Negotiating the Twentieth Century: A Historical Analysis of Camphill Communities

Zoe Brennan-Krohn lived in Camphill Ballytobin for two years before getting her BA in History from Brown University. She is currently teaching English at the University of Banja Luka in Bosnia-Herzegovina. This chapter draws on the findings of a thesis 'Negotiating the Twentieth Century: A Historical Analysis of Camphill Communities' submitted to the Department of History, Brown University, Rhode Island (2009).

Camphill: a personal introduction

Camphill communities defy description and categorisation. Camphill is a home for disabled children and adults; it is a radical experiment in shared living; it is a template for environmental sustainability; it is a historically–grounded and innovative project that in many ways turns the norms and expectations of our society's measures of ability, value and productivity on their heads. As well as all of these lofty elements, Camphill is also one of my homes, a place very dear to me. I lived in Camphill Ballytobin, in southeastern Ireland, for two years before starting college in the US, and have visited frequently since then. In Ballytobin, a wrought iron archway entwined with climbing roses leads from the car park onto the path that winds through the community. When I return to Ballytobin, walking under

21

this archway sometimes takes my breath away, because it is truly the entrance to another world.

There is something transformative about Camphill. A visitor there in the 1960s once asked the superintendent how he found such devoted and special volunteers to work with the disabled children. The superintendent replied that the young volunteers were as ordinary as any young people — their lives in Camphill made them extraordinary (Brüll, 2008).

This transformative experience certainly took hold for me. I moved to Camphill after finishing high school at Phillips Exeter Academy, an academically rigorous and intense boarding school. In Camphill, the currency of encounters among individuals was not academic prowess or sharp-edged wit, but something entirely different. It was an unquestioned respect, along with a sense of mutual empathy, shared purpose and inherent kindness. I could not have articulated this when I first arrived, but I certainly felt it. Finding my way through a community that often valued my heart over my head, and asked for emotional commitment above all, transformed me.

Disability and ability are viewed and valued differently in Camphill. If you visit a Camphill community, you will certainly notice that some people have strange behaviour; some use wheelchairs or do not speak; someone might have an epileptic seizure. It's not that these disabilities are kept secret. It's just that when you are in Camphill, the dry and scientific questions about diagnoses and IQ will recede from the forefront of your mind. Mostly, you will notice personalities, humour and individuals. Camphill is not a community *for* people with disabilities, nor does it push them to the margins. Difference is not ignored or rejected, but celebrated.

Although it may not be uppermost in our consciousness, disability is everywhere. Everyone knows someone who is at the social margins because of a cognitive or physical or emotional difference. Modern scientific enquiry generally pursues the cure and prevention of disabilities. Yet no matter how perfect prenatal genetic testing becomes, no matter how much we refine the tools to select against disability, there will *always* be disability. There will always be injuries; there will always be difference that we are unable to pathologise; there will always be neglect or trauma that leads to disabling reactions. No matter what breakthroughs the scientific community discovers, there must be equal energy towards accepting and embracing the differences that disability brings. Camphill is an effort to fill that role.

Researching as a Camphiller and an academic

The combination of Camphill's beauty and kindness, its dramatic founding and radically inclusive values, inspired me to conduct the research that led to my undergraduate history thesis, which is adapted here. I was curious about how Camphill's history could be relevant to its existence today, and how academic research might be valuable or useful for the many Camphillers who are looking to the future with both optimism and a degree of consternation.

I researched and wrote this piece as both a Camphiller and a historian, with the dual goals of finding historical insight into Camphill, and supporting its work and development in the present. I am, without a doubt, deeply committed to the ideals of Camphill, tremendously fond of its work and indebted to its people for much of my personal development. Yet I did not want to write a simple tribute to Camphill.

I became interested in this type of liminal research because I have noticed that it is not often present in work about Camphill. Research and scholarly writing about Camphill communities have tended to be written from an 'insider' perspective, both by and for people already familiar with, and committed to, the work of Camphill. I have read many of these books and articles with great pleasure, but I am not convinced that they are as helpful as they could be in the process of further opening channels of discussion and communication between Camphill and the mainstream world beyond it. Among Camphillers writing about Camphill, anthroposophical and academic histories and traditions are often collapsed, which can seem very natural: in daily community life, the physical and the spiritual are deeply intertwined and one cannot exist fully without the other

(Bock, 2004; Müller-Wiedemann, 1996). Yet for outsiders, this conflation is unexpected and can be difficult to accept.

I believe that research that examines Camphill holistically, yet does so using the tools and standards of academia, may play an important role in the negotiations of the 21st century. With the age of isolation long past, people who support alternatives such as Camphill need to be articulate about their work as it applies to parents, authorities, neighbours and peer institutions. I hope that this research can play a small role in this process.

Camphill's early history

One of the core arguments of my work is the idea that Camphill's origins were more historically grounded than its founders often realised. Camphill founder Dr Karl König often described the story of witnessing an Advent Garden in 1927 as the birth of the idea that became Camphill (Evans, 1982). Yet I believe that this story underestimates the influence of the Holocaust, the founders' flight from Nazi-occupied Austria and their status as refugees in Scotland. I suggest that these influences had a crucial impact on the development of Camphill, one that is often overlooked in histories of the organisation.

Camphill was founded in rural Scotland in 1939 by a group of refugees from Austria, many of whom came from Jewish families. The founders had all participated in the anthroposophical study group that Dr König had led in Vienna. All were students of Rudolf Steiner's anthroposophy and sought to implement this philosophy in a living community (Baum, 2004). Yet the influence of the war must not be underestimated. Where they had once been well-off members of Viennese society, the founders were now refugees in a rustic house hundreds of miles from home. Only one founder, Anke Weihs, was proficient in English. All of the founders had been forced to leave their homeland, which had been annexed by Hitler and was a hotbed of anti-Semitic fascism.

Camphill's commitment to embracing all people regardless of ability or nationality was an alternative to the Third Reich's categorisation and elimination of difference. It was a direct opposition to the trauma of World War II, which forced Camphill's Jewish founders out of Vienna in 1938. Camphill was founded in Scotland by refugees who consciously strove to embrace and welcome children with disabilities, who were, themselves, outcasts within Britain. Camphill's founding as a radical alternative to World War II laid the groundwork for the organisation's historical development, its delicate combination of innovation and constancy, and its simultaneous isolation and public engagement.

In a 1941 newsletter article, König recalled that at the time of their flight from Austria, 'the world seemed so empty and naked, so full of hate and destruction, and there was such a crying need to alter one's own muddling through a poor life, and to transform it into a real life.' (Scottish Christian Council for Refugees, 1941) The ideology of Camphill, the very antithesis of the fascist state, bolstered the group's commitment to their task in spite of the challenges and uncertainties they faced. As such, Camphill was founded as both a philosophically-oriented shared living community, and as a direct reaction to World War II. The dual purpose of its establishment has set the stage for Camphill's consistent existence at the threshold between isolation and public awareness. Camphill was imagined as a tangible alternative to fascism and Nazism, which demanded autonomy but also conversation with the world beyond.

These proactive and reactive elements of Camphill's founding have influenced its development in many ways in the last seventy years. The tremendous inner strength that was required of the founders in their flight and in building their new lives gave them the tools to develop Camphill based on a strong internal compass. In the case of education, this vehement independence proved to be a great asset when Camphill developed a method of educating severely disabled children decades before this idea would become common in the UK. On the other hand, this same trait of self-reliance meant that Camphill risked staying stuck in certain habits that, in hindsight, were clearly mistaken. The risk of this tendency toward isolationism was illustrated clearly in Camphill's early negative attitude toward parents of disabled children.

Education in Camphill

The educational developments in Camphill were a remarkable illustration of the potential of Camphill's autonomy. For most of the twentieth century, disabled children in Britain were widely considered to be ineducable, and legislation supported the segregation of people with disabilities for decades after Camphill's founding (Department of Health and Social Security, 1971). Compulsory institutionalisation for the 'mentally unfit' was the ultimate plan for most of the early twentieth century in Britain. Institutions were large, rural, and final places for disabled children and adults, designed to 'protect' society from a population considered disproportionately dangerous and demanding. IQ tests determined ability, and poor IQ scores, which were believed to foretell a life of poverty, crime and deviance, led to forced institutionalisation (Wooldridge, 1994).

Camphill's educational philosophy during these decades followed a very different path. The first step in its development as a school as well as a community came in 1948, when Camphill co-workers began teaching a class for non-disabled students, many of whom were children of Camphillers. There was considerable consternation about this project, which took attention away from the work with disabled children. A co-worker recalled that 'the sacrifice of work for the handicapped child in favour of the normal child caused those of us who took it on both sorrow and distress.' (The Cresset, 1961) Co-workers taught the classes at this new school — called St John's School — using the Waldorf curriculum established by Rudolf Steiner. The school was developed to fill a practical need, as many children of co-workers were of school age, and other schools were a significant distance away (ibid). In 1948, the Waldorf curriculum was considered unsuitable for most disabled children, although some of the more able pupils in Camphill were able to join St John's School in these early years (Robertson, 1949).

At the same time that this practical educational demand was being met, co-workers were becoming aware of the difficulties disabled children faced as they reached puberty. König described that 'their minds drowned into masses of body.' (König, 1952) He went on to explain that 'some of us could observe it only happened to those children of whom we thought a regular education would be of no avail.' (ibid) The establishment of a school in Camphill, alongside the realisation that the lack of education seemed to be a disservice for disabled children, came together in the 1951 decision to open the doors of St John's School to children with disabilities, even those who were widely considered unsuitable candidates for school (ibid). Within a few years, the school decided to arrange its classes based on students' chronological age rather than academic ability or 'mental age' as determined by IQ tests, a policy that directly opposed traditional conceptions of disability (ibid). This integration within classrooms was based on the realisation that children benefitted from having others with different abilities and challenges around them. Camphillers soon considered the experiment of inclusion at St John's School to be a success. König began to lecture about the nature of the Waldorf curriculum as it applied to disabled children, and meeting minutes reveal that co-workers were pleased with the accomplishments of the school.

Opening St John's School to disabled pupils in 1951 came twenty years before legislation would mandate universal inclusion in Britain regardless of disability. This change occurred with the 1970 Education Act and the 1971 policy paper 'Better Services for the Mentally Handicapped'(Department of Health and Social Security, 1971). The success and prescience of this process in Camphill illustrated the benefits of Camphill's flexibility and its distance from its conventional peers. Camphill was not an idea that arrived, fully formed, in König's imagination, or even in the first days or weeks of the founders' lives in Scotland. The founders were committed to a guiding philosophy and purpose but exercised a great deal of flexibility and capacity for change based on their experiences and the needs of society. In the case of observing the need for education for all children and the subsequent realisation of a solution, Camphill proved its potential as a forward-thinking leader.

Attitudes towards parents

In addition to the remarkable and prescient success of St John's School in the 1950s, however, Camphill's isolation and near-complete independence posed risks. While Camphill was clearly ahead of the curve in many ways, the community stood by certain outdated ideas longer than the mainstream, ideas that, in hindsight, seem clearly mistaken. A deep and even accusatory suspicion of parents was a prime example of a concept that Camphill stood by for a surprisingly long time.

For many years after Camphill's 1939 beginnings, long after the end of World War II, community members continued to identify themselves as alternative founders of a radical project in a hostile world. Within this identity, parents were perceived as potentially invasive outsiders. Seemingly unconsciously, parents were grouped with public authorities as potential threats to the evolution and strength of Camphill's alternative project. Part of this conflation of Scottish families and authorities probably dated from Camphill's earliest and most inward-looking period. Between the trauma of their exile and the strange task the founders had begun, the war years created a division between Camphill and the wider Scottish community. The early prevalence of German as a common language within Camphill furthered this separation.

Because the distinction between Camphill and its Scottish neighbours was based on identity as a Camphill insider or outsider, parents and authorities could easily be grouped together. Camphill, of course, only existed because of parents who sent their children to König and his companions. The land that became the first Camphill community was a donation from parents who supported the founders' work. Yet Camphillers were not inclined to feel beholden to those who had been generous to them. Like their attitude towards Scottish culture at large, the founders were not ignorant of the debt they owed to parents, but neither were they prepared to alter their work based on the wishes of outsiders.

In König's view, a common cause of disabilities was the actions and emotions of parents, a belief that was widespread in the 1950s and 1960s. König was fascinated by the concept that shock and trauma during pregnancy could cause a multitude of disabilities. Other conditions such as autism he believed to be the direct result of parental indifference or withholding of love.

This medical view of disability tended to neglect parents or even blame them. Camphill's early focus on medical work and research created a prescribed power dynamic that elevated König and his medical colleagues and diminished parents' roles. Nowhere is this more plain than in König's 1954 publication, *The Handicapped Child: Letters to Parents*. This book contains three letters to parents about their disabled children who either lived in Camphill or had visited König's medical clinic. In the chapter 'To the Parents of a Spastic Child,' König alleges that:

> Your bitterness grew, and your care for your child was so excessive that you made her entirely dependent on you. You meant well, but you did the worst possible for her. You fed and nursed her, and she became self-willed and egoistic and demanded your constant presence.
> (König, 1954: 12)

König's letter went on to describe the pupil's improvements since she had moved to Camphill, but maintained that after visits home her condition again worsened, which König attributed to her parents' own 'spastic minds and closed up hearts.' (ibid)

Yet this attitude did not represent the whole picture of early interactions with parents. As early as 1955, parents were organising events in local communities to raise money for Camphill (Council Meeting Minutes, 1955). Also in that year, parents' demands for homes for their adult children led to the establishment of Botton Village Community in England, a new departure within the Camphill Movement (Taylor, 1959). The founding of Botton Village was a major undertaking that was the product of collaboration between parents and Camphillers. It indicated König's responsiveness to the concerns and wishes of parents. In the same years that Botton was beginning, however, König continued to write about the association between shocks in pregnancy and disability, and espoused general parental culpability in the cases of many disabled pupils. In the decade after the 1955 founding of Botton Village, Camphill was in a sometimes-paradoxical grey area between rejecting and embracing parents. Although an improvement compared to wholesale mainstream rejection, Camphill's uncertain attitude was an example of its potential to falter in its independent innovation.

Camphill evolved incrementally and internally, and so its attitude towards parents are hard to track. By the 1960s, however, it was clear that these attitudes were changing. Parents were increasingly included in Camphill during open houses and children's frequent vacations at home. The clearest evidence that Camphill's indifference to parents was fading came in 1968, when the Easter edition of *The Cresset,* the journal of the Camphill Movement, was dedicated to parents. The dedication page described Camphill's debt to and admiration of parents, and the contents of that edition were devoted to experiences of parents and articles about disabled children at home. Morwenna Bucknall, the first British co-worker who joined the founders in 1942, wrote in the dedication:

> To you, the parents of our children, we wanted to
> dedicate this number of *The Cresset.* We must admit
> that many years ago, when the Camphill Schools first
> began, we were young and enthusiastic and convinced
> of our mission, but only gradually were we able to fully
> acknowledge that 'our children' are, after all, 'your
> children,' and it is our joint concern to help each of
> them to become their own true selves.
> (Bucknall, 1968: 4)

The progression of Camphill's views of parents is an unusual case study, as it finds Camphill to have been in agreement with mainstream opinions about what now seems to be an unquestionably misguided idea. Camphill's attitude of questioning norms did not seem to have permeated the concept of patient-doctor power dynamics and their implications for parents.

Camphill was working as an alternative, but a careful alternative: its mission was not to react against every aspect of public opinion or conventional practice. In many ways, this notion of a nuanced alternative was an asset to Camphill, and made its development and structure sustainable in a way that entirely reactionary organisations rarely are. Yet Camphill as a selectively alternative organisation also ran the risk of adhering to standards that were later overturned or found to be lacking by mainstream society itself. Early disregard for parents was a striking example of this risk.

Into the present day: inclusion and Camphill

Taken together, the parallel stories of Camphill's educational innovation and its interactions with parents reflect the complexity of the organisation's development in its first decades. Because the founders of Camphill were largely charting their own course, they were both innovative and stubborn in their own ways. In 1970, new legislation focused on the needs of children with disabilities and changed the dynamics of Camphill's interactions with mainstream organisations, parents and public officials. In the years since this legislation first mandated the education of all children, regardless of disability, Camphill has faced very different challenges and victories in its work. Even in these very different circumstances, however, Camphill's progress and development have continued to reflect the circumstances of its founding and early history.

The 1970 Education Act, which mandated that all children must be educated, regardless of disability, ushered in a new era of complexity. The years of relatively confident distance from the outside world were over. Camphill did not change suddenly, but it faced a gradual realisation that mainstream institutions and policies could no longer be entirely ignored. The days of seeing their work as the plain antithesis of the outside world were drawing to a close. Ann Walker, an educationist who has been involved with Camphill for many years, recalls this transition:

> Because [early Camphillers] were fighting a lone battle to provide for children that no one else provided for, they had to have this inner strength that comes from keeping yourself to yourself. Now they're not fighting that battle, but they still have a battle to fight to say that they have something worth offering, that not everyone is offering. What society really needs is a range of offerings that people can actually choose from.
> (Walker, 2008)

Since 1970, Camphill increasingly realised that its work demanded a meaningful dialogue with local authorities, politicians and peer institutions.

In recent years, debate over inclusion policy has become one of the central issues facing Camphill. Inclusion, or mainstreaming, policy is the belief that children with disabilities should be included in 'normal' schools under all circumstances. The underlying belief of inclusion policy is similar to Camphill's philosophy, as both share the goal of de-stigmatising people with physical and cognitive disabilities. Continuing a pattern that could be found in earlier government philosophies, however, the broad goal of inclusion soon developed into a standardised, monolithic template that was intolerant of any deviation. The well-intentioned and humane ideal of inclusion contained the risks of its non-negotiable and impersonal implementation for all people with disabilities.

For Camphill, the dogmatic pursuit of mainstreaming was a new theme that demanded a persistent alternative. Within the mindset of universal inclusion, residential special schools, like Camphill School Aberdeen, are seen as a discriminatory form of segregation and isolation. Even day schools entirely devoted to special education are seen as incompatible with inclusion policy. With the rise of inclusion as the dominant ideology, Camphill's work and structure were cast as outdated and discriminatory.

The decision to impose inclusion policy on every child marked a return to the ideal of a standardised, one-size-fits-all solution to disabled children, a pursuit that is still pervasive almost a century after it was first introduced. Stefan Geider, a doctor who first came to Camphill almost twenty years ago, has witnessed the advent and recession of various governmental ideologies. Inclusion, he observed 'was driven for many years in a [very] dogmatic way, and [created] so many casualties on the way ... organisations, schools, but also individuals, parents, children.' (Geider, 2008) Geider believes that this policy is beginning to relax its grip in recognition of its over-zealous pursuit, but still suggests that it will be many years before these changes make their way down to the level of individuals and local opinion.

Inclusion and mainstreaming are among the biggest unresolved issues facing Camphill communities in Britain today. Many experts and social workers deny the necessity of residential schools like Camphill on principle, but simultaneously strive to place children in such schools. According to inclusion theory, Camphill should not exist. It is seen as an illustration of the failure of mainstream schools to be open and accepting to all children, and a holdout from a bygone era of exclusion and control. In reality, children with complex needs, particularly those with behavioural and social difficulties, are routinely failing at normal schools and arriving at Camphill after a succession of such failures (Geider, 2008). Official scorn or neglect for Camphill exists alongside desperation on the part of parents and authorities to have a child admitted to Camphill.

Even as society's blanket solutions move towards more respectful and humane policies, Camphill is still questioning the key assumptions that stand behind these policies, namely the belief that there *is* an ultimate solution that will be right for all people and that can be universally applied. When the British solution to the 'problem' of disability was certification and compulsory confinement in hospitals, disabled people far outnumbered the availability of hospital beds. Camphill was struggling against the philosophy of eugenics and confinement, but its existence was perhaps less seriously threatened, as it was supporting children for whom governmental authorities could propose no practical options. Camphill was a living alternative to the prominent philosophy of those years, but the philosophy of institutionalisation could never realistically have been universally implemented.

These dynamics have changed in the last decades. The solution to the 'problem' of disability is no longer the unwieldy and costly plan of mental deficiency hospitals and permanent isolation, but rather mainstreaming and inclusion. At its best, mainstreaming demands significant resources in order to support students with and without disabilities in classrooms. Aides are needed to assist students, classes need to be small to accommodate a wide range of learners, and specialists need to be employed to develop education plans for the exceptional needs of disabled students. Yet in practice, mainstreaming can easily become a cheap project that lets governments and legislators shirk responsibility for disabled pupils and sends students with extraordinary needs into classrooms where teachers have neither the resources nor the training to adequately support them. Within the philosophy of mainstreaming, shoddy practice can be an inexpensive and seemingly easy way to deal with large numbers of disabled pupils. Because of the relative ease with which mainstreaming can be implemented, Camphill faces the possibility that mainstreaming may become the only accepted system of education in Britain.

The challenge to defend Camphill's relevance and value in a world that demands normalcy is very different from the founders' World War II challenge to defend the fundamental right of both Jews and disabled children to live. Yet in spite of the tremendous differences and changes of the intervening decades, Camphill has consistently created and re-created its identity to challenge what it perceives as the shortcomings of mainstream society. This flexibility and commitment to independent thought and development have been, overall, one of the greatest strengths of Camphill over the last seventy years. As Camphill's early attitude to parents shows, there have been moments of poor decisions as the product of this independence.

Looking to the future

From my perspective as both a Camphiller and a researcher, the clear challenges and unresolved issues of Camphill today continue to revolve around interactions and negotiations with the world beyond it. The early scorn for parents, legislators and peer institutions has long since faded, but the dynamics of navigating the ever-changing landscape of disability services while maintaining both external relations and an internal sense of purpose and commitment is an ongoing challenge.

Among Camphillers, the biggest questions focus on the future, not the past. There is real and valid anxiety about the changes that standards and laws are requiring of Camphill. A romanticisation of its history can be appealing, especially at a time when Camphill's work seems threatened. Yet the great successes in Camphill's history were the moments of flexibility and open-minded interaction. These moments will not look the same tomorrow, but the tools with which they have been navigated can be kept alive and flourishing in Camphill.

Camphill lives at the boundaries of tradition and innovation, of inward development and external change, of reaction and construction. These lines are necessarily fluid and complex. Camphill has been set apart by its commitment to staying abreast of these boundaries and constantly challenging them. This existence has looked very different in the years since 1939; at the same time Camphill has maintained its original goal in its broadest sense. History, of course, cannot tell us the future. Yet I believe, I hope, that the remarkable story of Camphill's founding and development may strengthen the process of navigating the challenges that lie ahead.

2. The Power of Organisational Myth: A Case Study

MANUELA COSTA

Manuela Costa is a qualified teacher and social worker who has been at Camphill School Aberdeen for 21 years. She is currently Care Co-ordinator at the School. This chapter draws on the findings of the author's MSc in Advanced Residential Childcare dissertation 'Camphill: An Island of Promise: Myth or Reality?' submitted to the University of Strathclyde (2008).

The Camphill Movement has a long history of progressive practice whether making provision for children, young people and adults with special needs, pursuing person-centred approaches to learning, adopting an inclusive decision-making management model or recognising the importance of investing in people through supporting the development of the nationally and professionally recognised BA in Social Pedagogy (formerly Curative Education) programme (Jackson, 2006). However, in recent years Camphill communities have been faced with serious threats to their future.

Given Camphill's progressive profile the question arises as to why there should be any threat of extinction. Whilst an answer to this question can be attributed in part to ideological, economic and political reasons that are related to discourses on inclusion, normalisation, and the free market economy, it is also the case that there is a perception of Camphill communities as islands remote from the mainstream, closed off from and resistant to external influences. However, the essential point here is not whether this perception is accurate or not but that it exists; that being so, it is the purpose of this study to identify how such a perception may have arisen and what are the implications. This is not simply a matter of cognition but, more critically, a matter of the dominant narrative which relates to a story that has been created and appears to be generally accepted which articulates the shared values of an organisation and helps toward the creation of its identity.

Narratives are powerful because they tend to be based on presumed certainties and they become part of one's identity. That identity is reinforced every time the narrative is retold. Those who hold power tend to be those who are seen as the guardians of the dominant narrative and that narrative comes to acquire a sacred and unchallengeable character. It is frequently based on a set of myths that embrace the psychological, sociological, cosmological and metaphysical truths surrounding a group. It also reflects the most important concerns of the people, it delineates their identity, illuminates their values and in so doing helps preserve the group's integrity and assures its continuity (McAdams, 1993).

My aim is to explore the origins of the Camphill narrative and the myths upon which it is based as they are revealed in the minutes of the Schools Community meetings which were held in the early pioneering years of Camphill. The study analyses this documentary material and draws from it the dominant themes that are then discussed in the context of the relevant literature on myth. The study concludes by looking at some of the possible implications for the Camphill Movement.

Myths: their power and function

Hughes (1995) has pointed to the power and influence that myths have in organisations and on the lives of those who work and live within them. The fact that myths often lie deep in the unconscious mind and are used without one knowing them to be myths makes them both powerful and dangerous. One of the most common and well-known myths in modern organisations is: 'This is how we always do things here.' This response is often encountered when practices, procedures or policies, which have been well established, are questioned. One consequence of a myth's power is the preservation of inappropriate cultures, the prevention of an acceptance of new ideas and the blocking of progress. Such myths are regarded as sacred and unchallengeable truths and are often deployed as a defence against change (Hughes, 1995).

Gabriel (2000) has argued that the most common underlying emotion involved in the process of mythologising and idealising the past is nostalgia. Nostalgia reveals the past in a glowing light and accepts the past as something which is irretrievably lost. Whilst the present is portrayed as impoverished and emaciated, the past is dressed up and embellished so that it appears triumphant. This idealised vision of the past provides individuals with an escape and refuge from the complexities of the present. The sense of loss involved in nostalgia has not been psychologically conquered. Nostalgia is used as a way of coming to terms with the present. In its acute form nostalgia can lead to a total inability to accept the present and to a morbid preoccupation with the past. Thus the feeling of nostalgia can profoundly affect and mould one's perceptions, interpretations and emotional reactions to present day realities (Gabriel, 2000).

Some of the elements in organisations that have been identified as attracting nostalgic feelings include totemic buildings and leaders, departed colleagues and certain ceremonial functions. Gabriel (2000) has argued that the constant idealisation of the past with its emphasis on community, authenticity, family spirit, warmth, love, personal care and protecting leaders lies at the heart of most nostalgic feelings.

This argument has been reinforced by Brown, Denning, Groh & Prusak (2005), who have asserted that stories about the past, which become embedded in legends and myths, can be so powerful that they constrain the behaviour of individuals within organisations. The stories help establish and perpetuate the organisational cultural norms. All these stories have an implicit message which may find expression in such statements as: 'We tried that and it didn't work.' And the reality is that if it *is* tried, it will not work (Brown et al., 2005). (The authors' emphasis.) In Poulton's opinion 'genesis stories' can become barriers to change and growth because people become locked in the 'genesis story' and cannot imagine themselves responding any differently (Poulton, 2005).

The power and negative impact that myths can have within organisations is addressed by Morgan's (2006) psychic prison metaphor. Plato first explored this metaphor in The Republic (1941). The story involves an underground cave with its mouth open towards the light of a blazing fire. Within the cave there are people in chains and the only thing that they can see is the cave wall in front of them. As they can only see shadows of people and objects projected onto the wall, the cave dwellers liken the shadows to reality; they give them names, talk about them and even link movements on the wall to the sounds from outside. If an individual were allowed to leave the cave, there would be profound consequences. There would be the realisation that the shadows are only reflections of a much more complex reality and that the perceptions of the cave dwellers were distorted and flawed. If the individual were to return, it would not be possible to live in the old way, since a different world had been experienced. If s/he were to share the new knowledge acquired, s/he would probably be ridiculed, since the familiar images would be much more meaningful for the cave dwellers than a world that they had never seen. The individual would no longer be able to behave with conviction within this shadowland, whilst the shadow folk would view this outside world as a dangerous place and one which should be avoided. This would in turn lead them to tighten their grip on their way of seeing the world. People and organisations find it difficult to change because they find themselves trapped within their own constructions of reality — their own shadowland (Morgan, 2006)!

In contrast to the negative impact that myth may have, Jackson and Carter (1984) have pointed to the positive and mediating function of myth. They argue that whilst individuals have a basic need to understand their condition, not everyone has an absolute need to understand everything. Myths provide explanations for events and realities and by so doing reinstate equilibrium, bring certainty and meaning to what otherwise may appear uncertain and meaningless (Jackson and Carter, 1984). Myths can also provide a way of: (1) coping with disruptive external and internal conflicts; (2) creating a sense of collegiality; and (3) perpetuating and reinforcing the values of an organisation (Sievers, 1986; Bowles, 1989; Boyce, 1996; Gabriel, 2000; Poulton, 2005). Such myths can be detected in the intentions embodied in mission statements proclaiming: 'Here is what we are aspiring to be.' They fulfil the need for people to have a vision of a better future. (Brown, et al, 2005: 30)

Myths can also be used to facilitate organisational learning. Cash (1997) has argued that organisations are often embedded in paradox. Increasingly government agencies in the fields of health, welfare and education have to act as profitable businesses and offer a service to the public. Cash cites caring industries as being there to 'assist the unfortunate at the stage when it is too late to prevent them being unfortunate.' (Cash, 1997: 160) Nevertheless by bringing to the surface these paradoxes and confronting the basic assumptions of the dominant mental models upon which they are based, it is argued that a higher level of consciousness is gained (Cash, 1997, Senge, 1990). Movva (2004) has reinforced the above argument by indicating that if the way organisational reality is constructed in the minds of organisational members fundamentally shifts, then the organisation goes through a process of transformation. Reflecting on old myths and creating new ones can raise the consciousness of people. Through framing and reframing reality, one can develop a shared vision that is likely to be understood, remembered and owned by all members (Movva, 2004).

McWhinney and Battista (1988) have described the above process as remythologising. Remythologising brings to consciousness the founding ideals that helped to create and sustain an organisation's identity and by so doing link the primal energy with present circumstances thus enabling organisational renewal. McWhinney and Battista have proposed three stages to this process: (1) bringing founding myths to organisational consciousness; (2) reviving founding myths; and (3) recommitting to a revitalised myth (1988).

Owen (1987) has argued that when environments become unstable or so radically altered that they can no longer operate effectively then the organisation has to seek a new path. Transformation rather than development is required because the environment is so unstable that the earlier form is no longer workable. However, development assumes the existence of a relatively hospitable and stable environment and involves making existing organisational forms function better so that it achieves optimal performance under the new circumstances. In order to highlight the difference between transformation and development, Owen (1987) offers us the image of the butterfly and of the tadpole. The butterfly starts out as a caterpillar, spins a cocoon about itself and after a period, emerges as a butterfly; in contrast to the tadpole which develops bit by bit — first losing its tail and then growing legs. If one were to cut the cocoon one would find a dissociated protoplasm. The caterpillar dissolves, returns to its essence and then is reformed and transformed into a butterfly. Assuming that it is better to be a butterfly than a caterpillar, it is clear that one has to allow the old form to dissolve and by so doing freeing essential energy, purpose or spirit to achieve a new form. Like remythologising, transformation also means an organisation going through a process of death, whether it is death of old ways of thinking, doing or feeling. In this process, the spirit and energy behind the myth is freed and old institutionalised ways give way to the new form that has been created.

Mission and vision

One of the clearest expositions of the purpose of Camphill, which captures a sense of an all-encompassing vision, is to be found in the Superintendent's Report for 1947/1949. In this Report Dr Karl König, co-founder of the Camphill Movement, made clear that with the number and variety of children in their care, a very special opportunity was presented to all who worked in Camphill. He noted that there was hardly a type of child who was not represented there and through that fact Camphill would be able to become a training centre for curative teachers and helpers. This same factor, the great variety and large number of children, gave the possibility of research into the nature and causes of 'mental deficiency' as very little was known about this condition. This was one of the tasks of the Camphill schools and to that end a research laboratory was to be established with the aim of studying more closely the psychosomatic foundations of 'mental deficiency'. Another task identified by König was seen as the most important one of all. This was to enlighten the public about the nature of the child in need of special care. In König's opinion, every one of the children at Camphill could be seen as a rebuke to mankind. Society had an obligation to make appropriate provision for such children; failure to do so was to betray the values of humanity.

> Everyone of these children is an admonition to mankind
> that our age is in danger of losing the values of humanity.
> These children are a strong warning not to abandon what
> is the highest ideal of humanity: the Image of Man which
> is still created in the 'Image of God.' This is the shining
> star which guides the work of Camphill.

The Schools Prospectus for 1948 expanded further on the perceived role for Camphill. What is particularly remarkable here is the contemporary resonance in much of what was written. It is worthwhile highlighting that this document was written nearly 70 years ago when most children with intellectual disabilities were receiving no education at all:

> Each child is an individual, and therefore needs a
> special and individual method, and not a standard
> method, which might be enough for the ordinary child.
> Therefore these children are in need of 'special' care, as
> they ask for their 'special' method of being trained and
> educated. It is with this that we are concerned — to find
> the Spiritual individuality in each child and out of this
> individual Spirit to assess the special method which he
> needs. Each child has not only the right to live, but the

right to demand that he is given all possible help towards bringing his potentialities to fullest expression.

Whilst the Superintendent's Report for 1947/49 and the 1948 Prospectus give the impression that the vision was to establish a residential special school, it is clear that by 1951 König had more ambitious aims. He saw Camphill developing into a centre for curative education offering professional training for doctors and nurses and possessing a range of on-site facilities including a hospital, X-ray unit and dispensary.

> ... there is hardly a type of child which is not represented to all who work here and through this fact Camphill is able to become a training centre for curative teachers and helpers. The same factor, the great variety and considerable number of children, gives the possibility of research into the conditions of mental deficiency.

But then in 1951 König signalled a possible change in direction for the role of Camphill. In the Schools Community Meeting for January 28, 1951 he reported:

> I had the idea that maybe the time has come when some of us must leave the idea of residential schools and have a kind of Camphill clinic in Glasgow. Each day a child could come for special lessons and treatment. In evening lessons for teachers and parents. On Sunday the children's service. We should have support of authorities and come into contact with Glasgow working class people.

König returned to the impact that his visit to Glasgow had had upon him in the School Community Meeting for February 15, 1952:

> We cannot leave the year 1951 without referring to the May conference in Glasgow. One thing became clear that we cannot restrict our work to just starting schools — we cannot only build islands when so much suffering

and misery abounds in the big cities and so many parents cannot send their children to us, some should start these social centres. I know it will hardly be possible to bring it about in a short time but it is an ideal for the coming year.

König was later to acknowledge in one of the Schools Community meetings that the courses for doctors that had been set up had proved a failure because Camphill was essentially a home for children and not a clinic. What is clear is that König and some of his colleagues saw Camphill as an experiment in creating a new social order, which, if it proved successful, could be adopted elsewhere. In 1951 König expressed, with remarkable prescience, his conviction that the Camphill model would eventually be found throughout the world.

Roles and responsibilities

During the period under investigation the vision for Camphill was very much the vision that König had laid out. What emerges clearly from examining the minutes of the Schools Community Meeting is the increasing frustration, and on occasions, anger displayed by König at the failure by colleagues to measure up to the demands of living in an experimental community. In the minutes for January 8, 1953 König stated that it had to be one of the tasks in the coming year, to improve the standards of Camphill in every respect and every housemother and housefather had a role to play in achieving that improvement. He pointed out that Camphill had an obligation to the local authorities that referred children to the School.

König felt it necessary to remind colleagues of their basic responsibilities. He indicated that the only way to help the children who attended Camphill was to learn to understand them with all their peculiarities. This could only be done in surroundings which were suited to them: a sheltered environment which was full of beauty, kindness and helpfulness. He went on to stress that the first thing for the children to learn was that they were not looked upon as outcasts or to be held as backward in comparison with other children. They should feel that the earthly world of which they were a part had room for them as well as for others and that their way of living was appreciated and their behaviour understood. Only when this was achieved would they gain in confidence and lose their distrust of the world. Curative education could then start but this had to be an education that not only developed intellectual faculties but also the whole being. Every aspect of life in the community played an important part in this balanced development of the children.

Based on the 1948 Schools Prospectus and the minutes of the Schools Community meetings of November 1952, January and February 1953, a picture of König's expectations of what co-workers should and should not do are outlined. König stressed that teachers should not be seen as adults who simply stand in front of the children but rather stand alongside them. They should not just be individuals who have received a special training but also be people with a well-adjusted personality. They should know not only how to teach reading and writing but also handicrafts and music, gardening and farming, painting and woodcarving. A distinction was drawn between the kind of professional specialisms that existed in the outside world and the problems that specialisms caused within the context of Camphill, where a range of diverse skills was sought and valued. In König's opinion, to handle a spade and to use a saw was as important as the ability to draw a picture or play an instrument. The teacher must live with the child, eat and sleep near the child, share the daily work and the daily joys. The warmth of the family and contact with the world were both necessary for these children. The children had dormant qualities which needed to be awakened before they could respond. Above all, the teacher had to keep the ideal of the whole man — body, soul and spirit — clearly in mind as Steiner had recommended.

In the Schools Community meeting of January 1951 König indicated that due to many human failures and human errors which all had been guilty of, the moral standard of Camphill had declined. By moral standard, König meant the way in which co-workers stood faithfully toward their work, the children and each other and to the ideals of curative education as described by Steiner. To the extent that people's innermost heart turned to these things and to the ideals of Camphill, people had not been entirely honest with each other. In his opinion the pioneering group had been a wonderful one, for it had been filled with courage, fire, zeal and determination. The group that followed was not up to the same standard. And so far as the present group was concerned, talk of their failures had been quite free and open and attempts had been made to instil something that appeared to be lacking. König was quite clear that the truth had to be spoken when the community met together: 'we must speak the truth when we meet here on the background of what we think and feel.'

In 1953 König directed his critical fire at the contribution of the house communities to the curative education endeavour. He argued that the communities were gradually becoming 'useless.' He made a plea that to the extent that they were engaged with children, they should concentrate on the sphere of curative education and the need for special individual handling of the children, as these fell short of what might be expected. More attention had to be extended to individual children in the form of special exercises so that their abilities could be enhanced.

Despite his sense of disappointment and occasional despair, König expressed his belief that there had been a marked improvement in human relationships. Some of his happiest moments had occurred during his personal talks with individuals and his having witnessed the changes that had taken place in them over time. By 1952 he had experienced a true spirit emerging that was shining forth from within individuals. He believed that those who wanted to develop into true human beings had that possibility in Camphill. He anticipated that there would be many tasks lying ahead and that great demands would be placed on the ability of the community to face these challenges.

Boundaries and relationships

There is evident confusion in the minutes concerning the respective roles and responsibilities of varying bodies within Camphill. At an early stage a distinction was drawn between the Schools Community and Camphill community. Whilst anyone working at Camphill could belong to the Schools Community, not everyone could belong to the Camphill community. What the minutes fail to reveal is the nature of that difference other than in the most simple of terms; namely, that the Schools Community was oriented to the outside world through the Schools Council of Management and that the Camphill community was inner oriented with possibly a closed membership.

In 1951 it was recorded that the only success Camphill had achieved in going out into the wider world was when it had been asked to do so. And it was accepted that this should be the guiding principle as far as further 'exports' were concerned. However later that year the view was expressed that Camphill was too much like an island and that members of the Schools Council should be made aware of what was happening beyond 'the island'. The minutes also recorded a degree of tension between what was seen as the farsightedness of the Council and the views of external members of the Schools Community and the rest of the Community, although it was conceded that Camphillers could acquire such views if they took enough interest! The minutes for November 21, 1952 noted that children who came to Camphill did so because they were unable to live in the outside world. It was necessary therefore to create an island where the world was kept out. Only when the children began to recover could they be sent to school and led back into the world again. It was noted how children were able to go home and fit into their old surroundings in spite of being out of the world whilst at Camphill. The task of Camphill was leading the children back into that outside world.

Discussion

In its most ancient and original sense, myth is reality: the unquestionable truth held by a group of people. The reality for the Pueblo Indians in New Mexico was that they literally believed they were the sons of the Father Sun, (Heller, 2006). The reality for people in Camphill is that a human being has a spirit which is not simply a 'product' of genes or the environment but is a 'product' of the stars. One interesting aspect of myth within Camphill is the belief that the rituals attached to myth are always performed for the good of humanity. The worship of the Sun by the Pueblo Indians was not just for themselves but for the whole world, for without their intervention it would be forever night (Heller, 2006). In Camphill in 1947/49 one of the most important tasks of the Camphill schools was 'to enlighten the public about the nature of the child in need of special care.' This was to be done in part by researching the causes of 'mental deficiency' in order that children would be better understood and in part by creating an environment whereby children's 'dormant qualities could be awakened.' It was König's conviction that 'each child has not only the right to live, but the right to demand that he is given all possible help towards bringing his potentialities to fullest expression.'

It is clear that König, together with his colleagues, intended to create a new way of life: 'We wish to create a new social order, which may influence social orders formed in a much bigger way in the future.' König was also clear how this new way of life was to express itself. In this respect the story is not dissimilar to the hero's mythic journey. König returned from internment on the Isle of Man in 1940 with a number of ideas that he claimed were revealed to him during the course of a spiritual encounter with Count Zinzendorf. This took the form of a dream in which Zinzendorf highlighted the need for the introduction of a Bible Evening.

Gardner (1997) has pointed out that myth in an organisation refers to that which is sacred and shared by a group of people; it is their reality and truth. It is an authoritative account of the facts which may not be questioned nor challenged, for myth determines the way things are done. Poulton (2005) takes this argument further by saying that not only does it determine the way things are done but it determines how people define themselves. He does not call this myth but rather the 'genesis story' of an organisation.

There seems little doubt that the Bible Evening is part of Camphill's 'genesis story.' The Bible Evening was created so that people could practise their spirituality by meeting at least once a week as spiritual beings; that's to say, meeting as morally and ethically developed human beings.

Meeting once a week and immersing oneself in the words of spiritual wisdom drawn from the Bible was only one way of practising one's own spirituality. Helping to implement the 'Christ impulse' was clearly and explicitly stated as one of the primary tasks of Camphill. According to König only those individuals who saw themselves as part of this mission could call themselves full members of Camphill (Müller-Wiedemann, 1996). In the beginning all saw themselves as part of a mission, not least because the early Camphillers began their shared life as members of an anthroposophical study circle and because König was personally drawn to the 'religious' expression of anthroposophy. This was such a vivid reality for König that not only did he arrange in 1942 for Camphill to become a member of the Christian Community but also he noted in his diaries that he expected Camphill to become a new sort of religious order (Müller-Wiedemann, 1996; McKanan, 2007).

König claimed that Camphill was not an organisation created for the purpose of disseminating Christian faith, nor was it there to propagate Steiner's teachings (Müller-Wiedemann, 1996; McKanan, 2007). However, it is quite clear that Camphill was expected to commit itself to anthroposophy. By insisting that only those who were committed to the 'Christ impulse' and anthroposophy could call themselves members of the Camphill community, König was helping shape Camphill's identity. He was also investing those who were committed to the 'Christ impulse' with the authority and responsibility to preserve that identity of Camphill as he had imagined it to be. The creation of these two communities — the inner-oriented Camphill community and the School Community — did not promote a sense of unity: one of the key aims of anthroposophy. What also seems not to have been recognised is that when König expected people conscientiously to attend the Bible Evenings, he was in fact violating his colleagues' spiritual freedom. It is quite clear from König's pronouncements that the inner community played a critical role in Camphill life and work.

Morgan (2006) has indicated that myths can have a negative impact within organisations in that people find themselves so trapped within their own constructions of reality that change is almost impossible. He uses the metaphor of the psychic prison: where people are imprisoned within their own realities and where people live in their own 'shadowland'. The notion of 'shadowland' is not dissimilar to the 'total institution' described by Goffman (1961) where individuals are divested of their individuality. This is not to suggest that this is what happened in Camphill, however it is quite clear that individuals were asked to make a series of 'sacrifices': sacrifice personal possessions, sacrifice their own needs in the interests of the organisation and in the interest of others. Camphill co-workers were asked to act like mythic heroes by giving freely of themselves.

Owen (1987) has argued that myth is not only the vehicle through which a culture's values, purpose and direction are realised but also the medium through which an organisation manifests its Spirit which is defined as 'that which underlies all that I am or we are. Spirit is man in his essence.' (Owen, 1987: 6) Owen has suggested that at the genesis of every organisation there is a moment when some individual or a small group of individuals has the kind of 'Ah-ha, I've got it' experience. It is the creative moment when something new appears as if from nowhere; what it is and what it will become are all unknowns. The individual may not know what to do precisely and where it might lead but something has happened which is hot, powerful and moving. It carries a high level of energy but little focus. This can be conceptualised as the primal Spirit.

Even though it is difficult to perceive 'high levels of energy' by just looking through the minutes of the School Community meetings, there is little doubt that this powerful and energising creative impulse was there, as otherwise it is difficult to see how Camphill came into existence and continues to survive. The energy that created Camphill was the conviction that all individuals have a spirit; a spirit which only needs to be recognised and given the possibility to express itself. This led to an investment in humanity and the celebration of the individual and of difference. But there was also a parallel conviction, which was that one needed to change the world. To that end it would be necessary to create a mini-world on its own, a different world where the 'spirit' would be able to 'shine' like a 'candle on a hill.' This metaphor was often used in explaining the origins of Camphill. Unconditional love, freedom and trust were its essential elements (Müller-Wiedemann, 1996).

Implications

What makes myths so powerful and dangerous is the fact that they tend to be buried deep in one's unconscious. From the point of view of those that own these myths, this is quite natural, for not only are they not conscious of their existence but are also oblivious to the fact that 'others' may see them as odd. As such, myths are regarded as unchallengeable truths and are often used to prevent acceptance of new ideas and to block progress (Owen, 1987; Hughes, 1995; Brown et al. 2005). Hughes (1995) and Brown et al. (2005) have claimed that if myths are ever challenged, the response tends to be the same and is expressed in such terms as 'this is how we always do things here' and 'we tried that and it didn't work.'

Gabriel (2000) has argued that myths can take the form of retrospective nostalgia – a form of organisational memory. Such nostalgia idealises the past and accepts it as something which is irretrievably lost, whilst the present is pictured as impoverished. With this form of nostalgia the sense of loss is never psychologically conquered, it uses the past like an analgesic, which numbs the pain and provides refuge from the complexities of the present. In its most acute form it can lead to a total inability to accept the present and to a morbid preoccupation with the past — so that buildings, particular rituals and charismatic leaders are identified as elements that attract nostalgic feelings. At the heart of these feelings lies an idealised past that is seen as authentic and caring, where there was the warmth of love, community and family spirit and the presence of protective leaders.

What the examination of the Schools Community meetings during the 1940s and 1950s reveals is König's clearly articulated and imaginative vision for the future but at the same time the existence of an organisational climate in Camphill that was largely unsupportive of the kind of changes he sought. This prompted him on a number of occasions to express his anger, frustration and disappointment with his colleagues. In other words, this was not 'a golden age'! At least, not in König's eyes! It can be argued that the situation has not changed, for the same conservative, introspective and exclusive attitudes found in Camphill in 1948 can still be detected in the Camphill of today!

The contradiction here is that in his frustration to lead Camphill in the direction he wanted it to go, König felt obliged to act in an authoritarian manner. Later in his life when he was asked why he acted in this way, he quietly responded that he was left with no choice! (Messenger, undated) This suggests that he had limited confidence in the ability of his colleagues to provide the collective and democratic leadership that was needed.

The fact that a significant number of the co-workers were at that time drawn from Central Europe and were living in a country whose language, culture and manners they did not share is likely to have increased their sense of physical, social and psychological isolation. The fact also that König was often away from Camphill for long periods of time probably contributed to the development of an introspective and closed community. With the death of König and later the death of Thomas Weihs, his charismatic successor, it could be argued that Camphill lost its way and when there is uncertainty, there is often an irresistible temptation to hang on to the past.

A number of authors have agreed that rigidity and preservation of lifeless forms will only lead to organisational death (Owen, 1987; Gabriel, 2000; Steiner as cited in Luxford & Luxford, 2003; Morgan, 2006; McKanan, 2007). Some have argued that only by contemplating death, can the possibility of survival be realised. McKanan (2007) has suggested that being ready to live in the face of death makes it easier to risk investing resources in 'touching the world' as well as remaining open to the possibility of resurrection. For Owen (1987) death is not a matter of choice, it is something that happens to all organisations, the choice lies in whether the organisation decides on death that leads to extinction or to resurrection.

For resurrection to happen, a process of transformation needs to be brought about which involves a search for a better way of functioning. This is not usually a process that the organisation itself initiates, as it is too painful (Owen, 1987). The essence of transformation is the odyssey of the primal spirit of the organisation as it moves from one formal manifestation to another. Transformation is different from development, as transformation requires the old to die and dissolve to make way for a new form. Owen (1987) has given the example of the transformation from caterpillar to butterfly. The only way to move from one stage to the next is to allow the old form to dissolve. Once the caterpillar dissolves and returns to its essence, it frees essential energy to achieve its new form.

There is some indication from research that the most successful communities (where success is measured in terms of longevity) are the ones whose practices demand that individuals subordinate their individual freedom to the welfare of the group, where loyalties that compete with group loyalty are discouraged, where there is total commitment to the prevailing ideology and where high walls are placed between the community and the outside world (McKanan, 2007). This may help to explain why Camphill has survived for seventy years. However to pursue this kind of community ideal runs the risk of sacrificing the real spirit and essence of what constitutes Camphill, which is deeply held beliefs in individual freedom and connection to the outside world. If Camphill wishes to survive, it will need to embrace living with instability. Rather than measuring success in terms of organisational longevity, it should judge effectiveness in terms of its attentiveness to, and realisation of, its larger goals.

The choices that lie ahead of Camphill are not clear-cut. It is not a matter of constantly adapting to external requirements like a subservient chameleon or sticking stubbornly to old ways and erecting even higher walls between it and the outside world. The most important thing for Camphill to realise is that it is not hostage to a cruel world that does not understand it but that it has an important and active role in helping to shape that world.

Working out of the principles of love and freedom is as relevant now as it was at the time that the Nazi regime drove König and his colleagues from Central Europe. The growth of a centralised state in the UK which is increasingly reliant on surveillance and inspection regimes is one in which individual liberties are being challenged. This is therefore a time when strategies to enable people to feel valued and fulfilled are needed. Camphill has a role to play here but if it is to do so, there needs to be the kind of transformation to which reference has been made.

One possible obstacle to organisational progress is the belief that there was once 'a golden age' and that any significant departure from what is generally perceived to have been past practice will be detrimental to the health of that organisation. Preoccupation with a notion of the past, thought to have been characterised by certainty, clarity of direction and purpose, merits challenge. As close scrutiny of the minutes of the Schools Meetings has revealed, there was considerable disagreement and confusion on a wide range of issues. Acceptance of the myth of a 'golden age' not only prevents Camphill from looking forward and responding to present and future needs but also represents a threat to its continued existence.

It is a matter of some surprise that no history of the development of the Camphill Movement has yet been written, notwithstanding its existence for seven decades. This short study constitutes one of the first attempts to take a critical look at the life and work of one Camphill community through scrutinising original documentary evidence held by that community. It is to be hoped that the publication of this study will stimulate future scholars to examine other facets of this unique community movement. The findings of such research can only benefit the Movement itself through encouraging those who live and work in Camphill communities to reflect critically upon the purpose of the Camphill enterprise. But those external to this Movement will also profit from such research, for the seminal ideas that König promoted and developed in the mid-twentieth century have an especial relevance and resonance today.

3. Sensing the Extraordinary Within the Ordinary

JOHN SWINTON AND AILEEN FALCONER

John Swinton is Professor in Practical Theology and Pastoral Care at the University of Aberdeen and Director of the Centre for the Study of Spirituality, Health and Disability.

Aileen Falconer is currently Registrar of the Council for Anthroposophic Health & Social Care. She has experience as an educator, researcher, complementary therapist and project manager.

Camphill is an international movement that seeks to enhance the lives of people with learning disabilities and other additional support needs by creating communities within which the contributions of all people are valued, developed and lived out regardless of intellectual or physical capabilities. The first community was founded in 1940 at Camphill House, just outside Aberdeen, Scotland, with the express intention of educating children with learning disabilities. At that time, children with such disabilities remained uneducated, either staying at home or being placed in a hospital. The founders of Camphill were led by an Austrian paediatrician and thinker, Dr Karl König. It was in 1927 that König, watching an Advent celebration carried out by children with special needs, felt deeply moved to commit his life to facilitating care and education for such children (Selg, 2008a: 28, 71). 'It was a promise I made to myself: to build a hill upon which a big candle was to burn so that many infirm and handicapped [sic] children would be able to find their way to this beacon of hope.' (Monteux, 2006: 20) To live as beacons of hope was, and remains, a primary raison d'être for the existence of the Camphill communities.

König built these initial communities on three primary tasks:

1. Hard work
2. Learning to live together
3. The study of anthroposophy
   (Weihs, 1975: 2-3)

These later gave rise to the threefold organisational structure underpinning the Camphill communities: economic, social and spiritual/cultural.

The third point is worth clarifying. König was inspired by Rudolf Steiner's philosophy of *anthroposophy* (Selg, 2008: 20–3, 145). Anthroposophy is a perspective on the world which is deeply spiritual. It derives from two Greek words: *anthropos*, 'human being,' and *sophia*, 'wisdom.' As theosophy ('theo' and 'sophia') means wisdom of God, or divine wisdom, anthroposophy means 'wisdom of the human being' or the wisdom that knows what it means to be human. In other words, it is a spiritually-orientated path of self-knowledge that leads to an 'awareness of one's own humanity.' As such it regards itself not as a system or doctrine but as a stimulus for individual spiritual development and discovery, which provides insights for renewing and recreating the foundations of our life and culture.

It was such a philosophy that kindled the conviction in König (and his followers) that those with disabilities had much to contribute if only their inner self could find expression. His intention was 'to create a community that would bring healing, help to those in need and protect their value and dignity wherever and whenever that was threatened. They also wanted to offer a counterbalance, however modest, to the events in Hitler's Germany.' (Monteux, 2006: 22) This last point is interesting. König was an Austrian Jew who, along with his family, came to Scotland as a refugee, fleeing from the Nazi regime and the impending dangers that he would inevitably have been subjected to. The suggestion that the Camphill communities were, at least in part, intended as a counterbalance to the Nazi's destruction, not only of the Jews but also of people with disabilities, is a fascinating and perhaps oft overlooked dimension of the ethos, formation and continued intention of the Camphill Movement: to provide light, respite and sanctuary in a hostile world.

Spirituality and the Camphill communities

The ethos of the Camphill communities has always been deeply spiritual. Historically the communities have drawn from and drawn together a mix of cultural, spiritual and religious traditions, including ancient Buddhist and Hindu wisdom, Judaism, Christianity, Quakerism and other faiths (Monteux, 2006: 19). However, whilst spirituality is diverse and eclectic, it was Christian principles that underpinned the early movement. Yet despite this emphasis on spirituality, little research has been done into what spirituality might mean for the people with special needs and the co-workers within the Camphill communities. The study upon which this chapter is based aimed to explore the significance of spirituality for those living and working within three Camphill communities in the United Kingdom: Newton Dee Village, Aberdeen; Botton Village, North Yorkshire and Camphill Houses, Stourbridge. The study used a combination of in–depth qualitative interviews and focus groups to explore the theme of spirituality with 74 people with special needs and 51 co-workers.

The aim of the research was:

- To listen to people's experiences and sense of the spiritual within their lives
- To hear how they understood and constructed the term 'spirituality'
- To understand the significance of spirituality for their lives and well-being

This chapter will focus on the ways in which people with special needs defined and understood spirituality, although, as mentioned, the study encompassed co-worker perspectives as well. The work with the co-workers will be published in the future. We will also explore whether or not König's three core foundational tasks remain pertinent.

Understanding spirituality

Tying down a precise meaning for spirituality is a tricky task in a cultural context where religion and spirituality aren't necessarily perceived as the same thing. The understanding of spirituality that underpinned the study could be broadly described in this way:

> Religiousness has to do with participation in the particular beliefs, rituals and activities of traditional religion. It can serve as a nurturer or channel for spirituality, but is not synonymous with it. Spirituality is more basic than religiousness. It is a subjective experience that exists both within and outside traditional religious systems. Spirituality in all of its forms relates to the way in which people understand and live their lives in view of their ultimate meaning and value. As such it includes the need to find satisfactory answers to ultimate questions about the meaning of life, illness and death. It can be seen as comprising elements of meaning, purpose, value, hope, love and, for some people, a connection to a higher power or something greater than self.

It will be worthwhile bearing in mind this broad definition of spirituality as we move on.

Sensing the extraordinary within the ordinary: the research findings

MORE THAN A CONCEPT: SPIRITUALITY AS A LIVED EXPERIENCE

The people with special needs we spent time with were quite clear that spirituality was important. That clarity was not manifest through definitions and concepts, but rather through actions and practices. Rather than offering speculative definitions of spirituality people tended to focus on their experiences of the spiritual; on the practical and pragmatic dimensions of spirituality that were rooted and worked out in the everydayness of their lives. It was as people identified everyday actions and practices as 'spiritual' that the complex meaning of spirituality became apparent and that spiritual well-being became a real possibility.[1] Spirituality was a lived experience rather than an idea or a set of beliefs. Spirituality certainly contained strong and, for some, very real elements of 'the unseen' and the transcendent. But even 'the unseen' was intimately interwoven with and deeply connected to the whole of a person's life. People expressed the spiritual in concrete terms, interlaced with tangible things such as work, relationships, community and nature; things which tended to be immediate and accessible to the senses but nonetheless mysterious and profound. The conceptual definition of spirituality was not of primary importance; the practices of spirituality seemed to be what were significant. Put slightly differently, spirituality found its definition experientially rather than intellectually.

A good example of this can be found in Rob's response to the question 'What is spirituality?' Rob replied: *'Well, not forthcoming ... cause I also clean in the church as well.'* At first glance this appears a rather strange and somewhat disconnected response. However, a deeper reflection might indicate that, for Rob, the meaning of the term spirituality was embodied in his regular practice of church cleaning; a task which clearly gave him a sense of value and a connectedness with his religion. Rob's response to a conceptual question was to root it in a practical task. Similarly when Derek and Fiona were asked to define spirituality, they responded:

> Derek: *Maybe going to church sometimes.*
> Fiona: *Work, leisure time, meetings.*
> Derek: *Like today's meeting.*
> Fiona: *Activity groups, school of learning ...*

Like Rob's response, it is easy to dismiss such replies as a consequence of people not really understanding the question. However, the consistency with which our participants responded in similar ways indicated to us the need for a different interpretation. People were conveying their sense that spirituality is not a concept, but an embodied practice.

For our participants then, spirituality related to a series of identifiable practices that may well have deeper conceptual meaning, but which were not primarily conceived of, or articulated, in that way. As we shall see, even the supernatural elements of people's spiritual experience — God[2], angels, prayer, afterlife — were not understood as simply dislocated experiences; their function was defined and grounded within particular contexts and life situations. As we shifted our attention away from the search for formal definitions and focused on its embodiment in the lives of the participants, it became clear that spirituality was in fact a significant dimension of many people's lives even if it was not always articulated formally.

INFORMAL AND FORMAL SPIRITUAL PRACTICES

Spirituality emerged as a multi-vocal term which was being understood and expressed in individualised ways, both formally, through religious and spiritual language, and informally, through certain modes of practice and experience that people were defining as spiritual. This observation helped us to develop a basic twofold structure for framing and capturing something of the essence of that which our participants considered related to 'the spiritual': *formal and informal spiritual practices.*

Formal spiritual practices are forms of action that are intentionally designed to express and develop a person's or a community's spirituality. These may be focused on religion or in a more general sense of transcendence and include such things as church attendance, prayer, bible study, meditation, celebration of festivals and formal worship.

Informal spiritual practices also comprise actions or series of actions that work together in order to cultivate an individual's or a community's spirituality, where spirituality is understood as a search to live and make sense of life in terms of one's sense of ultimate meaning and value. However, unlike formal spiritual practices, they are not necessarily intentional or structured by any particular tradition or formal sense of the transcendent. They simply occur as part of day-to-day life.

We might liken formal and informal spiritual practices to Viktor Frankl's idea of ultimate and proximate meanings and goals (Frankl, 1969). Ultimate meaning relates to a person's relationship with God or their faith in something beyond normal metaphysical boundaries. Proximate meaning relates to something one sets one's mind to do at a temporal level; a goal to fulfill, to achieve something for a particular cause or person, to care for one's family, friends and so forth (Frankl, 1969). Formal and informal spiritual practices function, roughly, along a similar dynamic although the two dimensions frequently interact in important ways. Thus, such things as searching-for-relationships, finding-meaning-in-work, and being-in-community took on particular spiritual importance (from the perspective of our participants) even though, when viewed from other perspectives, they may not appear to be explicitly spiritual endeavours.

INFORMAL SPIRITUAL PRACTICES: COMMUNITY LIVING

RELATIONSHIPS

We have already noted that community living has been, and continues to be, a fundamental dimension of the Camphill communities. Creating relationships of mutual trust is central to the ethos of these communities. It is therefore not surprising that it was community in general, and relationships in particular, that people identified as a primary mode of informal spiritual practice and expression. It was striking that almost without exception our participants seemed to relate spirituality to some kind of relationship and connection with others. For some that connection was with God or a divine being, but for others the word 'spirituality' was clearly and deeply associated with human relationships at a temporal level:

> So I mean it is not only in church and things like that [that we encounter spirituality] but when you meet another human being ... when you meet another person you're not just meeting a whole load of skin and bones and flesh and blood but you meet something and that must be something spiritual.

Relationships were perceived as more than simply social experiences. Encounters with others contained and reflected something of the spiritual. There was *'something more'*. We can begin to understand something of the nature of this 'something more' if we frame our participants' relationships within four key spiritual questions:

Who am I?
Where do I come from?
Where am I going to?
Why?

There is a sense in which these are the primary existential questions to which religious traditions seek to offer answers. They also sum up something central to the more general human spiritual quest. These questions are precisely the questions that a person's relationships provide answers to.

Who am I?

Relationships are fundamental to the way in which we understand ourselves and are intricately connected to the quality of our lives. Identity comes from encounter rather than through self-reflection. It is as we engage in relationships that we discover who we are. As we relate to one another so also do we bestow identity and value, or otherwise, on one another.

> Interviewer: *What gives you life, meaning and purpose do you think?*
> Matt: *Having friendly people around.*
> Interviewer: *Why do you think that is Matt?*
> Matt: *... em ... Stops you getting lonely...*
> Interviewer: *Doug what are the things that are important to you in life?*
> Doug: *Having friends and having a job, having a job, well friends and having a job and stuff.*
> Interviewer: *These are the two things that ...*
> Doug: *Stand out.*
> Interviewer: *Why are these things important Doug do you think?*
> Doug: *Because it, I just think, it just feels better, it feels good to have friends.*

Friendships give our lives meaning. To the question 'Who am I?' our friends respond: 'Someone worthy of friendship.'

Where do I come from?

Friendships and personal relationships thus provided our participants with a sense of connectedness; a sense of self-in-community. In particular, friendships over time seem to provide a deep sense of what we might call 'homefulness'; a sense that a person has roots that stretch beyond and before the present and which locate her in a place which she now considers to be home.

This sense of homefulness was particularly important for those who had lost parents:

> Interviewer: *Derek what about friends for you. Are they important?*
> Derek: *Yes they are, yes, yes. I've lost my parents. My father and mother are dead, I lost my godparents. My father said to me 'This is your home here in Botton.'*

For Derek, his friendships in the Camphill community of Botton and his father's 'instruction' that Botton should be his new home, enabled him to move on from that which once gave him security, identity and a sense of homefulness — his parents — to his new home with his 'new family' in the Camphill community.

Where am I going to?

Participants gave us the strong sense that they were embedded in a complex mesh of interconnected relationships as they went about the various tasks of living. This gave us an impression that people experienced a sense of being 'known by all' and also of 'knowing all'. This in turn contributed to a sense of security and safety, and, to a degree, a sense of shared direction and telos. This matrix of relationships, both within and beyond the community, provided the motivation for moving forward with life and offered the necessary support to do so.

> Interviewer: *What would you say is your source of hope in life? What makes you get up in the morning and motivates you to face the next day?*
> Duncan: *I suppose it is em I think it's to do well maybe I'm better, what motivates me is to I suppose to do as much good as I can for other people I mean.*

Relationships thus provided a context for meaningful contribution and a conduit through which the question 'Where am I going to?' could be worked out and answered.

Why?

Finally, relationships provided people with a context in which they could understand why we are here. Our participants gave a number of responses to the 'why?' of relationships. People expressed the belief that we are in a real sense made for relationships; that in relationships we find our meaning and purpose in life.

> Interviewer: *So are friendships important for you Brett?*
> Brett: *Ah yes. If you don't get on with people, you might as well forget it.*

For some this was bound up with being of service to others: '*Yes I think in a way he feels he needs to help me and I need to help him.*' Relationships provided an avenue for such fulfilment of purpose.

For others relationships were a solution to loneliness and other sources of disconnection:

> Interviewer: *In what ways are friendships important to you do you think?*
> Euan: *It saves you from, I think it saves people from, helps people to not be lonely and to avoid, you know, getting into trouble and things like that …*
> Duncan: *I suppose it* [friendship] *makes me more whole but I'm not sure how to explain that one, but that's a difficult one to explain I think.*

Bearing in mind the fact that loneliness, isolation and rejection are key challenges faced by people with special needs living in the wider community (Swinton & Powrie, 2004), this emphasis on relationships and their continuity over time within the Camphill communities is significant.

WORK

A second foundational aspect of community life that was highlighted as spiritually significant was work. Like relationships this emphasis seems in line with König's original intention for the Camphill communities.

Work as a source of meaning and identity formation

Work, like relationships, emerged as a significant aspect of meaning formation.

> Interviewer: *So what do you think your life would be like if you didn't have work then Holly?*
> Holly: *A complete and empty void. You'd be, it would be completely empty.*
> Interviewer: *So work's something then that helps you have a sense of meaning and purpose in your life is it?*
> Holly: *Yeah, exactly.*

Work also appeared to contribute to self-definition and self-identity for many.

> Robin: *My name is Robin Colville em my life is doing the bakery in the morning and the press afternoons.*
> Rhianna: *I'm Rhianna and I live in Botton for many years and my life is candle making, gardening around here.*

This identity-forming dimension of work was also important for another reason: it conferred on the individual an identity and value that counterbalanced the negativity of being a person with 'special needs.'

> Interviewer: *Why is it important for you Gordon do you think to be able to work?*
> Gordon: *Because I don't want to be seen needing, needing,*

> *my special needs being taking over. I come here to get on in*
> *my life to be able to have the same opportunities as*
> *my brother and sister.*
> Interviewer: *So you don't want to be defined by your special*
> *needs?*
> Gordon: *No I don't. No that's the whole point of coming to*
> *Camphill Houses.*
> Interviewer: *And work is one way of overcoming that?*
> Gordon: *Yeah. I don't want to be saying 'Oh he's in that*
> *centre or he's in that home.' I want to move on from that.*

This close identification between self and work seemed to enhance the creation of a positive self-identity through linking the self to something that is perceived (by self and others) to be of importance and value.

Working for others

One dimension of people's work that seemed particularly important was the fact that it was *purposeful*. In other words, there was a clear understanding that the work that people engaged in was *creative*; it was not just a meaningless task with no significant outcome. Rather it was goal orientated and people felt they were making a contribution to the wider good. The direct forms of service with which many people were engaged, made it easy to connect the work done with its value for others. '*I work in the garden, harvest all the vegetables, for the neighbourhood.*' This pattern of work-as-contribution was echoed throughout the study; people cooked *for others*, did housework *for others*, farmed *for others* and so forth. This is quite an interesting digression from the cultural norm which tends to focus on work-as-self-earning. The participants framed work quite differently: as *service*. Such an ethos of working-for-others is, as mentioned previously, central to the historical ethos of the Camphill communities and was clearly assimilated into the lives of the residents. As Keiran put it: '*We actually work for each other in the community.*'

Thus, the criticism that could be levelled at work or similar activities provided for people with special needs — that they are tasks designed simply to keep people busy, with no real meaning, purpose or value placed on the outcome, was not generally our experience in the Camphill communities. Here we found people engaged in their work with full knowledge of its significance and value to themselves, their community and society. However, we did find that in the 'non-village' community[3], which had been originally set-up with the intention that people would work in the wider community, the situation was slightly different. Here where the opportunities for work embedded in the community were more limited and less diverse, some were frustrated in their search for fulfilling and valued work, both within the community itself and in the wider local community. The positive experience of work evident in the village communities appeared to be harder to replicate due to the community structure and because people sought work in the wider society.

FORMAL SPIRITUAL PRACTICES: ACCESSING 'THE UNSEEN'

Whilst informal spiritual practices were clearly important and prevalent within the communities, there was also a strong element of formal spiritual practices that reached beyond temporal relationships towards God or some sense of the unseen. Here spirituality was developed in a more familiar cadence as participants drew on recognisable religious, theological and philosophical concepts, ideas and perspectives.

THE 'UNSEEN'

Spirituality as the 'unseen' dimension of existence was a common theme running through our conversations. As Olive put it:

> *Spirituality has something to do with what you can't see. But it underlies actually the whole of life because, I mean, where does life come from? It doesn't come from the earth. There must be*

something that's making it come from somewhere. It's a very
important part of life. I can't imagine life without it.

Here spirituality is understood in terms of an invisible and
creative force which brings into existence all of life and without
which life makes no sense. This life force is in a sense beyond
the present; and yet, is not really 'somewhere else.' Rather it is
here, amongst us, intangible to the normal senses, but accessible
and transformative via faith, as Donald notices:

… you can't see it … you can't see the second coming of Christ,
you can't see Him but you know that He's there. Even though
He doesn't walk amongst us now as He did 2000 years ago but
you know He's there amongst us somewhere doing, just showing
His presence is in the sort of spiritual realms rather than …
being on the earth a man like we are here now.

This is an interesting statement. Donald draws on imagery
from the Christian tradition to express his belief that God
is amongst us and that spirituality is unseen, but very much
present. At one level there appears to be what he describes as 'the
spiritual realms,' that is, a realm beyond the normal parameters
of human experience. But at another level, he seems to assume
that God (in this case God-in-Christ) is amongst us and actively
doing something. The paradox here is only apparent, as this is
precisely the type of teaching available within the Christian
tradition where God is assumed to be both present, through the
Holy Spirit, and absent, insofar as God remains mysterious and
'still to come.' The point to keep in mind here is that God is
both unseen and at the same time present and active.

GOD

One important aspect of the 'unseen' was people's perceptions of
God. All of the groups that we worked alongside had different
ideas about God. Some people expressed a strong belief in God:

> Euan: *Yeah I, I believe ... very strongly that there is a God and cause ... em ... cause that He created the earth, the earth, the world and I believe, I believe in that very strongly.*
> Keiran: *Well one thing I must say is that I've never heard God speak to me before and I've never seen Him neither but I believe He exists though because if God didn't exist we wouldn't exist.*

Here, once again, we have the idea of God as the creative force that lies behind all things and makes sense of the world: a God who is unseen and in a sense 'silent,' yet still an object that inspires and requires faith. As we began to probe a little further into precisely what people meant by the term 'God,' it became quite clear that, on the whole, people's ideas were shaped by traditional Judaeo-Christian understandings. God was perceived in terms of being the one who:

- Holds the power of life and death and the 'keys' to the future:
  I would say and ... em ... well ok I'm going to be 69 next year, 70. I don't know what's going to happen for later on. I'm afraid I can't answer that question. There's only one person who can answer that [laughs] and I'm afraid I can't.
- Is the all powerful creator of the world:
  He's meant to be the powerful spiritual being that created the earth ... That's what He is, I believe.
- Is good:
  He's good!
- Oversees human activity:
  Because God does look down on you.
- Is the power to whom you pray:
  Interviewer: *Can you speak to God or not?*
  Robin: *Sometimes.*
  Interviewer: *Sometimes. How do you do that Robin?*
  Robin: *Well, I pray a lot.*
- Is a source of personal support; father-like:
  Interviewer: *How would you describe your relationship with God or Jesus?*

> Felicity: *Probably like a father-figure really ... He*
> *seems to be there helping me ... if I, when I need Him ...*
> *It's nice knowing He's there ... to comfort me or support me.*
> • Resides in heaven:
> *I believe that He's up there somewhere.*

The apparent simplicity of these beliefs does not take away from their spiritual potency for individuals. Yet others, such as Gordon, had a more complex view of God and how He influenced life at a personal level:

> Gordon: *I see God as somebody who came on the earth 2000*
> *years ago and He ... He in showing you, in guiding you helps*
> *you to understand how to work with your spirit, He gives you*
> *the path what He feels you're suited to as a spiritual being.*
> *And you have to live that task and what He gives you to the*
> *best of your ability and you, whether you live it to the best of*
> *your ability is another question, but He gives you a task and*
> *you have to unravel, you go through your life unravelling, going*
> *through all these different tasks, going through all these different*
> *hoops and eventually you'll get to what hopefully, even if it's*
> *only partly, what God wants you to do.*

For Gordon life is viewed as a spiritual journey initiated by God, in which Gordon's responsibility is to discover his purpose and to fulfil it to the best of his ability. This concept that his life has a God-given meaning and purpose had positive consequences for Gordon's sense of self-worth and self-esteem. Gordon thus sees God, the 'unseen,' as continually interacting with his life.

A SPIRITUAL REALM

The idea of 'the unseen' also seemed intricately interlinked with the idea of a spiritual realm which stands outside of normal experience but which is, at the same time, deeply implicated within it. For some this realm was synonymous with traditional

Christian ideas about heaven; heaven or the spiritual realm being understood as a 'place' quite distinct from this world, where one goes when one dies.

> Norma: *The spiritual world is up there.*
> Interviewer: *So when people die then …*
> Norma: *The spiritual world that's where they go.*

For others, the boundaries between the spiritual world and the physical world were not at all clear with one regularly 'bleeding' into the other. This seemed to be particularly so during times of crisis where the spiritual realm was used as a mode of coping with trauma and distress.

SPIRITUAL BEINGS

God was perceived as unseen yet constantly active in the world. But God was not alone. It was clear that whilst traditional Christian ideas about God were important, they were not the only spiritual currency in the communities. People expressed beliefs that the world was populated by various spiritual beings and entities, all of whom in different ways interacted with the lives of the living. Luke's experience of angels helps to illustrate this point:

> Luke: *I got this angel and always … well … I mean sometimes I see it in the night time …*
> Interviewer: *At night time?*
> Luke: *Yeah and also … you think the angel is in you …*

This is interesting. For Luke angels are real spiritual beings with which he has direct contact. They are both external to him (he can see them) and yet in a strange way internal (they are within him). In line with many spiritual traditions, Luke's encounter with the spiritual is at one and the same time outside of him and yet also part of him; both transcendent and immanent. These spiritual beings were not passive. Rather they seemed to be actively involved in people's day-to-day lives, helping, guiding and looking after them as they negotiate the complexities of their lives.

> Amelia: *So I just got to know my guides, I got to know their names, and um, how they relate to me, and where they will touch me if they need to ask me a question. At the time that was how they did it, now I just turn to them and ask … But my guides help me, I do ask them a lot of questions and I use the tarot cards and things like that. But they listen to me and I listen to them. And they don't always give you the answers but they're there to step in and say, look sorry you're on the wrong direction, right if you don't listen to me now this is what we're going to do …*

The idea of a benevolent 'higher power' or 'spiritual being' who is involved with individuals' lives and well-being was something that came up regularly.

THE INDIVIDUAL SPIRIT

As well as spiritual beings, our participants felt that the existence of the human spirit was important. The spirit was understood as something that was individual and unique to each person, the 'something more' beyond the physical and the tangible.

> Donald: *What I'm saying is there's more to you and … this is what Camphill has helped me to understand more; there's more to you than just Donald Smith.*
> Interviewer: *What is that 'more' Donald as you understand it?*
> Donald: *I have a spiritual being.*

In line with our previous observations on relationships, it is important to note that this idea of the human spirit did not appear to be conceived in dualistic terms, i.e. that somehow the spirit is the *real* person and the body is simply a container for the spirit;

and that which we do with our bodies is somehow different from the spiritual. Rather, whilst linguistically recognising that differing elements make up the human being — body, soul and spirit — the inner spirit of the person was perceived as being something more than the physical or the psychological, yet intimately connected and indeed permeating both. In the same way as God and spiritual beings were intricately connected with the whole of people's lives, so also the individual spirit was connected to the whole of the person and from there into the world.

RELIGIOUS AND PHILOSOPHICAL FRAMEWORKS FOR UNDERSTANDING DEATH

In terms of formal belief systems, issues of death seemed to be an important focusing point. Our participants presented their views on death and the afterlife according to roughly three metaphysical positions:

1. Traditional Christian belief
2. Reincarnation
3. Uncertainty

Traditional Christian belief

Here the assumption was that people would go to heaven to be with God. There were no ideas of rebirth or entering into a spiritual world which interfaced with this world.

> Kevin: *My, my mother she's gone up to heaven now. I can see her no more now ... She's gone.*

In Kevin's understanding, once people die they go to live in a different 'place' — heaven. Those who remain alive cannot see those they have lost. They are not coming back. The living may move on to join the dead in heaven but the movement is one way, from life to death to new life in heaven. The belief in heaven emerged as a means of dealing with the separation from loved ones caused by their death and offered hope of being reunited with them in the future.

Reincarnation

For others, the belief in reincarnation was important in coming to terms with death. This was a commonly held belief that has its roots in anthroposophy, although it was adopted and interpreted in individualised ways by our participants. The main assumption within our participants' belief in reincarnation was that this current life is not the only life we shall live. The individual spirit of a person does not die when the physical body does but has the capacity to be reborn again and again, taking on different physical forms in a number of lives. As Alice put it:

> *Well reincarnation is really like if you ... em ... you come back as another person you have to be reincarnated and reincarnated but reincarnation for me is like ... if I came back ... if I started getting reincarnated so many times I would come back as another person.*

Others explained reincarnation in language which was more poetic and evocative:

> Lily: *Like in the summer, when the flowers die in the winter, the flowers come back in the spring and have new life.*
> Derek: *It's like the fir trees. You find that they, the trees shed their leaves down on the floor. You find after Christmas the trees are forming the buds and the leaves come back again.*
> Lily: *As I said, like a flower we come back to new life.*

These illustrations from nature offered to explain the life/death/life cycle and gave Derek and Lily a deep assurance of new life after death. New life is part of the natural order of things, as reliable as the seasons. As such, it is a deep source of hope.

It is important to highlight one thing. There was absolutely no suggestion that a person's current life state was in any way a punishment for past life or that reincarnation was progressive or a movement away from disability. Indeed our participants explained that it is the individual spirit that is evolving and changing, 'being perfected' through successive incarnations rather than the physical body.

> Gordon: *I believe you have several times in order to make that spiritual being absolutely perfect, as perfect as you can make it ... It's a learning curve to perfect that spiritual being so that one day you don't have to keep coming back to this earth.*

Thus, the idea of reincarnation was overwhelmingly conceived of as positive and life-enhancing. It seemed to offer people some form of security insofar as it emphasised and reinforced the idea that if things go wrong in this life, there is another possibility to do things differently and hopefully better in the next life. The idea of continuity and connectedness to past and future lives also seemed to help people to invest their present lives with meaning, purpose, hope and value.

Uncertainty

The final metaphysical position that people adopted in relation to the afterlife was one of uncertainty.

> Duncan: *On and off I've thought ... I have thought at one stage that death is the end, complete end. Now I've a feeling that there's more to it than that but how far do you go along the line? I think there is an afterlife but how to define it is actually very difficult now and I suppose that's the ultimate aim for me I suppose.*

Duncan did not know what lay after death but had moved from a position of agnosticism to a belief that there was 'something more.' A number of others could see the attraction of the idea of heaven and reincarnation as this 'something more' but also remained uncertain as to where they stood on the issue. Corinne had some doubt about reincarnation but did think about it and could clearly see it as a possibility: *'Em ... reincarnation; not entirely sure about it. But I do, I do often actually ponder and think about things like that, yeah.'* Lily was more forthright and expressed an obvious wistful longing to believe in it: *'Well I'm just hoping my grandma will come back the same way in the spiritual way come back down to earth.'* Lily's statement is really a hybrid between the Christian view and the views on reincarnation expressed by others. She wants her grandma to 'come down,' indicating that she is 'up there,' which is the type of phraseology used by participants to indicate the spatial location of heaven. She also wants her to 'come back,' but not in a new body or as a new person, but precisely as she remembered her. Lily, like many of us, brings together a number of spiritual perspectives in an attempt to cope with her loss.

Discussion

We began by suggesting that Camphill has traditionally perceived itself as being a place where the spiritual has particular significance. Our research has indicated that this remains true. However, the ways in which spirituality is manifested seem to be changing. Traditional Camphill spiritual practices have revolved around formal spiritual practices such as Bible Reading evenings, festivals and attending community church.[4] For those with whom we spent time, these modes of spiritual expression were less important and for some not important at all. Like many people in the Western world the people living and working within Camphill seemed to be expressing and living out diverse and individualised spiritual lives that may include, but are no longer necessarily defined by, formal religious or philosophical structures and assumptions. Even those who do engage in formal spiritual practices, such as those available through religion or anthroposophy, often fill these with new meaning and intention.

Traditional terms such as God and heaven find themselves filled with particularised meanings as people use and personalise that language to express the spiritual complexities of their lives.

König's three principles: hard work, learning to live together and the study of anthroposophy, continue to run implicitly and explicitly through the lives of the people with special needs that we encountered within the communities. The perception of spirituality expressed through relationships and work correlates closely with the first two of König's principles, and interpretations of 'the unseen' were, for some, clearly informed by anthroposophy.

All of our participants sensed the significance of community living for developing and sustaining their spiritual well-being. For some this was largely related to the particular Camphill community where they lived. But for most the idea of community living had a wider cadence; it extended to encompass a sense of connectedness, meaning and a valued place within society at large. The opportunity to find and hold a place of worth within that wider community was equally important in achieving and maintaining a sense of spiritual well-being.

The idea of work was also clearly important for our participants. As mentioned, work was considered to have spiritual connotations. Work was not busy-ness, but contribution; it was a source of altruism and a way in which people could tangibly sense that they were participating in and contributing to something much larger than themselves. In a real sense work was a place where the extraordinary was discovered in the ordinary. However, the spiritual function of work seemed to depend on whether people's experiences of work realised their inner aspirations and hopes; what they wanted to *be* rather than merely something they had to do. It was also linked to their perception of the work as 'meaningful' and 'purposeful.' Work that was 'created' not out of necessity for the work itself, but out of the necessity to find something for people to do, did not meet these important criteria. Work could therefore run counter to an individual's spirituality and spiritual well-being.

For a number of our participants their understanding of the unseen element of spirituality was deeply influenced by anthroposophy. This was particularly so with regards to reincarnation. Reincarnation is one of the key beliefs within anthroposophy. The founder of anthroposophy, Rudolf Steiner, considered each person to be unique. That uniqueness relates not only to a person's biological and genetic dimensions but also to his soul and spirit. Between death and re-birth, it is the individual spirit that searches for a place, a lineage, that will support its future incarnation. From the perspective of anthroposophy, what occurs in the present is formed in the tension between the past and the future. In other words, taken together the past and the future affect and shape our destiny in the present. Some events occur because of things that have happened in the past; but some events happen primarily to prepare us for the future. Free will is discovered as we live in the space between the past and the future. It is here that we create our destiny.

The participants in our study moved within this rather complex dynamic. Reincarnation helped them to make sense of the present, particularly around the issue of death. Some of our participants seemed to have a fairly sophisticated understanding of the anthroposophical perspective on reincarnation, largely in line with that of Steiner's, where reincarnation seemed to have a movement through time towards the development of an 'ideal spirit.' But others saw it slightly differently and tended to use the idea of reincarnation in ways not dissimilar to traditional understandings of heaven; that is, it provided hope that death is not the end and that there is life in some form beyond its borders.

Conclusion

In conclusion, spirituality seems to be alive, well and functioning effectively within the Camphill communities. It is shifting and changing but clearly important. It seems to function at a number of levels — social, psychological and spiritual. Our impression was that at all of these levels it is an aspect of people's lives that is significant for well-being and requires to be understood, listened to and facilitated. However, the issue of spirituality is not without its challenges. The key point is that these challenges are recognised and are met with strategies and approaches that intentionally seek to meet the deeper needs of all who participate in the communities. In recognising the significance of the spiritual, the Camphill communities are in a position where they can model important ways of caring for the spirit and show important leadership in a social context that is wary of the spiritual and unsure about how it relates to the complex practices of living and caring together.

Notes

1. Spiritual well-being may be seen to occur when a person connects with his spirituality in a health-giving way; in a way that supports his integrated functioning as a human being. As such it may be seen as the end result of how well a person's spirituality (defined as those aspects of a person's belief system that contribute to a sense of meaning or purpose in life) is integrated in his life and serves to allow him to make sense of and cope with life's experiences.

2. It is important to note that in the language and understanding of participants, the term 'god' did not always relate to a specific religious tradition, but rather often functioned as a free floating symbol or representative experience which had a profound impact on people's life experiences.

3. This was a mainly urban community 'without boundaries,' where the houses were scattered throughout, and integrated in, the local community context.

4. The Christian Community was established in 1922 under the leadership of Friedrich Rittelmeyer. Rudolf Steiner played a role in creating its constitution and forms of service. The centre of the community's life is a morning Eucharist, or communion service, known as The Act of Consecration of Man. The Christian Community has a creed that states the central truths of Christianity. For further information see: www.thechristiancommunity.co.uk

4. On Middle Ground: Camphill Practices that Touch the World

DAN MCKANAN

Dan McKanan is Emerson Lecturer at Harvard Divinity School, a scholar of religious movements for social transformation, and a friend of Camphill Village Minnesota.

For twelve years I have studied the Camphill Movement in the context of the broader phenomenon of 'intentional community.' Within that context, Camphill occupies a curious middle ground, not quite fitting into the categories observers often use. Many, for example, would classify communities as either 'sectarian' or 'secular,' distinguishing those that are wholly identified with a worshipping congregation from those that display little shared interest in matters of the spirit. Camphill is neither of these things. Though it cannot be separated from its roots in anthroposophy, Camphill welcomes villagers and co-workers who follow other spiritual paths, or none at all. Karl König explicitly disavowed the 'sectarian' label, explaining that Camphill 'works out of Christianity, not for Christianity.' (1993: 38)

Again, many would distinguish those communities in which shared life is an end in itself from places where communal living is merely an expedient means of running a school, farm or retreat centre. Camphill is often left out of general studies of intentional community because it seems to belong in the latter group. But most Camphillers would resist any separation of the work of curative education and lifesharing from the broader effort to build a Threefold Social Order. In cooperation with social welfare agencies, they are committed to providing the best possible care for persons with special needs; through the guidance of the Camphill community they are equally committed to 'light[ing] the way to a better future — a future where the work of healing the earth unites with the work of healing social life.' (Hunt, 2001: 115)

Similarly, Camphill embraces the whole of life — work, home, play and worship — without cutting its members off from deep interaction with friends beyond the community boundaries. In this way, it is unlike co-housing communities (which provide a shared home and nothing more) and equally unlike Hutterite communities that aspire to provide a fully enclosed social world. Unlike monastic communities, Camphill embraces family life, but its members rarely assume that their children will provide the next generation of Camphillers. And though Camphill aspires to be the seed of a new social order, Camphillers do not imagine a future that will be Camphill writ large.

Camphill's middle ground may be difficult to categorise, but it is not unique. Every point listed above applies to the Catholic Worker network of farms and urban houses of hospitality. These communities are rooted in Catholicism but open to all; they are devoted to caring for the homeless and to 'building a new society within the shell of the old'; they provide a venue for the full range of human activities but share these with 'extended community' members and neighbours; they welcome families but do not pressure their children to become Catholic Workers; and they envision a future in which their own work of hospitality will be dispersed among every household.

Similarly, a middle-ground ethos is ubiquitous within the most inclusive network of United States intentional communities, the Fellowship for Intentional Community. The Fellowship traces its roots to a cluster of Depression-era communities that shared a vision of small community as 'the best nest for incubating the good society' (Morgan, 1944: 5–6; see also Morgan, 1942 and Goodman, 1947). The idea was that the neighbourly practices formed in community would gradually diffuse to other groups and places. That vision helped inspire the 1960s wave of hippy communes and prepared the ground for Camphill's arrival in the

United States in the 1960s.[1] Recently, the Fellowship's magazine, *Communities*, has broadened its vision further, committing itself to 'life in cooperative culture' whether or not this takes place in formal communities.

'Middle-ground' practices can even be found in communities that seem quite different from Camphill. In principle, Roman Catholic monasteries exclude non-Catholics and non-celibate people, but in practice their sense of community includes students at the schools they sponsor, parishioners at the parishes they serve, and lay 'oblates' who bring monastic practices into daily life. And many nineteenth-century communities that dreamed of superseding the old civilisation wound up transforming themselves into informal neighbourhoods that embodied communal values in more modest fashion.

My book, *Touching the World*, celebrates middle-ground communities and their distinctive practices (McKanan, 2007). These communities can transform society as a whole because they provide multiple points of contact between the everyday lives of ordinary people and alternative practices of intentional community, inviting individuals and families to reshape their lives. I highlight four clusters of helpful practices: practices that honour the distinct vocations of individuals in community; practices that 'make room' for families, making communal life accessible to all; practices that link spiritual rootedness with an openness to people of all faiths; and practices that acknowledge that communities sometimes need to die and be reborn before their gifts can be fully realised.

Touching the World draws on interviews and participant observation conducted at Camphill, Catholic Worker and related communities. While researching the book, I explored parallel practices in a network of nineteenth-century American 'Associations,' most of which drew inspiration from the French utopian theorist Charles Fourier. In this chapter, I will recap the book's main arguments, with emphasis on interviews conducted at Camphill villages in the United States. Since readers of this book are likely to be unfamiliar with the Catholic Worker and Associationism, vignettes from three representative communities may help to set the stage.[2]

It is Saturday morning, and the kitchen at the Des Moines Catholic Worker house is buzzing with activity. Church groups, college students and Cub Scouts all appear at the door, either to drop off food or to help serve the daily meal. There are more volunteers than necessary, but each person has a story to share. An older man, wounded by a recent divorce, wonders if his faith is calling him to a change of lifestyle. A United Parcel Service manager, intrigued that one of his part-time employees is also a live-in volunteer at a homeless shelter, peruses the clippings about anti-war demonstrations that line the walls. A high school senior prepares for her trip to the Worker's sister village in Chiapas, Mexico. A father discusses anarchist philosophy while his twelve-year-old son plays chess with several homeless men he has befriended. A college professor, visiting to research a book, is invited into the game and soundly defeated. And Carla Dawson, who arrived at the Worker as a homeless single mother, tells stories, barks orders, stirs soup, and greets each newcomer with a warmth that seems born of lifelong friendship.[3]

Saturdays at Camphill Village Minnesota are usually quieter, but once a year this village of eighty people hosts several hundred visitors for its Open Day: residents of the nearby towns of Sauk Centre and Long Prairie. The visitors work hard on farms and in offices, spend their free time with their children, and worship at Lutheran or Catholic churches. A few Amish families, also from nearby farms, mingle with the crowd. Riding a hay wagon through Camphill's field, the visitors learn about a lifestyle that is both similar to their own and very different. The Camphillers share their love of the land and determination to preserve a beleaguered agricultural economy, but their farming is shaped by biodynamic principles that forbid chemical pesticides and require that planting and harvesting follow the rhythms of the heavens. Rather than travelling to an office, Camphillers alternate between work shifts in the home, the garden and craft shops that produce wooden toys, woven rugs and hearty cookies. They work as hard as their neighbours but receive no individual salaries. Perhaps most importantly, adults with developmental disabilities are at the heart of Camphill life, and on Open Day they are especially eager to show off the community they have built. Sarah, who has Down's syndrome, offers a boisterous hug to everyone she recognises. Mike, who grew up on a farm just ten miles away, beams with pride as he reports on the calves and baby goats born on the farm this year. Martha rocks back and forth, clutching her Cabbage Patch doll, as she makes a joke about the name of each person she meets. 'Is your name Daniel? Daniel have to tell another joke!'

Turn the clock back 150 years, and Martha would fit in at Brook Farm, a village of farmers and Transcendentalists located outside Boston. After serving a mostly vegetarian meal, the waiters sit down to their own supper. Others linger outside, waiting for the puns to begin. 'On this melon-collar occasion,' begins one as he places a watermelon rind around the neck of his companion. A young boy gets up from the table early; as the chief and only member of the Knife Scrubbers' group, he has a keen sense of his responsibilities. Community members listen irreverently as visiting intellectual Margaret Fuller gives one of her famous 'Conversations,' but they are all ears when William Allen, one of the few experienced farmers, teaches them the proper way to plant potatoes. The community's founder spends the day shovelling manure while his wife washes linens, provoking bemused speculation about whether less cultivated persons might have done the same work in half the time. Yet the whole community, children of privilege as well as workers bankrupted by the Panic of 1837, can come together with neighbours from the 'outside' for a festival of masquerades. [4]

The Des Moines Catholic Worker, Camphill Village Minnesota, Brook Farm and communities like them can easily be lifted up as heroic alternatives to a mainstream society corrupted by competition, consumerism and capitalism. They can also be dismissed as irresponsible utopians who prefer personal purity to social engagement. Neither view does justice to the mixed and mingled character of life in these communities. It is true that communitarians live in ways that are different from those of their neighbours. These differences can be heroic, self-righteous, or both at once. But Catholic Workers, Camphillers and Associationists also live *with* their neighbours. They worship together, serve together on school boards, share vegetables and political opinions and gossip. Community members are eager to share the insights they have gleaned from cooperative living, but they are also willing to learn from their neighbours. It is in this living together that intentional communities do the most to instil values of cooperation, equality and love in society as a whole.

The communal movements I have chosen to illustrate this thesis were built on diverse religious and ideological foundations. Catholic Worker founders Peter Maurin and Dorothy Day drew on the 'distributist' strand of Catholic social teaching, which emphasised personal responsibility, decentralism, and the link between worship and social justice. Karl König, the first leader of Camphill, was a disciple of Christian esotericist Rudolf Steiner, who also inspired Waldorf schools and biodynamic agriculture. Associationism blended the utopian theories of French socialist Charles Fourier with the zeal of New England pacifists and Transcendentalists.

The communities affiliated with each movement also vary in their structures and missions. Most Catholic Worker communities are houses of hospitality where persons experiencing homelessness join those who have chosen voluntary simplicity; others are small farms. Camphills are villages of fifty to a few hundred inhabitants in which persons with and without disabilities work together at farming, gardening and traditional crafts. Associations aspired to be economically productive townships in which manual and mental work would be shared and social hierarchies would dissolve.

All three movements defy the stereotype of the sectarian or utopian commune. Camphillers, Catholic Workers and Associationists are not escapists who create a private heaven while letting the world burn. Instead, they aspire to be 'a beacon for all on the path toward social renewal,' to 'create a new society within the shell of the old,' or to achieve 'Christ's idea of society' (Peabody, 1841). And they have rarely imagined that theirs is the only path to a new society. One long-time Catholic Worker reflected that 'there were times ... when I wondered if we, far from being a light unto the nations, were behaving even a notch better than the national average.' Such sober self-assessments go hand in hand with a determination to continue experimenting. This flexibility allowed Associationism to help launch the American labour movement, the Catholic Worker to transform the ways Americans think about persons experiencing homelessness, and Camphill to reveal the profound gifts of persons with disabilities.

Several clusters of practices help intentional communities maintain a flexible engagement with society. The first reflects the communities' fierce devotion to the diverse vocations of their members, recognising that only fully developed persons can change society. In the nineteenth-century Associations, vocational discernment was achieved through 'attractive industry': members performed those tasks for which they felt a personal attraction, and shifts rotated to satisfy the 'butterfly passion' for variety. Camphill has a similar structure; during my summers at Camphill Village Minnesota I often led a cooking crew in the morning and was a garden or garbage-collecting helper in the afternoon. In many Catholic Worker houses, no demands are placed on volunteers, who freely choose to cook meals, comfort depressed guests, or 'cross the line' to protest military installations. Such experimentation allows diverse vocations to emerge. Brook Farm formed labour organisers, journalists, the founder of a religious order and the pioneer of Boston's classical music community; Camphill and the Catholic Worker have inspired potters, weavers, organic farmers and entrepreneurs.

In my conversations with Camphillers, many told me that vocational search led them to community. When Mary Davis first learned of Camphill, she had just begun work as a physical therapist and was discovering that the institutional setting was not conducive to her ideals of healing. Rather than 'chasing a dollar all the time,' she yearned for a more integrative setting for healing. Camphill allowed her to solidify her vocation by 'explor[ing] how it would be to work with people in a healing way without the money factor and the income factor' (Davis, 2002). Mark Hobson and Ben Cownap similarly told of how their careers at the British agricultural ministry and the World Wildlife Fund clashed with their environmental ideals. Since 'sitting in an office wasn't my idea of what ecology was all about,' Cownap moved to Camphill Kimberton Hills in order to 'live ecology' (Hobson, 2002; Cownap, 2005).

Others stressed the ways community itself challenged them to explore new vocations. The twice-daily rotation of shifts in Camphill opens new vocational doors while satisfying the 'butterfly passion.' When Bernie Wolf arrived at Beaver Run in 1969, he was moved to see the skill with which co-workers cared for children, delivered lectures, and tilled the fields (Wolf, 2005). Joy Dean had just arrived at the Lukas Community in New Hampshire when I interviewed her, and her arrival there had allowed her to fulfil a lifelong dream of being a beekeeper. Her predecessor had kept a hive for the community, and he passed on a few tips to her. She wanted to know more, and so the community supported her in taking an eight-week course with master beekeepers. That reflected the community's general practice of supporting new initiatives and personal development (Dean, 2002).

Camphill supported Lois Smith in a lifelong vocational quest. When she came to Camphill Copake in her mid-twenties, she had just turned down a scholarship to study landscape design. 'People who know me at this end of my career,' she recalls with laughter, 'would probably have no concept that that could ever be on my mind.' Eight years later, she moved on to an Austrian Camphill that served developmentally disabled teenagers, many of whom also had mental illnesses. Eager for more 'tools' for dealing with mental illness, she decided to deepen her understanding of music. Visiting Camphills and other curative education centres, she observed how music was used in each place. This 'seed' allowed her to connect back to the time when, as a Jewish college student, her heart had been opened by the beauties of Christian choral music. Lois went on to Camphill Special School in Beaver Run, Pennsylvania, to explore techniques used in working with children. Eventually, she settled at Camphill Village Minnesota, where she combined the formal role of master weaver with the informal vocation of coordinating community music. The community enabled her to complete a master's degree in music and therapy, and Lois reciprocates with choral pieces for community festivals and celebrations (Smith, 2002).

While Lois's vocational quest led her to a deeper immersion in music, others have explored a series of temporary vocations. Liz Brett, who has lived at Garvald and Lukas, both therapeutic communities that are not officially affiliated with Camphill, told me that 'I've had incredible changes in my role in community.' Arriving at Garvald as a single woman with an art degree, she relished the opportunity to 'devote my whole being' to work with 'young, very lively children.' Later when she had settled into teaching and had begun formal Waldorf training, 'things really jelled' and she 'felt absolutely in rhythm with myself.' When the additional responsibilities of marriage led to burnout, she and her husband took a few years off in Australia. When they returned to Garvald, the community had begun serving adults, and she explored new roles as a workshop leader and houseparent. She continued in those roles after her move to Lukas, and when I met her there she was hard at work on a painting (Brett, 2002).

A commitment to vocation means that each community must accept, even celebrate, the decisions of individuals whose vocations lead them out of the community. 'The gold moves on and the dross remains,' observed Dorothy Day ironically. The 'young co-worker' programme run by Camphill, which attracts wanderlusting twenty-year-olds from around the world, means that dozens of people each year re-enter mainstream society with new ways of caring for others and honouring the environment. In other cases, veteran community leaders feel called to share their gifts in new contexts. 'It can be a wonderful thing,' observed Helen Zipperlen of Camphill Kimberton Hills, 'when people ... want to go off and do their own thing. When people used to come to me and say, 'I've absolutely had it! I'm going to leave,' I said, 'I'm not interested [in your criticism of Camphill] ... I'm interested in where you're going and what you're going to do. Sit down and tell me about it.' (Zipperlen, 2005)

Not infrequently, acceptance of individual vocations can lead to a 'revolving door' phenomenon. It is not unheard of for the entire membership of a Catholic Worker house to turn over within a year, leaving newcomers with little sense of tradition. Even the 'mother house' in New York City has had such years (Murray, 1990). Some Workers put a good spin on this by saying that instability 'makes us very flexible,' but it is draining to have to reinvent community over and over again. Other communities, including Camphill Village Minnesota, suffer from a steady decline in overall membership. This can make it hard to celebrate the new life directions of long-time co-workers with skills that are hard to replace. One Camphiller told me that while her own decision to move on was embraced, the community had a 'wrenching' struggle when another person wanted to pursue more schooling. But 'holding on to everybody you've got in desperation,' she reflected, is 'not going to be very attractive to people either.' (Anonymous, 2002)

One antidote to the revolving door is to create more opportunities for 'extended community' members who do not live full-time in community to participate in shared life. At many Catholic Worker houses, long-term neighbourhood activists initiate short-term live-in volunteers into the Catholic Worker vision. Another approach has been pioneered by Wisconsin's Community Homestead, which was founded by friends who had grown up at Camphill Copake. Seeking to blend their experiences in and out of community, they created a model in which many co-workers are employed full or part-time outside the community. 'I think everybody needs their own individuality,' Sheila Russell explained to me. The professional identities of individuals are supported at Community Homestead 'because that's part of them.' (Russell, 2002) Community life, added Richard Elmquist, 'can be a really scary thing ... if you're either in or you're out.' Communities that require a one hundred per cent commitment prevent many people from becoming involved at all (Elmquist, 2002). Allowing more flexibility also keeps Community Homestead in touch with professional colleagues who maintain conventional lifestyles.

Just as attention to individual vocation ensures that people do not have to choose between community life and their own identities, so the embrace of family life opens community to people who do not wish to sacrifice other formative relationships. The promise of Brook Farm, wrote Elizabeth Peabody, was that it would preserve 'the sacredness of the family' that had been violated by other communities (Peabody, 1841). Dorothy Day affirmed that 'the normal life in this world today and always is that of the family,' and that families might be 'Catholic Workers' simply by taking a single person into their homes (Day, 1963). Camphill has made the family a building block of its communal structure: each village is organised into distinct households, in which long-term houseparents (often a couple with children) anchor the life of disabled villagers and short-term volunteers.

Each community has honed distinct ways of making room for families. The Associationists imagined that they would liberate women by establishing communal kitchens and nurseries, but in practice most parents preferred to care for their own children and eat some meals at a family table. Many Catholic Worker families reconfigure communal space with each new stage of their children's development. Camphill parents, likewise, insist on having meals that are just for the family, or incorporate other community members into their family rituals. 'If we were reading stories in the evenings,' said Roswitha Imegwu, who grew up at one Camphill and raised her children at another, 'anyone else who wanted to share in that story could do that.' (Imegwu, 2002) Community parents have also found that children keep them connected to the larger society. 'Children are great community builders,' noted Catholic Worker mother (and grandmother) Willa Bickham. 'If you have a child, you go walking around the neighbourhood and talk to everybody.' (Bickham, 2000)

Camphill parents identify both benefits and challenges in raising children in community. Many appreciate the opportunity to live alongside others who share their values. 'We don't have to explain why we don't watch TV to our children,' noted Sonja Adams (Adams, 2005). They value the daily interaction with people of diverse cultures and abilities, and praise their children for the heightened 'consciousness or empathy for people' that results (Hobson, 2002). 'The children ... learn to read human beings pretty well,' said Diedra Heitzman (Heitzman, 2005).

Community parents place an even higher value on their communities' flexible approach to time with children. When I asked Mark Hobson about his experiences of parenting, he quoted an interview with John Lennon. 'He was saying, it's crap what they say about quality time. Children want quantity ... They want to know you're around.' (Hobson, 2002) Many community parents shudder at the thought of full-time day care, but they are equally troubled by the sexist implications of having a father who is always away at work and a mother who is always at home (Potter, 2000). Diedra Heitzman, who came to Camphill Kimberton Hills when her oldest child was six, found it a 'huge relief' to escape the isolation of being a stay-at-home mother without losing daily connection to the children (Heitzman, 2005). Peter Madsen, who cared for the garden at Camphill Copake, spoke glowingly of the pleasures of having one of his sons out in the fields with him and his work crew. 'Though it doesn't make my work any easier really, it's very nice to have them with me and seeing what Pop is doing, understanding what work is, learning how to help ... My favourite moments are when he just plays alongside and does his thing in the midst of us doing our thing ... This is archetypal, you know.' (Madsen, 2002)

Though community parents are pleased with what community brings to their children, they also stress the way family practices of nurture can infuse an entire community with nurturing care. 'If I'm in that caring, fatherly mode,' explained the Lukas Community's Mark Hobson, 'then I can also care for other people.' (Hobson, 2002) Families can break down the barriers between those who 'serve' and those who are 'served,' an important function insofar as the goal of Camphill and Catholic Worker communities is not so much to 'serve' the homeless or the developmentally disabled as to build shared community. After the birth of her first child at Camphill Copake, Laura Briggs came to rely on an older villager. 'You couldn't ask for a better nanny,' says Laura. 'She was just a natural ... If I was busy cooking, she would go and change the diapers, which she loved to do ... Being able to mother children was something she really longed to do and was never able to ... It was such a wonderful thing for her and so appreciated by us.' (Briggs, 2000)

Still, parenting in community is not all sweetness and light. 'What's most rewarding [about parenting in community is] that I get to be with my kids so much,' mused Peter Madsen. 'What's most challenging [is] that I don't get enough time with my kids.' (Madsen, 2002) The idiosyncratic rhythms of community life make it difficult for community parents to measure the quality and quantity of their family time against that of their mainstream peers. Some find that community pushes them toward more gender balance in their parenting style, as the masculine sphere of work is not separate from the feminine sphere of home. But it can have the opposite effect. Before founding Community Homestead, Christine and Richard Elmquist both had careers and 'tag-teamed the children.' Once they were in a community that did not separate work and home, Christine reports, 'I gathered up the children and released Richard to the community.' (Elmquist, 2002) This pattern may account for the traditional gender roles present in many Camphill communities.

A special set of challenges awaits those parents who do not begin to live in community until their children are school age or older. 'It's a real soul movement to open up,' explained Mark Hobson of Lukas Community, 'to let someone share your private space.' (Hobson, 2002) Sylvia Bausman came to Camphill Copake as a single mother with four young sons, and she reflected that when she placed her children 'into this new pond,' they were 'not in paradise. They [got] initiated, probably in ways that wouldn't have happened so soon if we had been a nuclear family.' (Bausman, 2002) Similarly, when Melanie Sabra came to Camphill Beaver Run, she expected that community life would be as wonderful for her nine-year-old daughter as for herself. The reality was more challenging, in part because most of the other co-worker kids had been born at Beaver Run and already had a well-established sense of cohesion. In response to these challenges, Melanie is clear that her daughter is still her top priority. 'In our busy community life,' she observed, 'one needs to consciously make time to be with one's own children.' (Sabra, 2005)

The key to a successful blend of family and community is to give each family the space it needs to grow — to 'make room' literally as well as figuratively. When I asked Willa Bickham and Brendan Walsh about raising their daughter at the Catholic Worker, they drew a diagram to show how their living space had evolved over the years (Walsh, 2000; Bickham, 2000). At Camphill Village Minnesota, the newest residential building was designed so that half of the upper floor could function as a distinct family apartment, less accessible to other household members. The Lukas Community took a further step toward family privacy by including a small kitchen within each family apartment. This gives each family a place for private breakfasts, or meals on their days off, though they are still expected to share a large daily dinner with the entire household. The arrangement also prevents an awkward situation that can be observed at many Camphills: parents allow their teenage children to prepare their own meals if they don't wish to eat with the entire household, but since they have no separate space to do so, they can be seen eating their private meals just feet away from the large common table. Still, the co-workers at Lukas definitely see their own arrangement as a trade-off. Nicola Hobson, who had lived in Camphill before coming to Lukas, said that, 'I don't know which one is better. If I ask my selfish one, I say this is great. If I think of the whole place, I think living closer together would be more fulfilling.' (Hobson, 2002)

Indeed, a necessary complement to the practice of 'making room' for families is a willingness to let the pendulum swing back toward more shared space. Camphill Minnesota's recently completed community centre, for example, includes a large dining area where the entire village shares one meal a week. Regula Stolz, who has observed three generations of parents during her time in Camphill, expressed mixed feelings about the trend toward more private time for families. Much of the change, she noted, was in response to reports from children who had grown up in Camphill, some (not all) of whom 'remember it very painfully.' (Stolz, 2002) For nearly all Camphillers, this awareness of hard lessons learned tempers any nostalgia about the 'good old days,' even as new and old co-workers are concerned not to let the pendulum swing too far in the direction of family privatisation.

Many Camphills are also learning to embrace the gifts of elders as fully as they've embraced those of children. Since Camphill was planted on this continent in the 1960s, the people who arrived as young co-workers in the early years are now reaching retirement age. As they discern what this might mean, they can learn from a wise generation of elders like Frank and Dorothy LeBar, who came to Camphill Copake after raising their children. Community life, Frank told me, 'is a great way to grow older, because one is constantly stimulated.' (LeBar, 2002) From the other side of the generational spectrum, Peter Madsen, father of two preschool sons, said that community life has taught him that 'development is eternal ... I have really gleaned that in a quite intimate way from having witnessed so many older or elderly people in Camphill, developing so fruitfully into their ripe old age.' (Madsen, 2002) 'I think any community that's really going to work,' Frank concluded, 'has to have the whole generations. You have to have babies coming along, and you've got to have some old folks like me and Dorothy.' (LeBar, 2002) Communities that find this balance offer a powerful witness in a society that segregates children in schools and day care centres, adults at overworked offices, and elders in nursing homes.

A third practice common to all three movements is that of hon-ouring diverse spiritual paths. All three movements I've studied understand themselves as Christian. Both Dorothy Day and Karl König were devoted to Jesus' parable of the sheep and the goats, with its lesson that 'inasmuch as ye have done it unto the least of these my brethren, ye have done it unto me.' But, with a few exceptions, their communities have not expected every member to share a Christian identity. As König explained: 'it is not our task to propagate [Steiner's] teachings; our endeavours are to help and to heal.' (König, 1993: 35)

All three movements have been pioneers in ecumenical and interfaith dialogue. The Associationists believed that the practice of gospel ideals would dissolve the artificial divisions of creed, and took pride in the presence of Jews, Catholics and freethinkers at their communities. Dorothy Day is known for the orthodoxy of her Catholic faith, but from the beginning the Catholic Worker has stood in solidarity with Jews and learned from Gandhi's nonviolence. Camphill has an even more intimate relationship with Judaism, insofar as many of its founders were Viennese Jews who had converted to the anthroposophy of Rudolf Steiner, and it draws as well on the Moravian tradition of Jan Comenius and Nikolas von Zinzendorf. When Camphill first arrived in North America, most of the villagers were children of Jewish parents, and a secular Jewish culture is tangibly present at Copake.

Many of the Camphillers I interviewed identified themselves as spiritual seekers or eclectics who were drawn first to the tangible practice of Camphill life. At Camphill Village Minnesota, Trudy Pax told me that she had 'visited a lot of communities where I liked the theory but not the practice. At Camphill, I didn't like the theory but the practice really worked.' (Pax, 2000) Tom Farr and Mary Davis testified that life in Camphill had deepened their practice of A Course in Miracles. Forgiving oneself and others is the heart of A Course in Miracles, Tom explained, and 'everyday Camphill provides another opportunity to forgive.' (Farr, 2000) Mary added that the course encouraged constant questioning, 'how I think about things,' and Camphill was like a 'huge mirror' that helped her see new things about herself (Davis, 2002).

Other Camphillers told stories of how they had initially found the theory of anthroposophy unappealing, but embraced it when they saw its daily embodiment. When Jan Zuzalek arrived at Camphill, she said to herself: 'I'm never going to join anything.' She had been drawn to Buddhism, but gradually she came to accept that 'for some reason I'm not in a Buddhist community.

And I do want a spiritual life.' Practising anthroposophical meditations, and becoming a Camphill community member, allowed Jan to deepen her spirituality and sense of connection to other Camphillers (Zuzalek, 2002).

Interestingly, all three movements have also allowed individuals of the 'dominant' tradition to follow wayward spiritual paths. Some Associationists became Spiritualists; others Roman Catholics. Camphill has encouraged its members to explore Buddhist, Jewish and Native American wisdom, sometimes from within the framework of Steiner's anthroposophy, but sometimes not. The Catholic Worker's emphasis on liturgy has led some members into Eastern Orthodoxy, even as others have repudiated what they see as the sexist and homophobic practices of Christianity. One Catholic Worker observed that, 'We've had people leave the Catholic Church. We've had people become serious Quakers while they've been involved with us; we've had people leave the Quakers ... If anybody is alive spiritually, they're searching.' (McKenna,1988) Similarly, many of the people I interviewed responded to transcripts by musing on their continued spiritual development and the fact that, 'you can't stick the same finger in the river twice.' (Sersch, 2005; Kavanagh, 2005; Smith, 2005)

Community life is conducive to spiritual searching because it forces people to put their ideals into practice. All Christians talk about welcoming the stranger and sharing their possessions; community provides concrete ways of doing so. Once immersed in this 'practice' of Christianity, some communitarians discard Christian creeds and rituals as pale substitutes for a fully Christian lifestyle; others become increasingly attached to the rituals; still others are drawn to traditions that offer different paths to the same practices. In almost every case, the spiritual journey leads the individual to make connections beyond the boundaries of the community, allowing communal ideas to diffuse into the larger society.

None of the practices I have described is without cost. They enhance shared life and draw vital energies out of the community. Most nineteenth-century Associations folded within a decade as a result. The Catholic Worker and Camphill have proved more enduring, but both are characterised by revolving door memberships and economic precariousness. If longevity were their only goal, communities would do well to build higher walls (literal and figurative) around themselves.

What Catholic Workers, Camphillers and Associationists have done instead is to remain open to death and resurrection. The Associationists first imagined they would change the world in a few years, but eventually concluded that their communities had 'tried to live before [their] proper time, and, of course, must die and be born again.' (Chase, 1857: 126–27) Dorothy Day affirmed that, 'We may seem to be constantly failing ... But unless the seed falls into the earth and die, there is no harvest.' ('Aims and Purposes' 1940)

Though the Camphill Movement has seen few communities close, its founding experience opened it to death and resurrection. As war refugees and near victims of the Nazi genocide, Karl König and his friends doubted that they would ever return home. In this 'boat of loneliness; a ship without a destination,' König thought of the future with despair: 'Will the fragments of my existence be put together again so that they may build a new frame?' More than a personal crisis, the war marked the death of the cosmopolitan European ideal they had been living in Vienna. König envisioned Camphill as a resurrected form of everything they had lost. 'Could we not take a morsel of the true European destiny and make it into a seed so that some of its real task might be preserved?' (König, 1993: 13–14)

This formative experience has made co-workers attentive to the villagers' experiences of 'exile' and social marginalisation. In addition, many Camphills have faced their own 'near death' experiences. In 1978 Camphill Beaver Run was audited by officials from the state of New York, who decided that they would no longer provide funding for children from New York to live at Beaver Run. Since New Yorkers accounted for about two fifths of the village's students, the Camphillers briefly imagined they would have to close. Instead, recalled Ursel Pietzner, 'We decided we would fight.' 'Affronted' by negative comments from the auditors, the Camphillers wanted, in Bernie Wolf's words, to 'establish some credibility.' In order to gain state approval in Pennsylvania, they sent most American co-workers who had bachelor's degrees to nearby West Chester University for special education certification. This increased workloads for everyone, but it was also an opportunity for the entire community to rally. 'It was very exciting, dramatic' to experience an idealistic community in conflict with a bureaucracy, recalled Wolf, while Pietzner described the episode as an 'inwardly and spiritually strong time.' (Pietzner, 2005; Wolf, 2005)

One consequence was that Beaver Run forged new connections to individuals and organisations beyond the village. Rallying to Beaver Run's defence, parents took on a more important role in the community. And the Camphillers who pursued special education certification began building connections with local professors. Today these connections are bearing fruit in Beaver Run's effort to provide formal college credit for its curative education seminar. 'The only way to allow our work to influence the work that goes on around us in the disabilities field,' explained Guy Alma, 'is for people to know us, to visit us, to study us, to understand us, to train with us, to build partnerships with us. There's a growing realisation that we'd like to have an effect on the outside world.' (Alma, 2005; Goeschel, 2005)

A similar crisis came to Beaver Run's neighbour, Kimberton Hills, a decade later. Several officials arrived from the state capital, demanding that the 'facility' be properly licensed. Helen Zipperlen, then one of the community's leaders, responded feistily. 'As far as we know,' she told the licensers, 'we're not a facility.' She showed them the community's files, in which 'villagers' and 'co-workers' (terms Helen prefers not to use) were intermingled. To Helen's surprise, Kimberton's board agreed to resist the pressure for formal licensure, and to this day the community maintains its independence by 'living up to pretty high standards' and fundraising to ensure that persons without private wealth are still able to live in the village (Zipperlen, 2005; Heitzman, 2005).

Kimberton's response to the challenge might seem the polar opposite of Beaver Run's. But in both cases, a challenge from the larger society forced the community to find creative ways of engaging that society. Kimberton may have refused to be licensed, but it embraced the opportunity to engage in constructive dialogue with the licensers. 'They would come down,' recalled Helen Zipperlen, 'and we would be very hospitable and offer coffee and walk around. They would usually depart totally confused.' With the support of a sympathetic official, Helen got a federal grant to write a report on non-bureaucratic strategies for keeping people safe. Inspectors, Helen insisted, are 'never the bad guy. These are human beings trying to do a job, and you can help them by being challenging.' (Zipperlen, 2005; Zipperlen & O'Brien, 1993)

Few people at Kimberton Hills feared that their conflict with the state would end their life as a community. But it forced them to confront their own death as a theoretical possibility, and at least Helen found this to be a good thing. Again and again, she asked other Camphillers to think about what they would do if the government forcibly took away all the persons with special needs. Would they go their separate ways, or would they find other ways to keep the Camphill spirit alive? Helen has never been fully satisfied with the responses to her question, but she relishes asking it. 'I'm never happy,' she said, 'when the question isn't there.' (Zipperlen, 2005)

A similar question is inescapably present at Camphill Village Minnesota, which has experienced a gradual decline in its population of both co-workers and villagers. Vacant houses often stand as visible reminders of the possibility that the community might not live forever. As the 'carrying' members of the community (that is, seasoned long-term co-workers) grow older, they have asked hard questions about what might happen if younger people do not arrive to take their places. The community has increasingly relied on the Camphill Foundation for assistance in recruiting and retaining co-workers, and the board has discussed everything from the possibility of raising an endowment large enough to sustain the entire community to the question of how to tell when it is time to die (Steinrueck, 2002).

It is significant that this 'near death' experience reflects

Camphill Minnesota's effort to touch the world. Camphill Minnesota has trouble recruiting co-workers because it is far from the centres of the anthroposophical subculture. Other Camphills attract families because of their proximity to thriving Waldorf schools, while Minnesotans must choose between home-schooling, rural public schools, and a theologically conservative Lutheran school. Cultural opportunities that other Camphillers take for granted require a two-and-a-half hour drive to the Twin Cities. Yet the isolation of Camphill Minnesota has forced the village to forge creative partnerships with local farmers, who are now beginning to use Camphill's processing kitchen to diversify their own enterprises. The Camphillers have even had some interesting contacts with the local Amish community. One can often see an Amish youngster or two hunting the pocket gophers that bedevil Camphill's fields.

All these challenges, says Beaver Run's Claus Sproll, reflect the fact that Camphill is now entering its third generation — something that rarely happens to a community movement. 'Now we are pioneering,' says Claus, 'and we have to redefine community.' The myriad changes underway may help Camphill avoid the fate of Shakers and other communal groups that responded to generational transitions by withdrawing from the larger society. 'The skin has got to be broken open,' Claus explained. 'The outreach and connecting [is] the health-giving thing.' (Sproll, 2005)

By facing death, communities plant seeds for the future. Too often, activists assume that we must either work 'inside' or 'outside' the system — either withdrawing into countercultural ghettoes or participating fully in conventional political and corporate institutions. Camphill, the Catholic Worker and Associationism point to a third way. It is possible to experiment with alternative social arrangements while maintaining a constructive dialogue with our neighbours. In a world threatened by ecological catastrophe, persistent poverty and a troubling new imperialism, such communities have a vital role to play in helping us all envision a new society.[5]

Notes

1. Camphill Special School at Beaver Run, Pennsylvania, for example, drew several of its early co-workers from Antioch College's cooperative programme, which like the Fellowship for Intentional Community was the brainchild of Arthur Morgan. Another intriguing connection is the work of Richard Gregg, a leading advocate of active nonviolence and intentional community in North America. In addition to spending years with Mohandas Gandhi in India, Gregg took the course in biodynamic agriculture with Ehrenfried Pfeiffer in Pennsylvania (Kosek, 2009: 224).

2. My thanks to Liturgical Press for granting permission for me to adapt portions of *Touching the World* for this chapter (McKanan, 2007).

3. Those who wish to learn more about the Catholic Worker would do well to begin with Rosalie Riegle Troester's magisterial oral history, *Voices from the Catholic Worker* (1993), or with the writings of founder Dorothy Day, particularly *The Long Loneliness* (1997). My own study, *The Catholic Worker after Dorothy* (2008) is the only book to attempt a (very brief) narrative of the movement's entire 75-year history; those who wish more detail about the early years should consult Mel Piehl's *Breaking Bread* (1982). The outstanding anthologies edited by Coy (1988) and Thorn et al. (2001) do for the Catholic Worker what the present volume does for Camphill, weaving together the perspectives of community members and scholars.

4. The definitive study of the Associationist movement in the United States is Guarneri (1991). Those who wish to know more about the Fourierist theories that inspired (and irritated) Americans Fourierists should consult Beecher (1986). Among Fourierist communities, Brook Farm has attracted more scholarly attention than all the others combined; the most recent general history is Delano (2004). Readers who wish for a broader picture of intentional community in the United States should consult Pitzer (1997), the website directory sponsored by the Fellowship for Intentional Community, and Timothy Miller's forthcoming encyclopaedia.

5. This chapter is dedicated to the memory of Trudy Pax and Jan Zuzalek and their decades of devotion to Camphill Village Minnesota.

5. Creative Living: Inside a Community for Children with Autism

Judith Shapiro is a post-doctoral resident child therapist at Kaiser Permanente Hospital in Richmond, California. She feels privileged to provide therapy and programme development for autistic children. This chapter draws on the findings of the author's doctoral dissertation 'Creative Living: Inside a Community for Children with Autism' submitted to the Wright Institute Clinical Psychology Graduate School, Berkeley, California (2009).

> Our task as educators will not be to help the child to become 'normal,' but to remove some of the rocks and boulders that lie on his path of development.
> (Weihs, 1987: 5)

Dr Thomas Weihs, a Camphill founder, asserts that the goal of education is to honour and facilitate each child's individual growth process (Weihs, 1987). It is an ambitious and process-oriented goal that contrasts the predominant outcome-based goals of many programmes for children with special needs.

A fundamental premise of Camphill is that the children are honoured as equal and valuable members of the community (Jackson, 2006). Children or 'pupils' live among aides or 'co-workers' along with 'house parents' or 'house coordinators.' (Hart & Monteux, 2004: 69) Some children go home to their families in the evenings or on weekends, but all are members of houses in which they eat meals, engage in social activities and often have independent responsibilities. According to the Camphill Rudolf Steiner Schools Provision for Autistic Spectrum Disorders (2007), the communities offer a number of elements that benefit autistic children specifically. This document states that Camphill offers autistic children a sense of security and predictability through regularly scheduled activities and meals; reduces anxiety by incorporating relaxation and non-directive therapeutic interventions; and incorporates sensory integration throughout the daily activities as well as in specialised treatments.

In this idiographic, phenomenological study, I joined one Camphill community as a participant-observer. I stayed in a house with twelve staff and seven children for three weeks, engaging in house activities, classes, therapies and festivals. The experience revealed that the culture of Camphill does not manifest as a collection of values or cognitive constructs. Rather, the therapeutic elements of the community are perceptible on sensory, emotional and relational levels. The Camphill community is an alternative society for both staff and children. Its members embrace pragmatic and abstract aims of daily living and of spiritual growth. The creative lifestyle of Camphill offers us an opportunity to challenge assumptions about normality, education, experiential learning and nonverbal life.

Five themes

Five interacting dynamics — Time, Nature, Spirituality, Community and Learning — emerge from the thematic analysis of my journal (a record of daily events and my reactions to them), conversations with staff, theoretical information imparted by members of the community, and post-travel reflection. Each category describes a dynamic that uniquely contributes to the quality of life at Camphill, and each one is crucial in creating a therapeutic or facilitating atmosphere. Together, these elements interact to create a current that flows through the community.

1. TIME

The dynamic of time is a critical element of the environment in this community. Like the others, it manifests as a psychological and sensory entity. Many children on the autism spectrum have a strong need to know what is going to happen next, and they feel overwhelmed by the choices they face in unstructured time. The schedule is designed to help the children feel comfortable, and to do so it must be adopted by the entire community.

The rhythm at Camphill is created in accordance with its members' physical and communal nature. Time is structured to honour human cycles of eating, resting and moving, with particular attention to circadian rhythms. One hour is dedicated for each meal. Exercise occurs after dinner. The blocks of time are directly derived from nature, in contrast to the blocks of time that are artificially constructed in a business day. Within the schedules, individuals have the freedom to respond to their own physical and sensory cues and move through the day at their own speed. And, interestingly, the community's rhythm interacts with that of the individual. Costa and Walter (2006) describe how the intention at Camphill is to set a rhythm through 'routine' and 'ritual' and to subtly break the structure by adding variation that children can handle (2006: 42). Pupils — and staff — follow a set, precise schedule. Within this structure the pupils are free to function at their own pace, with a supporting co-worker facilitating their movement through transitions.

While co-workers engage with the pupils' experience of time, there is a significant lack of personal time for them. Their day begins when they wake the children at 7 a.m. and help them get ready for the day. It ends when they finish helping the children fall asleep at 9 p.m. And of course, as one staff member says, you cannot tell a child living in your home that your shift is over. Co-workers might have a few hours break during the day. After hours, night nurses spend the night in each house, but a co-worker is on duty in case of an emergency.

The quality of time at Camphill is a complex combination of structure, openness and movement. It accommodates the needs of pupils, allowing them freedom to move at their own pace within a predictable schedule. This quality is facilitative to pupils, but it may also compromise the personal time and self-care of staff. However, the days feel long and filled with richness. The difference is perceptible when I take day trips to a local city, and when I visit both urban and rural towns upon my departure. The duration of my visit to Camphill feels much longer than three weeks would have felt in another context. This contrast is due to the powerful time dynamic of the community's atmosphere.

2. NATURE

Nature is the second indispensable element of this community. It is a central feature of the shared, external environment. It is also honoured as an individualised, internal experience of sensory processes. For small people, physical environments appear magnified. A creek can feel like a river, and a schoolyard can become a universe. To a child with autism, the sensory elements of these environments are even more pronounced. Yet it is not necessary to magnify the elements of the environment of Camphill in order to imagine its impact on the children. They are strikingly refreshing, soothing and welcoming. The physical environment of Camphill, both indoors and outdoors, is so pronounced that I feel physiological shock upon exiting and re-entering. I express my awe at the impact of the natural environment to a staff member. He agrees, and even suggests that the natural environment is the most significant element of healing in the community.

The community is situated twenty minutes outside an industrial city. The land itself is comprised of forests and hills dotted with trees. Inside are horse stables, streams, and farms with cows and produce. The narrow paved roads are wide enough for a car, a horse, a bicycle or a skateboard — and two of the three if all parties are vigilant. The school community is comprised of two estates. Each has a school, playgrounds and community buildings. Because pupils maintain the same classroom for the duration of their schooling, some children ride a small school bus back and forth. An able-bodied person can walk around one estate in five minutes and between the two in twenty.

When they leave their houses and go to school, the children are not confined within classrooms. Nature is incorporated into the school day. Second grade begins with a walk through a forest. I am moved to see a nonverbal, quiet child reach over and pick leaves as he walks. He brings each treasure of nature to his ear, rubs it around, and throws it to the ground. After watching him for a while, I pick up the same type of leaf and rub it next to my ear. I hear a soft, soothing sound, like a whisper. I am struck by this child's brilliance. It would never have occurred to me to explore nature in this way. The setting, and the use of it, gives him ample opportunities to explore the world through sound.

A number of unique therapies use nature as a source of healing. These therapies help children to feel comfortable in their bodies, as well as in their physical and social environments. One such therapy is horse riding. This activity incorporates exercise, deep pressure, balance, movement, and connection to an animal in an outdoor setting. The riding therapist finds that children who are lethargic or reluctant to participate in their daily routine are particularly motivated for riding.

She notes that she sees less aggression in the children than other staff who observe them in different contexts. Sitting bareback on a horse, I see children switch from anxious and irritable to calm and quiet within a matter of moments. Finally, this therapist notes that some children have a relationship with the horse whereas others appear to treat it as an object. Unsure of how the therapist would categorise one child, I watch him cling to the horse after the lesson in a full body hug. I wonder whether some children's ways of relating to this majestic animal might simply be less visible.

Perhaps unsurprisingly, due to exposure to animal training, this riding teacher uses the most behaviourist interventions I witness at Camphill. She tells children, 'pat the horse' or 'close your mouth' (personal communication, June 29, 2008) and leads the horse to trot (a highly desirable activity) when they do so. I learn that according to principles of anthroposophy, keeping one's mouth closed aids in balance and centres a person's body.

Thus, behavioural goals seem to align with the greater goals of holistic health and sensory regulation.

3. SPIRITUALITY

Spirituality manifests within this community as an ethos rather than as a dogma. Prescribed spiritual practices and philosophies are present, but they seem to provide a frame or a backdrop for the expression of core humanistic values. Because a large portion of the community is nonverbal, the spiritual element must be felt, rather than understood linguistically. Through their spiritual mindset, the community members embody and transmit the values of respect, trust and self-discovery. In addition, a number of unique therapies offer pupils a means of accessing the inner balance that is the goal of many spiritual traditions.

In this setting, spiritual beliefs and traditions are neither uniform nor based in a single branch of Christianity. One staff member suggests that the community offers exposure to the Christian religion while supporting other faiths. She notes that the widening demographic of community members has increased multicultural awareness and sensitivity. For example, after a religious service in celebration of St Johns Day, pupils and staff participate in a variety of cultural dances including the 'horah,' which is traditionally danced at Jewish weddings. Other faiths are not taught, but their observance is welcome. Conversations with staff also reveal that this community's spiritual practices do not necessarily stem directly from Steiner's beliefs but more from those of Camphill's founders. For example, one service incorporates the signs of the zodiac, as König referenced them in a play about St John. Steiner's own spiritual beliefs, stemming from a number of eastern traditions such as Hinduism and Buddhism, are also accepted and taught to varying degrees (Monteux, 2006).

The spiritual ethos, to a profound extent, is connected to the celebration of nature at Camphill. Community members describe a pantheistic sense that each child is a manifestation of God. They emphasise the unaffected, untouchable spiritual aspect of each child, and they do not claim power over the child's esoteric nature. They demonstrate the belief that spiritual life is within and accessible to the children. Their attitude of reverence and respect is transmitted to the children.

4. COMMUNITY

Community life is the unique contribution of König, Camphill's founder, to Steiner's model of curative education. As such, community is the defining feature of Camphill's identity. This element is emphasised in the mission of Camphill and it comes alive for its residents. Camphill does not feel like a residential treatment centre but rather like a community dedicated to people with special needs. The people without special needs make a significant commitment to share in the lifestyle of the community rather than separate themselves from it. Like the pupils, they also contract to live a new way, by the values of this society. As a teacher states, 'People meet the needs of the community and their needs are met by the community.' (personal communication, June 21, 2008) Although some staff members are officially employed, most live in exchange for food, accommodation and training in curative education.

A teacher states that the 'gift of Waldorf is a feeling of belonging.' (personal communication, June 22, 2008) She notes that as children have one teacher throughout their education, the teacher-pupil relationship becomes a source of deep connection and personal growth. Camphill also offers pupils ample opportunities to feel a sense of belonging in social activities such as song night and teen gatherings ('camp-chill'). In addition, children have roles within the house, taking on responsibilities to the best of their abilities.

Living in community is a far deeper and more complex social experience than what might be learned in a social skills group. Children with a variety of challenges learn to live together. Watching and helping each other, they must call upon their inner resources to cope with people who are as unpredictable as they are. One teacher suggests that children with social and emotional challenges thrive when they can help pupils with physical disabilities. Another observes that children with Asperger's disorder learn to be more flexible in such a varied environment. These interactions occur throughout the day and night. In this way, Camphill is a social learning 'playground' for children who might otherwise become isolated — often with videogames or television — at the end of the school day. Living in close proximity with so many people is quite challenging, but it is a powerful means of learning to be a social human being.

5. LEARNING

Learning is the final element that contributes to the environment of Camphill. In an educational atmosphere that honours experiential learning, staff members study curative education while learning by engaging with pupils in the moments of everyday life. They are informed by personal philosophies and theories outside of anthroposophy, and they exhibit both resistance to change and an attitude of ongoing learning.

Many people seem to embrace a non-pathological stance in conceptualising the children's presentations. A teacher and a therapist each target emotional states rather than developmental disorders as the source of their behaviours. In fact, one teacher argues that many people confuse anxiety with autism. He describes instances when pupils refuse to attend class, become violent, or remove their clothing in a public setting. In these examples, he points to anxiety as the culprit rather than autism or oppositional defiance. This subtle but important emphasis may stem from a multidimensional understanding of human processes. It may stem from reverence for the children as whole spiritual beings, or from a personal sense of the child's integrity.

Many children at Camphill receive therapies that are not unique to anthroposophy. Sensory integration, massage therapy, play therapy, art therapy and riding therapy have theoretical bases both within and outside of curative education. A number of therapists supplement their training by learning non-anthroposophical approaches, either prior to coming to

Camphill or after joining the community. Therapists may seek further education in order to become eligible for jobs outside of anthroposophical communities, or they may simply wish to incorporate new ideas.

At Camphill, change is met with openness as well as with resistance. One therapist makes a case for children to be able to bring special objects from their family's homes that are made of non-organic materials. She tells me she had to advocate for plastic toys to be allowed in the community. Despite tension around modifying traditions, individuals demonstrate an openness to learn. The massage therapist exhibits a sense of awe as she describes experiences in which she learns from the children, and she describes her work as a 'two way learning process.' (personal communication, June 2, 2008) She accepts that one will always make mistakes, and embraces the critical challenge of learning from them.

Particularly in schools, narrow-minded thinking on the part of adults can cause children to acquire reputations that they internalise. At Camphill, one way that teachers, therapists and co-workers maintain an open mind about the children is through a meeting called a Child Study. In this meeting, a pupil's co-worker, house coordinator, teachers and therapists meet to discuss their impressions of the child. They share insights and seek to create a set of consistent interventions. Professionals who witness the children across contexts, and engage with them in such distinct ways, have an incredible opportunity to learn from one another. If such meetings are conducted with genuine openness, the potential for appreciating the multifaceted dimensions of the children is quite powerful.

For children as well as staff, the most important life lesson is to engage with one's own development and to learn how to live with others. Taken together, these different philosophies and attitudes depict a simple and powerful goal of education. The goal is to learn to love the world, others and oneself within it. To thrive in these ways is not easy, nor is the end result static. It would be impossible, and irrelevant by these standards, to evaluate a child's progress by comparing him or her to other children, to a standardised target, or to a statistic.

Strengths and weaknesses

Each dynamic of Camphill's environment has advantages and disadvantages. The schedule of Camphill helps children to balance their physiological needs and its structure makes time less emotionally overwhelming. The co-workers' lack of personal time brings exhaustion and burnout into the shared environment. Spirituality at Camphill, embracing respect and honouring differences, can increase self-esteem and bring courage to individuals who are often under-appreciated in the greater society. Specific spiritual practices, such as services that reference Christianity, may be uncomfortable for children who come from families with very different traditions. The appreciation of nature, both within and outside of each individual, offers healthy sensory experience and makes exploration possible. Restrictions on what is brought into the community may limit children's exposure to elements of modern culture.

Experiential learning unleashes unlimited growth and discovery. Among the more rigid community members, the prescribed practices of anthroposophy may leave insufficient space for change and new ideas. Finally, community life offers children an opportunity to experience self-worth and connection in a way that is unmatched in an individualistic culture. And yet for children who are happy when alone, the shared living situation and the transmission of anxiety among community members may be too much. The impact of these elements is surely unique to each resident of Camphill. Moreover, it is not the aim of this hermeneutical study to qualify or measure the value of these dynamics. Rather, as a participant in the community, I explore the ways that I experience the tensions inherent in each. The five dynamics allow me to see new parts of myself. In a dance of solitude and company, structure and openness, activity and slowness, I experience the community as challenging and inspiring.

The dynamics of time, nature, spirituality, community and learning interact with one another to create the environment at Camphill. Time is structured according to natural human rhythms, and within the structure is space for the unfolding of relationships. Nature and spirituality are deeply intertwined, as the community's spiritual system is based on reverence for the divine inner nature of each individual. Community life feeds this universal respect, as pupils can experience themselves as worthwhile contributors to a common good. Community life is contained in a shared schedule, a shared sense of time, and shared priorities. Learning is based upon spiritual principles that emphasise the importance of nature and community as well as the rhythm of human development. Finally, the experiential emphasis at Camphill asks that the residents spend time engaging with community life, nature and spirituality in everyday moments.

Thus, the five elements cannot be thought of as individual parts that are mutually exclusive. Rather, they together constitute one larger dynamic that comprises the overall atmosphere and that can be experienced in a sensory way. Time seems to feel fluid rather than abrupt, and the natural surroundings feel refreshing and crisp. The emphasis on experiential learning keeps residents engaged in the present moment. The values of the community which are rooted in a philosophy that is grounded in sensory awareness are descriptive of how one should lead his or her life in order to develop as a whole, thriving spiritual being.

Discussion

Camphill is not a school. It is society. The pupils' presentations are no more distinctive than the community in which they live. Camphill embodies a vision that is abstract and concrete, material and spiritual. Staff members dedicate their time and energy to upholding this vision by creating and living in a new paradigm. The boundary in which healing takes place is not a frame around an adult and child, but rather it is a frame around an entire community. The result is a shared reality for pupils and caretakers, one with a unique sense of time, nature, spirituality, learning and community. It is moving to step into this reality, to enter a natural environment in which children with special needs and openhearted adults share a holistic and creative lifestyle.

This research reveals that the aims of Camphill education are multidimensional. Many teachers and therapists hope for pupils to appreciate and enjoy the world and themselves within it. According to Steiner's theory, the goal of education is intrinsically linked to the aims of human development — in its physical, emotional and spiritual manifestations. But the objectives of any spiritual system are outside the linguistic confines of a materialistic model.

Outcomes are not necessarily seen and to expect to see them would be missing the point. Rather, staff members at Camphill visibly trust that by honouring children in the present moment, natural processes will allow them to develop to their full potential. Within the community, I observe goals that are less abstract. A large portion of energy is directed toward helping children with their adaptive functioning. Co-workers help pupils learn to walk to class, bathe, and eat with a spoon. These pragmatic objectives are significant, and they may facilitate a child's independence in the future. In addition, if a child accomplishes a task of daily living, he or she may experience a sense of pride. The child may enjoy the surroundings and their connection to it, even for one moment. Thus, pragmatic goals and psycho-spiritual aspirations overlap, and they can be held in mind simultaneously. Further research might explore how staff members and parents weigh and integrate them.

According to a staff member, the cost of sending a pupil to Camphill for one year is the striking equivalent of 180,000 US dollars. It is important to consider the fact that due to current economic trends, many children referred to this community are those who will never be able to function independently as adults or to attend integrated schools. Perhaps, because these children have been deemed ineligible for integrated services, they have been liberated from a set of societal expectations. No one is trying to streamline them. Adults may have different expectations for their futures. What, then, do the pupils and their families hope for? Where do the children — now young adults — go upon graduating? Some people live in anthroposophical communities for their entire lives. Others adopt a more mainstream lifestyle.

The experience of the children *after* Camphill is not captured in this study. A follow-up phenomenological study of the lives of Camphill graduates would deepen the results of this research. In addition, if possible, it would be valuable to include pupils' reflections upon their Camphill years.

The results of this idiographic study are unique to the time, place and individuals involved. They cannot be generalised to Camphill communities worldwide, nor are they replicable within this community. The house described is not a representative sample of the community. Each house has its own character, and residents suggest that the two estates have distinct sub-cultures. The duration of my stay limits my ability to observe changes in the children over time. Follow-up studies would enrich this research by offering a longitudinal perspective. It is also difficult to distinguish between the values of Camphill and those of the socio-political context in which it resides. Waldorf methods seem to be more accepted in this country than in the United States, making it more viable for federal funding. This school meets the national curriculum standards, which, according to one staff member, do not emphasise standardised testing. Though a teacher suggests that the national trend is to increase emphasis on standardised achievement, the influence of national policy is not visible to me. The creative, spiritual model so contrasts the current trend in California public schools that if curative educators have made compromises, they are not apparent. My personal culture, upbringing and disposition impact the elements of Camphill that I perceive to be most compelling. For example, my upbringing on the east coast of the United States and my acclimatisation to fast-paced urban life impact upon my perception of time. For some co-workers, communal life is less of an adjustment, and in discussions with them I appreciate our varying points of reference. I do not live with autism or with another challenge that is represented among the pupils at Camphill. The subjective element of this study does not decrease its validity. It mirrors the uniqueness of each individual's sensory experience. It honours a phenomenological approach that, in allowing clinical material to emerge, parallels clinical work within the field of psychology.

Embracing phenomenology

The phenomenological approach to this research mirrors the experiential emphasis at Camphill. This approach offers the field of psychology a bridge between the experiential nuances of clinical work and scientific empiricism. In the dominant 'discourse,' language is privileged over experience. However, the theories that inform Camphill and the phenomenological methodology used in this research acknowledge and honour the unlimited dimensions of human experience that are often lost because they cannot be articulated in words.

Embracing the power of phenomenology also honours the experience of nonverbal children. Their worlds are rich with sensory information, with relationships, and with alternative forms of communication. Perhaps it is actually easier for them to remain focused on the present moment if they do not have word-thoughts getting in the way. This experiential research seeks to explore *their* process. Nonverbal children show me ways to fully engage with my surroundings. By using my own sensory system as a primary source of information, listening to leaves and to physiological changes within myself, I experience Camphill in ways that are not accessible in literature. I learn about Camphill through my physical and emotional participation. I am not separate from the research; the data takes shape within me, rather than outside of me. It simmers, cooks, dwells and deepens. At times, I feel lonely, homesick and out of place. At others, I feel I am part of something greater than myself. This profound sense of connection, and the collective commitment to holistic health, is absent from my reality at home. In fact, when I describe my clinical work to one staff member, we marvel at how odd it is to drive to an office building, offer hourly therapy, get into a car, and drive home. The experience at Camphill causes a shift within me, one that causes my life at home to feel stranger than this new one. When I return, I feel a sense of urgency to write everything down immediately, to describe all the moments. It is concerning that the experience might fade with time. How can I capture the sensory qualities of this environment? Is it possible to articulate my sense of immersion in the community? The memories are poignant, but their integration is equally important.

Applications

This experience continues to teach and guide me in an ongoing learning process. It lives within me as a means of considering what is therapeutic, both personally and professionally. The thriving community of Camphill serves as a new reference point from which to juxtapose other models. Seeing an attitude of reverence for difference on such a massive scale helps me encourage parents to reject pressures to change their children. I also recognise that it will be powerfully healing to conduct a therapy session with a young client outdoors, rather than in an office with sealed windows. The expansive, balancing elements of nature will facilitate the therapeutic process irrespective of the words that pass between us.

The experience offers me perspective in my ongoing work with teachers, parents and children who are trying to find their way within the educational system. I would like to invite parents and teachers to try new approaches by asking different questions. Is the social environment of a school setting conducive to the relational needs of a particular child? Is respect an ethos of the community? Is the rhythm of the daily schedule helpful for the child? In what ways does he or she move her body during the day, and when? Does he or she exhibit joy? Does the child have an opportunity to try new things, to discover new talents or abilities? What are the expectations of the child's accomplishments, and why?

No environment and no intervention will have the same impact on two children. I cannot say how the five dynamics at Camphill impact children on the autism spectrum, but I can be sure that it is different for each child. Some might experience the communal atmosphere as comfortable or overcrowded. The house may feel containing, confining or expansive. Along with their sensory systems, the pupils bring their own reference points from their environments of origin. The contrasts may be welcome for some and challenging for others. The children are similar in their means of coping with uncomfortable sensations, but they are no more uniform than the rest of us. Instead, if we focus on the questions that are relevant to the children, we can give them the opportunity to grow and explore.

Changing the dialogue

This research suggests that dialogues of education and mental health need to shift away from the topic of normality. In our society, to be 'normal' is to look and act like other people. People feel pressure to conform in order to be accepted. Tremendous value is placed on a relative term that costs people their individuality. In a society that honours difference, people need not spend their entire lives trying to be similar to others. At Camphill, children with a wide range of distinct abilities and challenges learn from one another by engaging with their differences. People appreciate one another because they are unique, not in spite of that fact. The community joins the child in navigating landscapes of emotions and sensations rather than wiping out symptoms of a disease. We can learn the most from each other when we do not let expectations limit us. By holding a respectful, open attitude in all of our interactions with autistic children, we can join them in discovering their unique and exceptional talents. Unfortunately, it is extremely difficult for people to accept that there are beautiful things that they cannot experience. But if we do not do so, the risks are very high. Steiner cautions us as he writes:

> ... we have in mind something that is normal in the
> sense of being average. At present there is really no other
> criterion. That is why the conclusions people come
> to are so very confused. When they have in this way
> ascertained the existence of 'abnormality,' they begin to
> do — heavens knows what — believing they are thereby

helping to get rid of the abnormality, while all the time
they are driving out a fragment of genius.
(Luxford, 1994: 10)

In a race to make children look the same, we risk extinguishing
the development of their special abilities, and we miss the
tremendous opportunity to share their company. Whether or not
they live in a community, autistic children can all thrive within
our society. I have been moved and privileged to work with
children on the autism spectrum both within this community
and outside of it. As many autistic children act without regard
for social norms, they are in essence nonconformists. Their
presence asks us to examine our own attitudes and assumptions.
We must challenge ourselves to do so, and to help alleviate their
suffering while letting them be free of the need to conform. Let
us learn from them, and let us learn with them. In their sensory
sensitivities, these children have much to teach us.

6. Camphill: Children, Childhood and Disabled Identity

CHRIS WALTER

Chris Walter has worked in Camphill since 1980 as house co-ordinator and teacher. He is currently tutor and lecturer on the BA in Social Pedagogy. This chapter draws on the findings of the author's MSc in Advanced Residential Childcare dissertation 'Camphill: Understanding Children and Childhood' submitted to the University of Strathclyde (2010).

> Is there anyone who can recover the experience of his childhood, not merely with a memory of what he did and what happened to him ... but with an intimate penetration, a revived consciousness of what he felt then — when it was so long from one Midsummer to another?
> (George Eliot, 1985: 123)

The subject of individual and social identity is of pressing interest for many people at the beginning of the 21st century. This is perhaps understandable at a time when so many historical certainties about gender, class and disability are being questioned (Bendle, 2002). Individuals seek for a clear foundation for their identity, their sense of themselves, whilst at the same time boundaries around their identity become ever more fluid and permeable. This chapter considers Camphill's distinctive contribution to this debate.

This study used documentary research to analyse Child Study reports within Camphill over a seven-year period from 2001 to

2008. These are internal meetings of co-workers to evaluate a child's progress and formulate new common aims in house, class and therapies. They are viewed as important learning situations for all Camphill co-workers for here they can meet the 'heart of Camphill's therapeutic work and endeavour.' (Hansmann, 1992: 127) As such they offer a valuable opportunity to discern certain fundamental aspects of Camphill's understanding of the child.

Social identity

According to Jenkins (2004) the concept of social identity was initially developed in social psychology by Tajfel and Turner. They considered processes of social categorisation in an effort to understand discrimination between groups. They argued that the categories we use to define identity in everyday life, such as class, 'race' and disability are culturally constructed. Fundamentally, our social identity entails an understanding of what it means to be human, the similarities and differences which unite us and also separate us (Hockey & James, 2003; Jenkins, 2004). It is important to realise that power relations are fundamentally implicated in this process as identity is often socially institutionalised in hospitals, schools, social work and similar settings.

The identity of children with disabilities has increasingly been subject to debate over the last thirty years. Special education has historically taken a medical and behavioural approach which stressed the importance of diagnosis and individualised behavioural programmes (Molloy and Vasil, 2002; Thomas and Loxley, 2007). This has become characterised as the medical model and has been criticised for its over-emphasis on individual deficits. By way of contrast, writers such as Abberley (1987) and Oliver (1990) have developed a social model of disability which argues that disability is socially produced due to discriminatory practices towards those who have different kinds of bodies and abilities. They distinguish between impairment such as lack of mobility which is merely a bodily difference and disabling factors such as inadequate facilities and oppressive attitudes.

There is a danger however that this approach minimises the actual 'lived experiences' of individuals with disabilities. As Shakespeare (2006) has pointed out, while it is important to challenge social injustice it is also vital to realise that whilst individuals are not determined by their disabilities they are profoundly influenced by them. A child who has autistic features can experience profound suffering due to sensory issues such as the noise in a busy shopping arcade. This is clearly not only a social construction but also a painful sensory experience. Shakespeare claims that society needs to understand these sensory issues and adjust their views accordingly. Over the last seventy years Camphill has set an example of such an empathic approach. In doing so it has sought to value the contributions of each individual child. From this point of view the child with disabilities has a high degree of social status in Camphill.

The anthroposophical view of the child

At the beginning of the twentieth century the focus of child psychology on the scientific study of childhood influenced the work of the developing Child Guidance movement with children and families. The 'backward' and 'delinquent' child (Abrams, 1998) was studied in relation to normal development and was increasingly targeted for specialist support with an overwhelming emphasis on medical diagnosis and categorisation. Although this attention to the disabled child's needs was in some ways a positive development, it maintained the child's social identity as a potential threat to society which was in need of control and remediation. This extreme view was promoted by the eugenics movement and was still being advanced by distinguished scientists in Britain as late as the 1940s (Hubbard, 2006).

By contrast, Rudolf Steiner, the Austrian philosopher and founder of anthroposophy, was giving a series of twelve lectures in 1924 on the subject of curative education for 'children whose development has been arrested and whom we have now to educate — or again, to heal, in so far as this is possible.' (1998:17) The term 'curative education' is a direct translation

of the German *Heilpaedagogik* which means 'healing education.'
(Monteux, 2006) He saw himself as developing the work of
earlier nineteenth-century continental pioneers such as Seguin
and Pestalozzi who had advocated an education which addressed
more than just the intellect. He thus positioned himself quite
consciously against what he viewed as modern, materialistic
views of disability as a purely medical problem. Following on
from Steiner, König drew on anthroposophical insights to frame
impairment holistically as part of an individual's life narrative
thus providing it with a spiritual meaning and purpose.

Perhaps the most significant contribution that anthroposophical
understandings have contributed to this issue is the recognition
that each individual person has a 'spiritual core' of essential
humanity which cannot be reduced to a materialistic analysis.
This is a profoundly ethical perspective on the human being.
Camphill co-workers attempt to form an ethical relationship
with the child where they constantly struggle against what
Mason (2002) terms our habitual tendency to fix the other
human being into a category. This essential humanity is
viewed as embodied in a unique and differentiated manner
within each individual human being. Each person's experience
of themselves and of the world around them is consequently
highly individualised and personal. Curative education is thus
engaged in the difficult task of synthesising this universal
spiritual narrative with a recognition of individual difference and
diversity. This is a complex balancing act which calls for a high
degree of ethical awareness.

It is important to place these aspects within their historical
context. König opposed the medical model of disability with
its emphasis on standardised testing and individual pathology:
'... we are not pronouncing an absolute ... it can always only
be a subjective interpretation.' (1989: 17) However, the children
were often discussed in terms which to some extent jar with
21st century understandings. There was an emphasis on the
archetypal tendencies of particular disabilities, and children
were grouped in houses in such a way that they would balance
out each others' difficulties. This emphasis on mutual help and
support was innovative, yet one can trace in König's writings a

tendency to generalise about particular groups such as cerebral palsied and autistic children. This ambiguity is evident in a lecture König gave in 1958 where he praised the change in societal attitudes so that children were no longer seen as human outcasts but were looked upon as sick human beings who, like all other children, had a right to be educated and to be given the appropriate treatment.

However, due to the anthroposophical emphasis on development as a gradual process of embodiment, the child is generally not viewed in a deterministic manner but is seen as constantly changing. König observed that: 'childhood, from beginning to end, is nothing but transformation.' (1964: 81) Camphill co-workers consequently do not view developmental difficulties as pathological inabilities without any possibility of change but rather as barriers to growth which can be lessened through curative educational approaches. König stated that the task of curative education: 'is to apply such methods as to restore the disturbed equilibrium in the developing child.' (1964: 9) Whilst this language may give the impression that the child is overly passive within this process, my experience has been that co-workers try again and again in daily life to discern sparks of individual initiative in the children.

Early in his career König was deeply influenced by an Advent celebration he witnessed involving children with disabilities at the Sonnenhof, an anthroposophical curative home in Switzerland (Müller-Wiedemann, 1996). König believed that this experience represented a powerfully symbolic moment for the future development of Camphill. A mossy spiral was set up in a room in the Sonnenhof with a large candle in the centre. Each child, alone or with guidance, walked through the spiral holding a small candle which they then lit from the large 'candle on the hill.' This image spoke deeply to König as it echoed his spiritual conception of the child engaged in a struggle to maintain its 'inner flame' through the vicissitudes of life. In addition, he felt that the children's task was deeply connected with his own life's purpose:

> And suddenly I knew: 'Yes, this is my future task! So to awaken the spiritual light inherent in each one of these

children that it will lead them to their true humanity —
that is what I want to do!'
(Müller-Wiedemann, 1996: 68)

König's decision to create a shared living community in
Scotland together with children with a variety of disabilities
stemmed from this intense idealism. He was also building on
his previous experiences in Pilgramshain, a curative educational
home in Silesia. Writing in 1960, König placed the authentic,
respectful encounter with the child at the centre of the
community's ideals: 'To serve and not to rule; to help and not to
force; to love and not to harm, will be our task.' (König, 1993:
14) From the inception of this project the children were not
viewed as essentially different from the Camphill co-workers.
Thomas Weihs, another of the early pioneers, put it thus in an
address to parents:

> In their one-sidednesses, they have shown us the glory
> of the total human potential and they have given us the
> opportunity of helping others in a way that has helped us
> to develop our own integrity, maturity and fulfilment.
> (Quoted in Hansmann, 1992: 31)

It was a basic principle of Camphill's work that the co-workers
should learn from the children, as they had much to teach the
adults who looked after them. Co-workers were expected to
reflect on how their biography had led them into a particular
encounter with a child. This was not seen as a chance happening
but rather one that was intimately connected to each adult who
had decided to undertake this work.

In order to maintain this intimate 'closely knit fabric of human
relations,' (ibid: 11) König insisted that co-workers should live
with the children, eat with them and sleep by them and share
their daily work and challenges: they must be placed in family
groups so that the children would not become institutionalised.
This would be a new form of family, not based on blood ties
but on what a later writer termed: 'the spirit that unites us.'
(Hansmann, 1992: 40) It was viewed as part of the educational

task of healing to 'include everyone, children and adults, into our house communities and imbue them with an experience of a spiritual family.' (ibid)

In 1951 this aspect was further developed when the decision was taken to educate the co-worker children together with the pupils, at a time when many children with disabilities were considered ineducable. König later extended this close identification with these children to the view that they too were refugees from an unsympathetic society, occupying a position as outsiders on the boundaries of 'normal' life:

> We had learned from Rudolf Steiner a new
> understanding of the handicapped child ... At the same
> time, we dimly felt that the handicapped children, at
> that time, were in a position similar to ours. They were
> refugees from a society which did not accept them as part
> of their community. We were political, these children
> social, refugees.
> (König, 1993: 9)

In contemporary language, one might say that König recognised that both groups had been socially excluded due to no fault of their own. In this statement he consciously linked the children's social identity to that of the adults whose task was to care for them. König also pointed out to parents in 1964 what adults needed to learn from children in their care.

> That is what our children constantly bring home to
> us. They show us the other side of life, which is just
> as necessary and important as that in which we are
> immersed every day. Here too our children are our
> teachers. They help us — through their daily appearance,
> through their hardships and tribulations — to keep the
> spiritual spark of our souls awake and not to forget the
> oil in our lamps. Our children are not warriors but
> gentle, though constant, admonishers in the great battle
> of the history of mankind.
> (Müller-Wiedemann, 2006: 476–7)

König was convinced that the wider society lacked understanding of the essential nature of the human being due to an over-emphasis on abstract, intellectual knowledge (König, 1942). He drew on Steiner's complex writings for his view of childhood as a process of embodiment into earthly life but framed it in overtly religious language:

> We are all prodigal sons who have gone astray among swine, but in every child anew an inner guide arises who wants to lead us into that kingdom out of which we came and to which we long to return. This is the true image of eternal childhood.
> (König, 1994: 109)

Childhood was often referred to by König using the language of nature. He referred to the 'nesting powers of the world' which protect the unborn child and he used the metaphor of the 'garden of childhood' to capture childhood innocence, vulnerability and potential. He considered the task of the curative educator was to stimulate the sprouting forces, the new shoots of childhood potentiality but also to tend and weed, to prune out the wild growth. Nature portrayed in this image appears to have an ambivalent potential — positive growth and chaotic weeds appear to be equally possible. The curative educator appears to be immersed in this world of childhood, patiently guiding and training children in the way they should go. The garden metaphor appears to imply however that the plants are somewhat passive, dependent on the skills and expertise of the gardener!

This symbolic significance was nowhere more evident for König than in his understanding of the life of Kaspar Hauser. This child of noble birth was abducted and secretly imprisoned in a dark cell until he appeared on the streets of Nuremberg in 1827 unable to read or write. In 1959 König wrote that Kaspar Hauser: 'is in every respect the image of innocence and moral integrity.' (Müller-Wiedemann, 1996: 208) Two years later he explicitly linked this figure to children with disabilities in the following manner: 'If we contemplate the destiny of Kaspar

Hauser in the right light, we know that handicapped children touch our hearts in a similar way. They too remind us of our better selves.' (ibid: 212)

Camphill consequently has developed a particular understanding of children with disabilities which rests on a view of childhood as a time of innocence and vulnerability requiring adequate protection until such time as the children are able to manage more independently. König again and again linked the work to the wider struggle against the dehumanising tendencies in contemporary society which he believed endangered children and childhood. In a number of lectures he pointed to his view that modern adult life paid insufficient attention to the needs of the developing child for security, imaginative play and sensitive understanding. This view of childhood has contributed to the manner in which children with disabilities are highly valued within Camphill culture. Co-workers attempt to separate children's essential humanity, their spiritual essence, from the particular disabilities they struggle with. In doing so they try to ensure that a particular disability does not become the totality of a child's identity. Fundamentally, human development is a mysterious and individual process (Fewster, 1990). Human beings are thus a complex blend of capacity and incapacity, of resilience and vulnerability. As König has written:

> You have to appeal again and again to that immortal individuality which is present in every single child, no matter how ill.
> (König, 1989: 83)

However, it is important to challenge certain aspects of this view of childhood which at times can appear to over-emphasise children's vulnerabilities and dependence on adult protection. Jenks (2005) takes as his starting point the need to question familiar, taken for granted concepts about children and childhood. Childhood is seen as socially constructed and culturally relative, having both biological and social aspects. He argues that we cannot imagine what a child is except in relation to how we see our social identities as adults. These identities are complex and shifting in the early years of the 21st century. How we represent the child is therefore influenced by a range of narratives that live in our particular culture and most of all by our own childhood experiences. We are all 'experts' on childhood as we have all lived though the experience; the challenge perhaps is to maintain an appropriate distance from those experiences. Consequently, in understanding children we consider similarities and differences from our own experience; we construct their identity in relation to our own. Jenks proposes that views of childhood have become a way of exploring: 'missing, unexpressed and disempowered aspects of ourselves.' (Jenks, 2005: 150) Evidence for this within a Camphill context might be drawn from König's view that the children with disabilities who came to Camphill were in a position similar to their own: they, too, were refugees from a society which did not accept them. König develops his view of the mutuality in the relationship between adult and child to the extent that the child with disabilities appears to almost have redemptive qualities.

One of the most significant narratives underlying current representations is a view of childhood innocence and goodness. Meyer (2007) presents research using discourse analysis of media articles and focus group interviews about child protection scandals. Although conceding that it is difficult to generalise from a limited sample, she suggests that underlying common anxieties is a moral rhetoric about childhood which is profoundly ideological. Childhood innocence is an incontestable good in this narrative which considers that modern developments such as computers and video games have contributed to the loss of childhood. Burman (2008) however argues that this rests on an assumption of a romantic, pre-social child dating back to Rousseau's call for a return to nature in children's upbringing. During the nineteenth century, nature was increasingly seen as a positive force and identified with all that was fresh, pure and innocent in children. Anthroposophy can arguably be located within this idealist tradition which finds resonance in the writings of the American authors Emerson and Thoreau.

The development of Child Studies

König's intense efforts in the pioneering years of Camphill were indeed part of a wider project 'to enlighten the public about the nature of the child in need of special care.' (König, 1948 cited in Costa, 2008) Curative education was fundamentally different from current approaches although it could draw on these. This is evident in the way König refers to the College Meeting: an in-depth 'symposium' attended by doctors, teachers and carers involved with a child. Here the attempt was made to form a holistic, non-theoretical yet detailed picture of the manner in which the precarious balance between the spirit and the body of a child had been disturbed by their impairment. These considerations were indisputably embedded within an anthroposophical understanding: 'The fundamental indications that Rudolf Steiner gave on the being of man are the compass we follow.' (König, 1960: 32–33) König's comments about the purpose of College Meetings appear to point to a closely intertwined dual purpose. They were seen as the central expression of the Movement's striving for Anthroposophia and the means to realise necessary curative and educational treatment.

There are a limited number of accounts of these meetings from visitors over the years. Perhaps the most illuminating of these was written by Julius, an experienced anthroposophist (Julius, 1949). He appears to have struggled to categorise the College Meeting, remarking that it was something between a talk and a seminar-training-course. Teachers and carers shared their observations and interpretations which König then summarised to build up a picture of the child and his problems. Julius concluded by reflecting on the valuable opportunity the Meeting afforded for a large group of individuals to practise its capacities of perception and insight.

König conducted what he termed clinical examinations on an annual basis in the pupils' residential houses. They were viewed as an opportunity to assess a child's progress from a multi-disciplinary perspective and formulate new aims in house, class and therapies. Although teachers, carers and therapists were all invited to contribute, these 'clinics' were coordinated by the doctor who took a central role. This was originally König but over time other doctors were also responsible. The child was usually invited into the meeting for a brief conversation with the doctor about their progress. Knowledge about the clinic's aims and methods appears to have been passed on primarily through an oral tradition, in common with many other aspects of Camphill's work. Over the last few years, the format and aims of these meetings have subtly adjusted in line with the changing demands of residential childcare. An aspect of this change is signalled by the change of name to Child Studies, which has a slightly less clinical, medical connotation. Practice remains somewhat uneven across the organisation however, particularly in relation to the involvement of parents in these meetings. Although this is beginning to change, parents are not invited as a matter of course and often are not made aware of the content of these meetings. Consequently the Child Study in its current form presents an ambiguous picture, being an 'open' setting within the community which any co-worker can attend if they wish, yet being apparently 'closed' to parents and indeed to the children who are being discussed. I was to experience again and again during my research this contradiction between apparent openness and the exercise of professional 'expert' power.

Developing inclusive practice

Camphill has developed an understanding of the child's identity, which rightly stresses its vulnerability and need for a protective, rhythmical environment. Co-workers appear to be sensitised to these aspects and efforts to support and ameliorate them are repeatedly reported in Child Study notes. Camphill is able to draw on a wide variety of medical, educational and therapeutic resources in meeting these needs and the notes repeatedly demonstrate how participants were extremely willing to adjust to the child's changing needs. Special programmes are developed, individualised approaches discussed and attention is directed to many different aspects of a child's environment including their diet, sleeping, physiological processes and leisure activities. Through all of these efforts children clearly make progress, becoming more able to participate meaningfully in daily activities. In this way, each child is socialised into Camphill culture and generally appears to benefit from an enhanced sense of belonging. It could be argued that this aspect is related to Camphill's distinctive contribution to work with children with disabilities: the development of a sense of belonging within the community based on co-workers' empathic identification with children's support needs. Because of Camphill's particular philosophy these needs are viewed holistically: attention is paid to spiritual, psychological and social needs as well physical and behavioural issues.

Whilst these aspects are clearly welcome, Camphill has perhaps over-emphasised children's individual problems in the past and not paid sufficient attention to their strengths. There is clearly a danger of placing too much emphasis on a child's vulnerabilities and need for protection which leads co-workers to miss aspects of a child's capacities and strengths. Much attention was paid in the Child Studies documents to the pupils' challenging behaviour: this involved aggression, threatening behaviour and also self-harm. This attention was very understandable as these issues can be extremely destabilising for children and adults alike. In one of the meetings a co-worker claimed that a pupil was 'out of control' and had taken to lying down in the road when she had a temper. Her aggression was clearly provoking much anxiety; the worry was stated that she might destroy the whole house. Participants were clearly encouraged when pupils were more settled, 'stable,' calm and able to manage their programmes. There was less unanimity however about pupils' strengths and abilities.

Over the last decade however it appears that this view of childhood is beginning to change as participants in Child Studies become increasingly open to other points of view on a child's needs. There is an increased emphasis on children's competences, wider contextual aspects such as the family's perspective and the individual child's own view of their needs. These developments have accompanied the gradual dismantling of firm boundaries between the community and others who are significantly involved in the children's lives such as parents and professionals. It is also much more common to hear examples of how children themselves see their own needs. Co-workers are increasingly willing to take on these perspectives and adapt to the way they sometimes challenge their professional views. In this sense these developments involve a realignment in the way the group sees its own professional authority.

This paradigm shift was evident in one of the recent Child Study documents when the group realised that they needed to understand a child's 'language' and even wondered how much they should try to convince him when he clearly had his own views. Whereas in earlier meetings there was a tendency to pathologise the individual's inflexibility as stubbornness, now the group tends to realise that he can move on. Rather than attempting to change the individual, the group is increasingly able to reflect on its own responsibility to change their own potentially inflexible attitudes and to accept difference. Whilst maintaining its duty of care for each child, the Child Study appears better able to accept that its judgments will be provisional and are open to be contested by other perspectives. This appears to be a reflection of wider developments in the Camphill culture. Camphill's philosophy has always emphasised the spiritual potential of each human being but sometimes this has been less obvious due to a preoccupation with individual deficits. Consequently this development towards a more consciously strengths-based approach appears to echo König's original intentions whilst integrating more inclusive contemporary understandings.

The concept of mutuality in relationship, of co-workers learning from children and adapting to their needs, is part of Camphill's distinctive contribution. This has drawn on a spiritual view of the individual based on anthroposophy so that children in many ways have significant social status in the organisation. However, the vulnerability of children with disabilities has also historically been interpreted within Camphill as indicating their need for protection and reliance on adult guidance and authority. This perception, whilst in many ways legitimate, has contributed to a hierarchical social space for childhood where adults are assumed to be the experts on a child's needs. In the contemporary climate of care Camphill professionals are rightly challenged to work much more inclusively with children and their parents. One of the significant recommendations of the research undertaken is that the school should actively consider how to incorporate the views of children and parents in Child Studies. As the school begins to develop a distinctive social pedagogical perspective in its work with children with disabilities, a closer and more inclusive involvement with parents would be a natural development.

7. Whaur Extremes Meet: Camphill in the Context of Residential Childcare in Scotland

MARK SMITH

Mark Smith is a lecturer in social work at the University of Edinburgh. Before that he was a practitioner and manager in residential childcare settings for almost twenty years.

Back in 1919, Gregory Smith coined the term 'Caledonian antisyzygy' to reflect the internally-conflicted national character of the Scot. The poet Hugh MacDiarmid speaks of needing to exist at the point 'whaur extremes meet.' In literature the Caledonian antisyzygy is probably best exemplified in Robert Louis Stevenson's characterisation of Dr Jekyll and Mr Hyde. But it is not just in literature that this juxtaposition of opposites is evident; it also emerges in the wider Scottish body politic. Thus, a country that boasts a philosophy and a system of juvenile justice that is recognised internationally as enlightened and progressive also manages to imprison more of its adult population than almost any other European jurisdiction.

Extremes came to meet when, fleeing the Nazis, a group of Central European intellectuals arrived in the Aberdeenshire countryside in 1939 to set up a community for children with special needs. The idea of curative education was not one that Scottish dominies would have had much truck with. Scotland didn't do 'fancy' when it came to education (Jackson, 2006: 12). In fact it did the opposite. 'Chalk and talk' was the norm with an emphasis on mechanistic learning and tight discipline (Scotland, 1969).

That the band of foreign settlers might think that the Northeast of Scotland might provide a hospitable environment to set up an alternative community reflects something of a triumph of the will. A couple of decades later another freethinker, A. S. Neill, turned his back on the kailyard culture of his Forfarshire upbringing for Summerhill in Suffolk to take forward his experiment with 'free' education.

For much of the seventy years since the arrival of the original settlers it is probably fair to say that Camphill has existed on the margins of Scottish education and social work. Its separateness was in many respects maintained internally by a purist adherence to anthroposophical principles and a deliberate sense of offering a counter-culture to mainstream society as Costa discusses in an earlier chapter. It is only in recent years that extremes, if not exactly meeting, may at least be coming gradually closer together to a place where Camphill might be considered to have something to offer residential education and care. In this chapter I attempt to locate Camphill within wider developments in the Scottish scene. In so doing, I identify some of what I consider to be key developments and ideas in respect of residential childcare and education before concluding with some more personal reflections on the possibilities Camphill may offer to think about residential childcare in a different way.

The Scottish context

While its dissonance with its surroundings was always likely to elicit some suspicion, the community ideal proposed by the Camphill pioneers was not altogether new to Scotland. Indeed a sense of collectivism and collective responsibility is imbued within Scottish approaches to social welfare which Checkland (1980) argues exist on a continuum reaching back to the Reformation. Following the Reformation the Kirk assumed responsibility for education, poor relief and public works. Education and welfare were thus brought together under a common structure. Parochial approaches to social welfare were largely family and community based (Abrams, 1998). The social climate engendered by the Reformed Church was, on the one hand, democratic and collectivist, on the other, narrow and morally authoritarian.

The philosophers of the Scottish Enlightenment nurtured a collectivist ideal, demonstrating a 'well-developed sense of human mutual obligation.' (Paterson, 2000: 39) The Enlightenment, while a wider European phenomenon, exhibited some particular features in a Scottish context. Specifically, it encouraged a practical approach to ideas rather than elevating them to lofty principle. This was particularly true of the common-sense philosophy associated with Thomas Reid at the University of Aberdeen. Common sense required a dialectic between expert knowledge and the instinctive sense of the common man, which encouraged 'an anti-individualism, almost a kind of socialism.' (Davie, 1991: 62)

The early years of the nineteenth century witnessed the rapid urbanisation and industrialisation of Scottish society. Parishes, with roots still in rural and small town settings could no longer fulfil their erstwhile responsibilities for the education and care of vagrant or orphan children, tens of thousands of whom had relocated to the burgeoning cities. An evangelical wing of the Church of Scotland, concerned with what it considered to be the complacency of the established Church, sought to take the Christian message into the cities. Tensions between the traditional and evangelical wings of the Church of Scotland led to the Disruption of 1843, whereby over one third of the ministers and elders of the Kirk seceded to form the Free Church of Scotland. Key figures in the Disruption and subsequent social movements included Dr Thomas Chalmers and Dr Thomas Guthrie. Guthrie is perhaps best known for the spread of 'ragged' or industrial feeding schools across Scotland, two of which continued to bear his name in Edinburgh until the 1980s. In many respects, the 'ragged' schools provide a fascinating illustration of the durability of Scottish Enlightenment thinking. Problems such as delinquency and responses to it were rooted firmly in the context of social conditions and community responsibility for the rehabilitation of those beyond the norms of civil society (Seed,

1973). This persistent strand of social thinking re-emerges especially in the Kilbrandon Report (1964), which I will return to.

The 'ragged' schools

The first industrial feeding (or 'ragged') school in Scotland opened in Aberdeen in 1841, under the patronage of Sheriff Watson. The school sought 'to feed, train in work habits and give basic education' to the children who attended. While this basic aim was modest the schools were in other ways very progressive. They were characterised by an aversion to institutional care and sought to operate, primarily, as day schools, with a view to strengthening family ties. Children unable to return to their families in the evening were boarded out or occasionally offered respite accommodation on school premises. Proponents of the 'ragged' schools explicitly eschewed the English 'hospital' model of care, which involved removing children from their families.

When current policy concerns identify the importance of interdisciplinary working, it is interesting to note that in the 'ragged' schools teachers undertook a role in visiting families to reinforce the social and religious messages children had learnt in school. A particularly prescient feature of the Aberdeen schools was the establishment of a child's asylum committee in 1846, which according to Seed:

> ... resembled a modern children's hearing. The criterion was whether children were in need or whether they had committed offences. The committee was composed of representatives of the local community appointed by the Town Council, the parochial boards, the committees of management of the industrial schools and a representative from a multi-purpose charity known as the 'house of Refuge ... The great advantage sought here was to avoid stamping the child for life with the character of a convicted felon before he deserved it.
> (Seed, 1973: 323)

The rescue period

While the concern of the pioneers of the 'ragged' schools was to maintain family bonds, the dominant concern in the second half of the nineteenth century became the 'rescue' and removal of children from poor families and surroundings. Orphanages of varying sizes (and not necessarily catering only for orphans but for children removed, for a variety of reasons, from their homes), generally run by Christian philanthropists, sprang up across the country. This era is perhaps best characterised as that of the large 'children's village' such as Quarrier's at Bridge of Weir, founded in 1878, and Aberlour, founded by the English Episcopalian clergyman Charles Jupp in 1875. The focus of many of these institutions was to ensure the moral and religious propriety of their charges.

Boarding out remained the most common response to children's care but in line with the 'rescue' philosophy they were sent further afield, often to isolated farms or crofts in the Western Highlands and Islands. Children who offended could be committed by the courts to Reformatory Schools (successors, along with Industrial Schools for non-offenders, to the 'ragged' schools). While there may have been pockets of more enlightened practice in residential institutions, the norm was probably one characterised by austerity, discipline and hard work with 'brutal punishments, Spartan diets and austere living conditions.' (Heywood, 1959: 189, cited in Butler and Drakeford, 2005: 177) A primary focus on moral propriety and on saving the souls of children placed there left little time or inclination to address any emotional needs they may have had.

At its most extreme, the 'rescue' philosophy was manifest in the emigration of children to the Colonies in pursuit of a better life. This is a period in welfare history that can be judged harshly when set against current day understandings of the importance of contact with birth families. However, for the governors of many charities and schools, emigration represented the chance of a fresh start and a new life. Indeed assisted passage to the Colonies was held out as a goal for the better-behaved and better performing boys and often involved parental consent (Harris, 2009). As a practice it continued from the 1860s until it eventually died out as late as the 1960s.

The influence of psychoanalytic thinking

The emergence of psychoanalytic thought in the early twentieth century marked a shift, although perhaps only at the margins, away from a focus on the soul towards the psyche. It led to a questioning of some of the more traditional and authoritarian ways of responding to children and led to some interesting experiments in child rearing and education. Perhaps the best known of these are Neill's Summerhill, established in 1921 and Kilquhanity in the Southwest of Scotland, opened in 1940 by John and Morag Aitkenhead. These schools known as 'free schools' sought to allow children to develop free from the constraints of adult or societal oppression. Whilst the ideas behind Summerhill and Kilquhanity remained minority ones, the influence of Freudian psychology was also apparent in the growth of the child guidance movement, which emphasised the importance of working with children in the context of their family relationships. In keeping with Scotland's educational tradition, the child guidance movement was rooted within the field of educational psychology (Yelloly, 1980).

The Children and Young Person's (Scotland) Act 1937 established separate juvenile courts, which were required in their proceedings to 'have regard to the welfare of the child,' thus marking the formal embodiment of the 'welfare' principle, which has been central to subsequent childcare philosophy and legislation. The 1937 Act also brought together industrial and reform schools under the new title 'approved' school. The passage of the Act coincided with the start of the Second World War, which saw a significant increase in the use of 'approved' schools, largely to deal with problems of social disruption caused by the War (Struthers, 1945). Voluntary bodies, many of them Catholic religious orders, catering for the growing Catholic population, largely of Irish descent, managed most of these schools.

Although legislation provided school boards with the powers to set up appropriate education for children with less severe disabilities (The Education of Blind and Deaf-mute Children [Scotland] Act 1890, and the Education of Defective Children [Scotland] Act 1906), children with serious disabilities were usually placed in hospital settings. It was not until 1945 that there was a clear requirement for these children to be educated (Furnival et al, 2001).

The Clyde Committee and the post-war years

In the aftermath of the Second World War, The Clyde Committee (1946), reporting in response to concerns about the welfare of children in foster care, criticised large-scale institutional living and proposed that provision for children should be provided in smaller units, located nearer to centres of population. Clyde and its English equivalent, the Curtis Report (1946), which were influenced by the thinking of the child guidance movement, proposed the family as the preferred unit of care. Substitute care where it was required was to be modelled on family life. These recommendations were enacted in the 1948 Children's Act, which established local authority Children's Departments. The 1948 Act resulted, by the early 1960s, in the development of family group homes, where groups of children were looked after by 'auntie' and 'uncle' figures, ostensibly modelling the experience on family living. Many residential schools moved at this time away from large institutional arrangements to a cottage-living model where children were cared for in smaller groups by housemasters and housemothers.

Significantly then, the post 1948 developments marked an ideological shift away from the kind of large village community that the Camphill pioneers had, only years earlier, set out to establish. But there were also countervailing trends. In the mental-health field the therapeutic community, associated with another Scot, Maxwell Jones, highlighted the importance of group living in recovery from mental illness. The therapeutic community also took root in childcare, although perhaps more in England than Scotland. Therapeutic communities challenged the separation of a medicalised form of treatment from care, being premised upon the idea that disturbed children needed a round-the-clock psychotherapeutic 'milieu' in which care workers provided healing environments and experiences in the course of their everyday interactions with children.

Kilbrandon (1964) and the Social Work (Scotland) Act (1968)

The Kilbrandon Committee (1964), set up to inquire into problems of juvenile delinquency, is, arguably, the high point in Scottish welfare provision. The committee accepted growing evidence from the developing social sciences that it was not helpful to separate young people who offend from those deemed to be in need of care and protection. In both cases something had gone wrong in the child's upbringing, reflecting unmet needs for protection, control, education and care (Smith & Whyte, 2008). The thinking of the Kilbrandon Committee was strongly educational, reflecting its aim of achieving social wellbeing and social cohesion through what it called social education: education 'in its widest sense.'

Kilbrandon proposed the integration of social welfare and educational services within a new field organisation, the Department of Social Education located within the Department of Education and staffed mainly by social workers. However, the social work lobby, which was becoming increasingly influential, adopted a number of Kilbrandon's ideas but, in this process, the educational rubric within which they were set was weakened. Social work ideas were advanced in a White Paper, Social Work and the Community (1966), which thereafter became law in the Social Work (Scotland) Act (1968). The 1968 Act established professional social work rather than the social education departments envisaged by Kilbrandon. Provision for children and young people was located within new generically structured social work departments.

The Social Work (Scotland) Act also heralded the introduction of the Children's Hearings system. Children can be referred to a children's hearing on a range of different grounds, only one of which involves offending, the others reflecting their need for welfare or protection. Philosophically the system works on assumptions similar to those that characterised earlier Scottish approaches to welfare, namely that the underlying needs of children who offend and those in need of care and protection exhibit greater similarities than differences. Where Kilbrandon had envisaged children's hearings to involve panels of experts and to operate within a broadly educational model, under the 1968 Act, hearings were constituted of a panel of three lay volunteers, emphasising, once again, the principle of community responsibility for children in trouble.

Residential childcare within social work

The new social work profession claimed residential childcare as its own. However, the intention to bring residential schools into the social work fold did not happen. Special schools, following the 1968 Act, became identified alphabetically according to their positioning on a Scottish Education Department list; approved schools became List D and schools for children deemed to be maladjusted, List G. Tensions emerged and were played out in newspaper correspondence at the time between the new social work profession and the educational establishment, which argued that provision was being removed from a universal service and located within one the basis of whose claims to address delinquency were at best untested. Nevertheless, the 1970s witnessed important developments in residential education in both Scotland and England. In Scotland the development of the List D Schools psychological service provided the schools with an impressive body of knowledge around assessment and care planning rooted within a developmental model (Martin & Murray, 1976, 1982).

Much of the suspicion levelled at social work by educationalists was perhaps understandable. At an ideological level, social work was influenced by the literature of dysfunction, deriving in large part from Goffman's (1961) critique of institutions and by related theories of normalisation (Wolfensberger, 1972). The underlying ideological and policy thrust of these movements was in the direction of closing, or at least minimising the use of, residential care provision. A former List D Schools psychologist noted that:

> ... the whole attitude towards residential care changed with the introduction of the Hearing System and Social Work. The Social Workers as a profession always seemed to be very hostile to residential care. I think it had something to do with the training and the way that attitudes developed towards separating children from their own natural family.
> (Vallance in Harris, 2009)

This anti-institutional bias was given a shot in the arm with the publication of the 'Children Who Wait' report (Rowe & Lambert, 1973). This installed substitute family care as the placement of choice for children deemed unable to continue to live at home. 'Children Who Wait' was particularly influential in embedding a strong preference for fostering within social policy discourse despite the fact that significant criticisms can be levelled at the report as a piece of research (Kelly, 1998). The report saw the beginning of what became known as the 'permanence movement' in childcare. In its aftermath all local authorities developed 'permanence' policies, centred around family placement, which developed to include fostering as well as adoption, a fact that is not without some irony given the number of foster care breakdowns and placement moves that have resulted from this policy.

Around the same period, in the field of special education the Warnock Report (1978) 'signalled the beginning of the inclusive education agenda' (Pirrie & Head, 2007) which has gathered pace to a point that recent legislation (Standards in Scotland's Schools etc. Act, 2000) speaks of a 'presumption of mainstreaming.' Thus, both social work and education policy and discourse could be seen to render the special residential care and education offered at Camphill seemingly anachronistic.

With the professionalisation of social work the nature of care shifted from what was essentially a private and largely domestic task to become more public and ostensibly professional. It also marked a shift from what was still a largely religiously run or influenced service to a (often aggressively) secularised one. The new 'professionalised' care that continued to exist in local authorities saw a shift away from the 'aunties' and 'uncles' and live-in staff who had been at the heart of the family group home system to what Douglas and Payne (1981) term an industrial model. In this the personal and professional selves of carers became separated, on the one hand by structural changes such as the introduction of shift systems and on the other hand by discourses that made particular assumptions of what it was to be 'professional.' Thus, ensuring that children had clean socks and brushed their teeth regularly was not considered to be 'professional' but counselling them around particular difficulties was. A simplistic reading of Biestek's (1961) exposition of the casework relationship introduced notions of 'professional distance' to be maintained between the carer and the cared for. Erstwhile notions of care became suspect; social work discourses of independence, empowerment and anti-institutionalisation became totems of a profession that could consider itself 'so tainted by its associations with care that the word should be expunged from its lexicon and its rationale.' (Meagher & Parton, 2004: 4) Interestingly, contemporary commentators observed that neither staff nor residents have really benefited from the introduction of industrial practices and conditions to human service organisations and that staff, through no fault of their own, have given up trying (Douglas & Payne, 1981).

The next layer of threat to any conception of care emerged over the course of the 1980s and 90s as neoliberal political and economic ideologies took care into the marketplace (Scourfield, 2007). Neoliberal ideology has little room for care with its connotations of dependency, valorising instead independence, autonomy and competition. Managerial ways of working, predicated upon concerns for economy, efficiency and effectiveness, imposed more rigorous external control over residential childcare, often exercised by managers with little or no experience of the field. Indeed the term 'care' was even removed from legislation following the English Children Act, 1989 and the Children (Scotland) Act 1995. Children were no longer considered to be 'in care' but were 'looked after and accommodated,' terms that speak of instrumentalism and impermanence.

The 1990s, partly as a result of the crisis induced by revelations of abuse in residential care, saw the reawakening of political interest in the sector. In 1992, Angus Skinner the Chief Inspector of Social Work Services for Scotland produced a review of residential childcare, 'Another Kind of Home.' This set out eight principles of practice: individuality and development, rights, good basic care, education, health, partnership with parents, child-centred collaboration, and a feeling of safety. The Skinner Report was important in a number of respects, not least, was its recommendation to create a central resource point for those involved in residential care (Skinner, 1992). This led to the inception of the Centre for Residential Childcare (CRCC) in 1994 which became the focus in Scotland, and indeed more widely, for the development of practice in residential childcare. In 2000 the CRCC was expanded to become the Scottish Institute for Residential Childcare.

Political interest in residential childcare has undergone different phases. The election of the New Labour government in 1997 spawned a massive increase in regulatory regimes, which entrenched managerial and bureaucratic ways of working (Humphrey, 2003). This trend was reified in 2001 in legislation to regulate care across the different jurisdictions in the UK, establishing regulatory bodies and inspection regimes to assess the quality of care, measured against identified care standards. Warmly persuasive terms such as 'inclusion,' 'personalisation' and 'improvement' became totemic but ultimately slippery and self-referential ideas. So too did the idea of the state as the corporate parent of children in care. But while legislative tendrils came to envelop care, legislation singularly failed to give any idea what it might mean to care and be cared for.

It is not just legislation that defines care but, perhaps more importantly, ideas. Dominant ideas in relation to children in recent decades have been those of risk and protection and rights. In residential childcare, ideas deriving from risk and protection discourses dominate practices of care. They inhibit what ought to be everyday recreational and educational activities, requiring that staff undertake disproportionate and prohibitive risk assessment schedules before they can take children for a picnic or go paddling on the beach (Milligan & Stevens, 2006). At another level they cast a veil of suspicion over adult/child relationships. This suspicion is evident in prescriptions and injunctions applied to staff boundaries (particularly perhaps related to aspects of practice around physical touch).

The other central principle applied to residential childcare is that of children's rights. The rights discourse, as it has developed, is consistent with wider neoliberal positioning of the individual (Harvey, 2005), reflecting an 'increasing recourse to law as a means of mediating relationships ... premised on particular values and a particular understanding of the subject as a rational, autonomous individual.'(Dahlberg & Moss, 2005: 30) As such it can be inimical to conceptions of care that stress interdependence, reciprocity, mutuality and affective relations.

The reality is that despite the political gaze focused on residential childcare and its promise of improvement the sector as a whole is struggling. Its population has plummeted over the past thirty years, although this decline seems to have bottomed out. And despite policy assertions to the contrary (Skinner 1992) residential care is rarely seen as a long term or indeed a positive option for children; the reality is that it is often a residual service dealing with those children and youths who cannot be maintained in any other resource. The upshot of all of this is captured by Cameron, who claims that:

> ... the concept of care within public care for children
> has been rarely seen as visible ... poor outcomes, lack
> of investment in staff training, increased pressure to
> marketwise care services have all contributed to a
> narrowing of what we mean by care, a lowering of
> expectations of what the state can offer in terms of care.
> Of particular note is the marked contrast between the

potential for care within families as centring on control and love, and the optimum expected from state care which is around safekeeping. Care as used in legislation seems to have been emptied of its potential, a dried up expression for how to manage an underclass of disadvantage.

(Cameron, 2003: 91)

Personal reflections

It is not just academics like Cameron who identify problems with current residential childcare. As I engage with practitioners I pick up an existential awareness that things are not as they could be. The following are some of my own reflections on the state of residential childcare in Scotland, generally, and then more specifically in relation to Camphill and the possibilities it may offer to hold a mirror to a different kind of public care.

My initial reflection is rooted in a sense that something odd has been going on for the past twenty years or so. Pictures painted and assumptions made of residential childcare being at best an unfulfilling experience and at worst an overtly abusive one do not fit with my own experiences; nor are they borne out in my ongoing PhD research, which seeks to chart changing discourses of care in Scottish residential schools through the voices of those who worked in them. Those voices tell a very different tale to that of the unreflective and oppressive establishments of public and professional lore. One of the words that crops up in the course of my interviews is 'curiosity.' In the 1960s and 1970s the schools attracted a number of bright idealists, driven by social conscience, but also by a spirit of wanting to understand why children behaved in the ways they did rather than just responding to these behaviours. They had little to draw upon — psychological understandings were in their infancy, at least when applied to the practice of care and education. But they were curious. That curiosity led them to innovate, to experiment with different approaches; there was something of a pioneering spirit around and several respondents have identified their involvement in new ventures as among the most rewarding experiences in their professional lives. That sense of being pioneers is one that resonates with a Camphill tradition. It is one that is deadened by the weight of the regulatory burden placed upon staff in the present climate.

The dissonance between dominant and largely negative professional views of residential childcare leads me to conclude that the shift away from care is best understood as an intensely ideological project, one which, according to Garrett (2008) is required, within the dominant neoliberal frame of reference, to reveal failure in order to provide a rationale for privatisation. This rationale is, at its core, motivated by cost but also reflects a conceptual failure to identify a wider moral or relational purpose for care. This failure has led care to be misconceived as a technical/rational rather than the moral/practical endeavour that it irredeemably is (Smith, 2010).

Reflections on Camphill

My first experience of Camphill came when I visited with a group of students studying for the MSc in Advanced Residential Childcare at the University of Strathclyde. The sense I picked up there was in many respects reassuringly familiar in that it brought back some of my own early experiences of residential care, working for another kind of community, a List D School run by the De La Salle Brothers. I wrote about my thoughts of this visit to Camphill in a piece for the journal of the International Child and Youth Care network, CYC-online. I reproduce some of what I said at the time below.

> When there you quickly pick up a sense of being part of something bigger than yourself. This is evident in the rituals such as holding hands and singing grace before and after meals. Of course rituals like this, as well as affirming a spiritual dimension to the school's philosophy, also play an important symbolic and practical role in marking the beginning and end of mealtimes. We were

discussing how we had lost such rituals in most residential facilities. They were considered institutional, possibly even religiously divisive or just too difficult to struggle to maintain. Mealtimes then stop being part of the community life and become potential flashpoints to get over and done with as quickly as possible.

Personally I found Camphill to be a welcome and challenging antidote to the reductionism that characterises so much of residential childcare. In this managerial age we seek to pathologise particular bits of a kid; cognitive, behavioural, social or sexual and then apply some quick-fix (and often ill-conceived and poorly understood) 'professional' intervention. Camphill affirms the dignity of the 'whole person' and the potential they have for growth alongside others in community.

Camphill adopts a similarly affirming view of those who live and work in the community. Again in this climate where we can be led to suspect the motives of anyone who wants to work with children, Camphill assumes a basic altruism and goodness among co-workers. That basic message of trusting that workers are motivated to do good seems to me to be a far better starting point for the provision of care than our current fixation with rooting out bad apples with resultant climates of fear and recrimination.

(Smith, 2005)

A more official involvement with Camphill came when I was appointed external examiner for the BA in Curative Education (now Social Pedagogy), a qualification run by and for staff in the Camphill communities and accredited by the University of Aberdeen. We speak in social work about the need for reflective practice and writing but most social work academics would attest that this is something that students and practitioners struggle with; it is far easier to write about the latest assessment tool or intervention programme and to keep any notion of 'self' safely in cold storage. Students on this course are refreshingly, at times disarmingly, reflective in their writing. And the focus of their writing is the practical task of caring, from baking bread and carving wood, to negotiating with residents over wearing a coat in wet weather, to falling out with co-workers over the tensions that emerge in everyday living. This, rather than the reductionist and soulless vocational qualifications that have become the norm in residential childcare, is the kind of educational experience that workers in residential childcare need if they are to develop in the job.

The change of name from BA in Curative Education to BA in Social Pedagogy is perhaps another straw in the wind suggesting that Camphill is becoming more mainstream — this time in a wider European context where social pedagogy is the discipline underpinning direct work with people. It is an approach that is attracting more and more attention in the UK. Again, Camphill is in a position to be in the forefront of any emerging social pedagogic paradigm here. The change of name is perhaps also indicative of Camphill reaching a stage of its development where it can look to other traditions without these being seen as a threat to its anthroposophical roots. Indeed the involvement of Camphill staff on wider Scottish initiatives such as the MSc in Advanced Residential Childcare represents a process of mutual enrichment for residential childcare.

Whaur extremes meet

Some obvious conceptual similarities emerge between European and Scottish approaches to work with people, which Camphill may be in a position to bridge. Perhaps the most obvious of these is the focus on a sense of community; in Camphill's case a particular geographical and physical sense of community and in a wider Scottish context a sense of civil society. Human beings have responsibilities to the communities in which they live, but similarly, these communities have responsibilities towards their members, a basic tenet that can be cast aside within a neoliberal paradigm. Another similarity is the focus on upbringing within both European and Scottish traditions. In Germany the term for a pedagogue *erzieher* translates to 'upbringer,' capturing the holistic nature of the task as involving all aspects of a child's growth and development. In this sense it echoes the centrality of the concept of upbringing in the Kilbrandon Report.

But there is perhaps something more profound going on, something that takes us away from the Enlightenment's dominant legacy of rationality, bureaucracy and care as mere duty, towards an appreciation that the qualities of benevolence, sympathy and community identified by the Scottish philosophers need to be reclaimed within some understanding of what it is to care and to be cared for. There are signs that this shift is beginning to come about. Smith and Smith note that:

> ... when we enter into more bureaucratic arenas helping tends to be stripped of much of its moral dimension and utility. It also loses touch with a great deal of the supporting language and thinking. Words like boundary, client, delivery, intervention and outcome replace the discourse of friendship, association, relationship and faith. (Smith & Smith, 2008: 153–4).

More hopefully, the same authors go on to note that 'bureaucratic professionalism may well be working itself into a corner. We hope more will have the courage to develop spaces where helping is on a human scale.' (2008: 154) Throughout its existence Camphill has held on to the conviction that caring is a moral rather than a bureaucratic activity and that helping must be on a human scale. In that sense it is ready to catch the tide of emerging academic if not yet professional discourse and to hold a mirror to a different kind of residential care and education across Scotland.

8. Social Pedagogy: Past, Present and Future

CLAIRE CAMERON

Claire Cameron is Reader in Education at the University of London. Her professional background is in social work; her main areas of interest are the children's workforce and social pedagogy.

In 2007, the English Department for Education and Skills (as it was then known) issued its White Paper for children in public care, *Care Matters: Time for Change*. It was a landmark publication. For the first time, an English government committed itself to substantial funding to explore the effectiveness of social pedagogy in residential care. Social pedagogy, or variants of it, has been well-established in continental European countries for many years. Originating in Germany in the nineteenth century, it was first defined by Karl Mager in 1844 as 'the theory of all the personal, social and moral education in a given society including the description of what has happened in practice.' (Winkler, 1988: 41, as translated by Thomas, 2000) This long evolution in continental Europe, largely in parallel with other 'people' professions, such as teaching and social work, was not mirrored in the UK. Here, we have only recently encountered the field of social pedagogy and the occupation of social pedagogue, although there are professional traditions with commonalities. In this chapter I will seek to document the origin and character of social pedagogy and identify some of the commonalities with parallel developments in the UK. I will then look at reasons

154

why we might be interested in social pedagogy and give some examples of social pedagogy in practice.

The origin and character of social pedagogy

Although there are earlier references, social pedagogy is a tradition that emerged from nineteenth century Germany. Lorenz (2008) refers to the particular conditions at that point in time, when the nation state was fragile and faced the need for both social integration, given the prevailing socio-economic divisions, and cultural integration, given the deep regional and religious differences. Social pedagogy provided 'the means and the method through which the integration of modern societies could be brought about.' (Lorenz 2008: 631)

Social pedagogy, which translates best into English as 'education in the broadest sense of the term,' has evolved in most continental European countries, and right to the fringes of Europe — from Israel and Palestine to Finland and Portugal. As Kornbeck (2002) points out, the variants, such as continental social work (e.g. *Sozialarbeit* in Germany), and socio-cultural *animateurs*, as found in France and Spain, are important, representing differing perspectives on questions such as who to work with, on what basis, and with what kind of interventions and values. Lorenz (2008: 633) refers to the many possible applications of social pedagogic practice: 'pedagogy, as such, is always more than schooling, is always the totality of lifelong educational processes that take place in society,' including informal learning within families, from peers, and more formal contexts such as leisure or community activities, as well as learning while an adult. What was significant from the point of view of developing social pedagogy within welfare services was that early on social pedagogy was identified as a method and approach for all children, as everyone requires educational guidance for the development of their potential, and for children who were experiencing some kind of difficulty, for everyone has the potential to develop further. This meant that work with children and young people experiencing difficulty could be conceptualised within a normative framework of *all* children's experiences. This universalist orientation was, and is, matched by a holistic perspective on children: 'the pedagogue sets out to address the whole child, the child with body, mind, emotions, creativity, history and social identity. This is not the child only of emotions — the psycho-therapeutic approach; nor only of the body — the medical or health approach; nor only of the mind — the traditional teaching approach.' (OECD 2004: 19)

As seen from a UK perspective, social pedagogy represents a distinctive approach to human services work that contrasts quite sharply with the conceptual frameworks used in the UK and other English speaking countries. On the basis of a study exploring social pedagogy and residential care across five western European countries, Petrie et al. (2006) identified a number of principles of social pedagogy. These were: a holistic approach, attending to the many dimensions of the child (or young person/adult); a focus on social relations between the child and adult, and nurturing that relationship; a concern to share the 'lifespace' with children; to be highly reflective and thoughtful practitioners, applying theoretical understandings, and contextualising judgments; employing practical and creative skills as a part of self expression and mutual, authentic learning with children; working with groups as a resource; valuing children as competent, 'rich' participants, with voices and rights; and valuing team work, including work with parents.

The work of the pedagogue is often referred to as involving the whole person: the *head*, knowing and making use of theories, through reflective capacities and situated judgments; the *heart*, offering constructive, dependable and authentic relationships that involve the 'personal' and not the 'private' self (Bengtsson et al. 2008); and the *hands*, which represents the action in social pedagogy, the 'being with' others, and which often involves quick decisions as well as practical and creative activities with individuals and in groups that help to build self-esteem and extend relationships.

Overall, social pedagogy is a field of theory, policy and practice that encompasses work with children and young people, and also adults and older people, usually in group settings. It is a field that focuses on, specialises in, actual practice. Lorenz (1994) reminds us of a further dimension to social pedagogy. This is its relationship with transformative social action on the one hand, and engaging with normative societal interests on the other. Should social pedagogy be aiming at the emancipation of individuals and groups — as Diesterweg and Natorp argued in the nineteenth century — or is it concerned with effective social control through taking its values to all sections of the population through practice in services children, young people and adults attend? In other words, social pedagogy's roots in professional practice must be seen in its democratic and ethical context: it has the potential to be emancipatory or oppressive.

Commonalities with practice development in the UK

Despite the distinctive character of social pedagogy, the evolution of ideas about practice in continental Europe and the UK has some common threads. As Lorenz (2008) pointed out, those defining the field in Germany had contact with contemporaries shaping social work in the US and the UK in the early part of the twentieth century, and common lines of thought developed. Well before the twentieth century, an early example of pedagogic thinking was that of Robert Owen. Owen developed, in 1812, a community in New Lanark, Scotland, with the explicit aim of emancipating working people, through the means of education, reorganising working practices and improving housing. Of particular note were Owen's thoughts on education: schools were to encourage children to form their own opinions, and to be governed by kindness and love (Petrie & Cameron 2009). This concern with transforming the lives of poor citizens through education would have found favour with the German pedagogic thinkers of about the same time, and, indeed, later were to influence the work of Camphill's founder, Karl König.

We can point to similarities with traditions in youth and community work, where mutual informal learning, based on respectful social relations, and the importance of young people's or community members' voice in shaping the service are long standing ingredients. Eichsteller (2006: 17) points out that 'the philosophies of youth work in Britain and Germany are generally similar' and CPEA (2007: 31) argued that 'any good youth work in the sense of being community based, centred on voluntary engagement, association and relationship, starting where young people are' is consistent with a social pedagogical approach. The English Government (DCSF 2008) recently committed itself to developing a youth professional status underpinned by a social pedagogic approach, reflecting a perception of commonalities between the two traditions. Furthermore, a report for the Children's Workforce Development Council (2009: 3) on the implications of a social pedagogic approach for youth work supported this idea: 'much youth work training ... has a strong focus on enabling practitioners to critically reflect on their practice, and on developing skills in relating to, and communicating with, young people.' In several European countries, parallels between youth work and social pedagogy are well established as higher level training for youth workers is through social pedagogic qualifications or courses (Qualification for Youth Workers 2001 IARD study). According to Higham (2001) the Connexions service, with its Personal Adviser, is an example of a UK approach with some parallels with social pedagogic thinking. This service was designed as a comprehensive, universal and non-stigmatising way of guiding young people in their educational and employment choices, retaining them in education and assisting with any health or social difficulties through the expertise of a generic adviser who was not a teacher.

The relationship between social work and social pedagogy should also be mentioned. The development of social pedagogy and social work has been intertwined in Germany, with joint degree programmes, whereas in the UK, social work has developed independently of social pedagogy. Higham (2006: 20) pointed out that in the early twentieth century there were two contrasting approaches to social work in North America and the UK: a casework approach that focused on individual causes of social problems and a community action and education approach called 'the settlement house movement' that was aimed at addressing structural issues in society. By the mid-twentieth century, the casework approach influenced by Freudian thinking was dominant but in the subsequent decades concerns with addressing social disadvantage and discrimination reappeared, as well as concerns with the rights and empowerment of service users (Higham, 2006). Social pedagogy, as we have seen, had similar perceptions concerning the causes of difficulties, but developed an integrated, relationally-based approach to methods of intervention that combined a focus on individuals and groups, with a concern for transformative social processes. Smith (2009) argued that there was a 'social pedagogy moment' in Scottish thinking about working with young people when the Kilbrandon Report (1964) explicitly identified supporting upbringing as part of the educational role of social workers. But it was 'never really embraced by social work ... bringing up children was not deemed sufficiently professional.' (Smith 2009: 172). More recently, social workers in the UK have more explicitly adopted a case management role, focusing on legal and organisational aspects of working with clients, with untrained or less well trained support workers undertaking most of the relational work. As Boddy and Statham (2009) point out, the relational role is given more prominence where social pedagogues are employed as specialists in direct work with children and families. In their study, Boddy and Statham (2009: 7) found that in Denmark, France and Germany, 'social pedagogy was not seen as an alternative to or substitute for social work' but as a complementary profession, each with a distinctive knowledge base.

Another area of overlap between UK practice and social pedagogic practice is with the therapeutic communities. Therapeutic communities were designed to offer a physical space or environment where the group, located within a psychotherapeutic framework, is valued as well as each individual. This approach is underscored by theories of attachment where the therapeutic task is to provide a safe environment in which to explore and forge beneficial rather than destructive attachments (Campling, 2001). The reflective, 'culture of enquiry,' group-based, democratic approach has much in common with social pedagogy. Diamond (2009: 4) argued that social pedagogy's use of everyday interactions and events as a joint focus for developing and sustaining authentic and meaningful group and individual relationships also has much in common with therapeutic childcare's use of 'planned environment therapy' and 'milieu therapy.' Such relationships, under therapeutic childcare models, 'allow the child to "work through" disturbed and confused attachment issues,' help them to (re)establish relationship building skills, and to understand their traumas with a new perspective. But social pedagogues do not see themselves as therapists *per se*. Nor do they invest to the same extent in attachment theory. Pedagogues would see relationships in terms of presence, or 'being there,' and authentic co-construction of meanings in an activity or time spent together. Pedagogues would support rather than replace specifically therapeutic interventions and would rarely focus on building up a single attachment relationship on the model suggested by Bowlby and Winnicott.

We can see much common ground between the theory and practice in the Camphill approach and that of social pedagogy. The founders of Camphill were highly influenced by social pedagogy and this is reflected in its philosophy and values and its emphasis on relationships, creating and sustaining a community. The founders were concerned with the development and support of the whole, multi-dimensional, physical, creative, spiritual and intellectual child (Jackson, 2006). In its multi-disciplinarity, and its combination of theory and practice and reflecting on practice, the Curative Education degree programme curricula developed at Camphill has much in common with those following social pedagogy degree programmes in other parts of Europe (Cameron, 2006).

Montessori schools are a further example of continental pedagogy that is well established in the UK. They developed from the work of the Italian educator Maria Montessori and are based on the principle that children are competent, self-directed learners and that when provided with a sensitive and suitable environment they will achieve self-determination and self-realisation. Finally, the Early Childhood Studies degree programmes were seen as benefiting from continental pedagogy's multi-dimensional approach to working with young children (Calder, 2006). In sum, many of the ideas and methods of social pedagogy are present in the UK services and approaches to working with children and young people but they have rarely been recognised as such.

Why are we interested in social pedagogy now?

The Thomas Coram Research Unit (TCRU) has a long tradition of cross-national research in children's services and two particular individuals stand out for bringing the continental field of social pedagogy to our attention. In the 1980s, Professors Pat Petrie and Peter Moss were responsible for coordinating European Networks, for out-of-school play, and for childcare services, respectively. Through these networks, it became apparent that the central occupation involved in play and early childhood care and education was, in many countries, a pedagogue, social pedagogue or educator and Petrie and Moss wrote extensively about these services and roles (Petrie, 2001; Moss et al., 1999). During the late 1990s, in the face of mounting concern with the largely poor outcomes for children in care, the English government began to look at European practice and commissioned TCRU to conduct a series of studies of children's services in continental European countries with a history of social pedagogy. The study of residential care (Petrie et al., 2006), comparing residential care homes and staff, and child outcomes in England, Denmark and Germany, proved influential in government thinking. This study found that the characteristics of staff were very significantly related to the much better outcomes for children in residential care in Denmark and Germany compared to England. Staff in the continental European countries were likely to have had an extensive professional education, usually to degree level, to be committed to their place of work and find the work rewarding, especially working in a relational way with children.

Almost all the Danish staff interviewed found relations

with staff groups enjoyable. Pedagogues noted the rewards of companionship with young people often expressed as 'being there' or 'being together.' Both Danish and German pedagogues appreciated their work conditions which promoted a 'constructive environment' where staff could have peer supervision, and could debate approaches to practice in particular contexts. One pedagogue in the study said they had regular meetings 'where you are not afraid of saying when you have made mistakes' and can learn from colleagues. Another distinctive feature of working as a pedagogue was being able to exercise professional judgment, introduce new ideas, and, if persuasively argued, effect change in the organisation of their work. A Danish pedagogue summed up the impact of this democratic approach to residential care practice when he said: 'it is a house where it is good to be; you are recognised and tasks are delegated.' (Petrie et al., 2006: 61) There were other distinctive features of residential care in the social pedagogic context. Young people tended to be in residential placements longer in Denmark and Germany, and to be more likely to have a key worker than in the English homes. Strikingly, the young people in the Danish and German residential care homes were more likely to be in education if they were under the age of sixteen, and were more likely to be in employment if they were over sixteen, than those living in the English homes. Furthermore, in the English establishments, young women were more likely to have had a pregnancy in the year prior to the research and residents were more likely to have a criminal record than their counterparts in the Danish and German homes. On all these indicators, correlational analysis showed the important role that pedagogues were playing in the more positive outcomes for young people. Most interestingly, a higher staff to child ratio corresponded to poorer child outcomes, perhaps because, where there are many staff and very few young people, it is difficult to form meaningful and personalised relationships, and there may be a fragmentation of knowledge of, and responsibility for, the young people (Petrie et al., 2006: 109).

The findings from this study posed a fundamental challenge to practice with looked-after children; the continental European way of working appeared to do so much better with residential care than the UK, where residential care was staffed by a head with a social work qualification and around a third of staff having no relevant qualification at all, and a further third having only a Level 3 qualification, well below that of their colleagues in Denmark and Germany. At the same time, children's policy, set out in *Every Child Matters* (DfES, 2003), appeared to be advocating what social pedagogy was delivering in other countries: namely, a multi-disciplinary, joined-up approach, informed by a common core of knowledge and skills that focused on positive outcomes for all children, with disadvantaged children identified within a mainstream context which was termed 'progressive universalism' by the Labour Government (HM Treasury and DfES, 2005; DCSF, 2007). Consultation papers on workforce reform referred to the social pedagogue as a promising occupational model to pursue for both early childhood care and education and for work with looked after children (DfES, 2005). But there was scepticism about creating a new profession. Although the thrust of *Every Child Matters* was about the integration of skills and knowledge across care and education, the notion of a core integrated worker was not pursued, instead a further specialism was introduced with the adoption of a graduate level early years professional (EYP) (DfES, 2006). The professionalisation of residential care practice was given little specific attention and was retained as part of social work and social care.

Nevertheless, interest in the potential application of social pedagogy to 'care' services in the UK began to grow and three feasibility and implementation studies were conducted (Cameron, 2006; Cameron and Petrie, 2007; Bengtsson, 2008). Cameron (2006) tracked the impact of Danish students of social pedagogy (termed 'pedagogue' and 'pedagogy' in Denmark to reflect the generic training and application of their work) while on six-month practice placements in early childhood and residential care services in England. The study involved interviews with heads of establishment, staff and students at the beginning and end of the placement period and the students' Danish tutors. Through desk research the views of professionals and students from a range of backgrounds and settings who were interested in social pedagogy were also examined in the study. These individuals were drawn from youth work, social work, housing, schools, residential special education as well as early childhood care and education and residential care.

The study found broad enthusiasm for introducing social pedagogy into England, with general agreement between UK and Danish practitioners and tutors on the principles, and the knowledge base forming cornerstones of practice. Moreover, the Danish students, by embodying a different approach to practice, were capable of stimulating debate among staff groups, with the possibility to effect change in practice. Appreciation of the potential for, and understandings of, social pedagogy grew over the six months of the placement. One pedagogue illustrated her methods when she said, 'I am not afraid to address subjects they [the staff group] do not want to speak about. I asked questions about one young person leaving [the residential care home] and that led to a long discussion about how the young people felt and the staff feelings about it. It was very positive. I'm not scared of asking about challenging subjects. In pedagogic education you have to not only describe the work but also the ways they feel about it. Here they tend to spend a lot of time discussing daily routines.' The manager of this residential home described the staff discussion referred to above as 'one of the best staff meetings ever.' (Cameron, 2006: 50) This focus on the discursive and analytic, a skill that stems from pedagogical methods in the educational programme to become a pedagogue in Denmark, is a critical and distinctive practice method.

Cameron and Petrie (2007) investigated training profiles in England, specifically the NVQs for practice and management in residential care homes, and social work degrees in Denmark. Again, there were broad areas of agreement, especially in the topics studied. What was different were the methods and depth of study expected from students in the two countries. In particular, the NVQ system in England, based on demonstrating competencies, was quite different from the Danish approach. The Danish pedagogy curriculum involves theory and practice drawn from pedagogy, sociology and psychology and cultural studies; Danish culture and communication; studies of the individual, the institution and society; practical study in either health, the body and exercise or music and drama or arts and crafts or science and technology. Teaching methods usually include problem-based learning in groups, which was much less emphasised in the NVQ system. Studying the expressive arts is rarely, if ever, found on 'care' courses in England. Cameron and Petrie (2007) proposed a qualifications framework for introducing social pedagogy into England that would take practitioners from a Level 3 qualification through a holistically oriented Foundation Degree programme in working with children, to a top-up BA year specialising in social pedagogy and then a number of post-qualifying awards and MA options in social pedagogic leadership and management and practice. Finally, Bengtsson et al. (2008) undertaking an action research study examined two approaches to introducing social pedagogy in residential care in England. The two approaches were in-service training and practice-based observation and enquiry. Again, the findings were broadly encouraging but difficulties in fitting an analytic, reflective and change-oriented approach around the organisational conditions of residential care were apparent.

These small-scale implementation studies were important in exploring training and practice options for introducing social pedagogy, and they laid the ground for investment in a 'Care Matters' pilot programme for social pedagogy in residential care. At the time of writing this chapter the pilot programme is about halfway through its three-year duration. Thirty children's homes are involved, either because they have recruited social pedagogues, nearly all from Germany, or to act as a means of comparison. The programme is exploring different ways in which social pedagogues can contribute to a change in thinking about practice. This is throwing up many issues. For example, does the organisation of children's homes allow sufficient time for staff to analyse and discuss practice, or to develop and sustain meaningful and authentic relationships with children based on shared activities and understandings? Is there sufficient recognition of the role that the expressive arts and outdoor activities can play in working with children and young people and how are staff skills in these areas nurtured? How can regulatory requirements, such as record keeping and case planning and review, incorporate a more developmental and goal-oriented method, to make them more useful in the longer term to the young people as individuals? How can social pedagogy be 'visible' in a children's home?

One response to this last question in one children's home was a 'social pedagogy tree project.' The social pedagogue took the lead in creating a garden sculpture that was a visible representation of participation, creativity and team work. Instead of having fixed days or times for the activity, resources were constantly available, to encourage participation at moments when the young people wanted to get involved. The manager of the home claimed that the tree project gave everyone involved an opportunity to understand social pedagogic approaches through the very visible and physical experience of the tree sculpture (Cameron et al., 2010). The issues emerging from the pilot programme are wide ranging and offer an opportunity to reflect on the prospects for fundamental change in residential care homes, as well as the more specific social pedagogic direction of change that is being attempted. Evaluation of the programme is underway.

However, in the longer term, importing German social pedagogues is not sustainable. Making social pedagogy a reality in children's services will require investment in education and training on a national scale and at all levels of training. One local authority, Essex, has adopted a plan of work-based social pedagogy training for all residential care staff, supported by senior managers and so called 'change agents.' After one year, practitioners reported sustained changes to practice. For example, one worker noted that, 'if you enable the children to attempt to resolve their own conflict a solution is often found. It might not always end in the way that you would have expected or hoped. However, the process is important as it gives them the beginnings of developing the tools that will take them into adulthood.' Another said that, 'through group meetings and active listening we have focused on finding out how the children feel and have empowered them to make decisions alongside the adults.' (Holtoff & Eichsteller, 2009)

Social pedagogic work-based training for residential care workers has been taken up by employers in Scotland and Northern Ireland as well in England. Although clearly valuable, and stimulating much interest, work-based training is not equivalent to a full-time professional award at BA level, which would be required to make it comparable to continental European countries. Although routes to accreditation of this training are being explored and adopted, this is very much in the embryonic stage at the time of writing. Initial work on a Level 3 diploma in social pedagogy has begun and there are some BA programmes with explicit attention to social pedagogy, and an MA in Social Pedagogy has been launched at the Institute of Education, University of London. The curriculum of the BA (Honours) in Social Pedagogy at the University of Aberdeen which is co-run with Camphill School Aberdeen is clearly a model that can be used in the development of educational programmes for social pedagogy. However this programme would have to be adapted for more mainstream applicability.

The time is advancing when, in conjunction with the findings of the pilot programme, a national strategy to introduce social pedagogy will be necessary. Such a strategy will need to take into account the multiple players in work with children, including regulatory bodies, qualification and awards bodies, employer and higher education bodies. A first step is to decide whether social pedagogy is to be developed for all direct practice work with children in care and education settings (outside classroom teaching) or just with 'looked-after children.' As noted, social pedagogy has a mainstream applicability in other countries but the development of the EYP has taken the early childhood care and education workforce in a particular direction. Second, it is important to establish the scale of demand for social pedagogy programmes by mapping the qualifications profile of the current children's workforce onto the national qualifications framework and the social pedagogy qualification framework. Currently, the major demand is for courses pitched at Level 3, but more advanced courses are also needed. Third, a major issue is generating the teaching capacity in colleges and universities to deliver social pedagogy educational programmes. This could be done by investing in exchange programmes with continental European partners and English-medium taught courses in other countries. A fourth step is to revisit the national minimum standards and inspection requirements for children's services to ensure they are compatible with the principles of social pedagogy, and the organisational conditions that flow from these principles. A fifth step is to develop a framework for endorsing the curricula on social pedagogy programmes, to safeguard its integrity and ensure it meets quality standards. Many more steps will follow. An important development in the last year is the inauguration of two networks to further interest in social pedagogy. These are the Social Pedagogy Development Network, which brings together those interested in policy, practice and training, and an International Centre for the Understanding of Social Pedagogies at the Institute of Education, University of London, which is focused on theory and research.

Social pedagogy in the UK is fast establishing its place as a foundation for direct practice with children in care, and its relevance for work with all young people, and in some circumstances, adults. There are still sceptics, and there is a long road to travel to the wholesale adaptation of what we know of social pedagogy into a pedagogic care and education profession for children in the UK. However, in this chapter I hope to have shown that social pedagogy is not so very 'foreign' and that it offers a policy, practice and training coherence with many points of familiarity and, also, constructive challenges, for our children's workforce.

9. The Development of the BA in Social Pedagogy

ANGELIKA MONTEUX AND NORMA HART

Angelika Monteux has been a teacher and house co-ordinator in Camphill since 1973. In 2000 she became Camphill Director of the BA in Curative Education/Social Pedagogy.

Norma Hart trained as a social worker and is currently Senior Lecturer and Programme Director of the BA in Social Pedagogy, University of Aberdeen.

From the beginning of his work in Camphill, Karl König was concerned to establish an appropriate form of co-worker training, which included relevant areas of study and ways of enhancing the personal development of the individual student. In 1949, these approaches were formalised into what came to be known as the Camphill Course in Curative Education. This course, which he developed at the Camphill School in Aberdeen, was unlike any other course in either teacher or childcare training. And this was reflected in the title of the training: *Community as a path of learning.* Great emphasis was placed on the importance of personal development and learning gained in practice within a community living framework.

Students were expected to be fully engaged in community life and to show commitment to the work with the pupils in the houses, classes, craft workshops, therapy sessions, on the land and in a wide range of social and spiritual activities, such as Sunday services and seasonal festivals. This learning gained from daily life and practice, as well as through artistic activities, was an essential part of the training. The theoretical content was firmly based on anthroposophy, on the wealth of research and medical knowledge of König and other founder members. This form of training answered the longing for meaning and understanding in what they were doing, as memories of some of the early students illustrate.

> Next to looking after my seven boys, training to learn Music Therapy for deaf children, I also had to replace Morwenna Bucknall in her class ... The work was hard and absorbing and the friendships among us were one of the sustaining factors. I experienced every day as a privilege: this was a promising establishment with its own training course.
> (Bock in: Nauk, 2009: 35)

> In the course of the lessons which took place during rest hour for the children, an amazing and inspiring new world opened up for us ... Dr König's lectures in which he shared his deep insights into the background and challenges of 'our' children were very moving. We also had lectures by Thomas Weihs, Carlo Pietzner, and others; eurythmy lessons with Irmgard Lazarus and lyre playing with Susie Lissau (later Müller-Wiedemann) were a wonderful artistic accompaniment.
> (Nauk 2009: 16)

Twenty five co-workers completed the first course in 1951 and of these more than half continued to live and work in Camphill (Nauk, 2009).

The Seminar, as the course was usually called, soon expanded from a two to three-year course leading to the Camphill Certificate in Curative Education. Each year of the course had a special emphasis: during the first year the students learned about childcare in the home, were immersed in artistic activities and learned about the history of curative education, the main characteristics of a range of disabilities and were guided in developing observation skills. The focus of the second year was on the classroom: learning about Waldorf education and studying child development. It also included an introduction to an anthroposophic understanding of the physical, mental and spiritual aspects of the human being and the evolution of human consciousness. In the third year, a study of the senses and life processes, diagnosis and practical experience of therapies was introduced. Throughout the Seminar, artistic activities were provided for the students.

An indication of student numbers in the early years shows how central to life and learning the Seminar had become. Between 1955 and 1962 a total of 209 co-workers participated in the Seminar of which 111 successfully completed the course (Weihs, 1962). The rich content of the Seminar, combined with the challenge of community living, inspired and enabled many individuals to take what they had learned into new situations, to build new Camphill communities and establish curative education wherever it was seen to be needed.

Although the training work was initially focused on children in need of special care, König had a more encompassing vision:

> We only need to define the concept of curative education widely enough to see its true purpose. It is more than just practical child psychiatry and educational and psychological efforts to handle maladjusted children and 'dropped out' young people. Its intention is to become a global task to help counteract the 'threat to the individual person' which has arisen everywhere. The 'curative-educational attitude' needs to express itself in any social work, in pastoral care, in the care for the elderly, in the rehabilitation of the mentally ill and physically handicapped people, in the guidance of orphans and refuges, of suicidal and desperate individuals, in the international Peace Corps and similar ambitions.
> (König, 2009: 42)

This vision of the original Seminar has been highlighted by Müller-Wiedemann:

> In spite of the partly specialised subjects in the
> Training Course, the Course as such can be regarded
> as a 'Menschen Schule' — a 'School of Humanity' in
> which new human faculties can be acquired, where the
> fundamental spiritual value of the human being can be
> regained, both of which may also lead beyond the scope
> of education only.
> (Müller-Wiedemann, 1963: 37)

In order to learn how to apply this 'curative educational attitude' in different situations, particular importance was attached to the students' personal development and finding their own inner path. This is clearly reflected in the following statement by Thomas Weihs (1962) when describing the Seminar:

> An all-round 'human schooling' is needed as a result of
> which the student finds he has changed, his sense of value
> is different, new powers, new gifts are at his disposal.
>   Although the Training Course at Camphill is based
> on the teachings of Rudolf Steiner and the subsequent
> research carried out here, students are left free to assess
> the merits of Rudolf Steiner's philosophy themselves.
> Whatever a student's basic creed or outlook may be,
> few have failed to recognise the profoundly educational
> character of such a Training Course.
> (Weihs, 1962: 75)

When the Camphill Movement expanded into new communities in other countries, the Seminar retained its basic three-year structure. Whilst in some communities this training continues to follow closely the original framework and content, in others it has adapted to different circumstances and cultural influences. For example, the Friends of Camphill India community in Bangalore has established a training programme in curative education and social therapy. This is offered to the co-workers and people from various walks of life, who are either qualified professionals or people hoping to start curative work or parents of children with special needs.

The seed planted by König a long time ago has sprouted and grown in many ways, as is shown in the emergence of various other Camphill Seminars: for example, the Adult Communities Course, Kate Roth Seminar, Youth Guidance Seminar and Mental Health Seminar.

Although all these courses and seminars are appreciated and have succeeded in offering valuable insights and learning that help the professional development of participants, questions have arisen concerning their future, as the demand for professionally recognised training and qualifications challenges this form of 'in-house' training. For how long will they be relevant? Will they have to be replaced by other accredited courses? One possible answer is to use existing Camphill courses for the purpose of continuous ongoing learning, complementing official training; another answer is to go through the process of accreditation, which the Seminar in Aberdeen has successfully done.

The BA (Honours) in Curative Education/Social Pedagogy

In Aberdeen the original impulse for co-worker training has undergone many changes; in breaking this new ground it has continued the pioneering spirit and energy of the founders of Camphill. The Seminar, as it was taught in the Camphill School Aberdeen, was successful for many years until changes in government policies and regulations in the 1980s led to demands for new ways of training and the necessity for registration with accredited professional bodies. Other forms of professional training, such as in social work or special needs, were not delivering the specific knowledge and skills needed for work in Camphill settings. So began the search for a positive solution.

In 1995 the process of seeking accreditation for the Seminar started, with the support and encouragement of friends from outside Camphill. This involved working out a curriculum and writing up courses in a language that could be understood by the academic world. In 1997 this resulted in the Curative Education Awards Scheme — BA Degree in Curative Education, which was delivered in a partnership arrangement between the Northern College of Education, Aberdeen and Camphill Rudolf Steiner School. It was validated by the Open University.

This first version of the BA programme was closely modelled on the original three-year Camphill Seminar. Whilst little change was needed to the content, the teaching methods had to undergo significant change in order to develop a creative dialogue between the anthroposophical and other professional theories and approaches to practice. Students were strongly encouraged to adopt a critical and reflective attitude when exploring these different approaches. In spite of some initial hesitation and even defensiveness by Camphillers, it soon became clear that through the process of dialogue, questioning and critical reflection, both teachers and students could reach a deeper understanding of anthroposophy and curative education, and at the same time become more open to, and appreciative of, other ways of thinking and working. Many students have indicated that they found this to be one of the most important aspects of their learning: engaging with a wide range of ways of knowing and understanding the world and humanity. By acquiring confidence and competence in the knowledge, skills, attitudes and values of the curative educator, they could engage on a secure basis with other professionals.

In 2002 the Northern College of Education merged with Aberdeen University and the BA in Curative Education (BACE) was welcomed into the School of Education. At this point a number of important developments took place. An increasing number of students drawn from Camphill communities providing services for adults applied for entry into the BACE. This had two consequences. Firstly, the content of the programme had to respond to the learning needs of students who were working with adults. This necessitated expanding the course across the whole life course. Thus the concept of Curative Education was extended to include essential aspects of social therapy and youth guidance.

Secondly, the increasing popularity of the BACE led to the growth of a network of 'partner communities' spanning the whole of the UK and Ireland. To keep tutors and students fully informed concerning the delivery of courses and issues relating to student support and assessment, it was necessary to heighten general awareness and establish clear channels of communication. Further levels of complexity were added by the introduction of block teaching in three- to five-day day workshops in the later stages of the programme; this was partly to facilitate the development of an 'accelerated entry route' for experienced co-workers from any community in the UK and Ireland through a portfolio credit claim.

This was an important opportunity for experienced individuals who had carried responsibilities as house co-ordinators, teachers, therapists or craft instructors but who were now required to add an accredited and professionally recognised qualification to their internal Camphill training if they wanted to continue with their work. Having accepted the need for further study, many were reluctant to take up non-anthroposophically recognised forms of training and were glad to enrol on the BACE programme, whilst others decided to follow the SVQ or social work qualification route.

Another important step in the development of the BACE was gaining professional accreditation. This was almost more difficult to achieve than academic status, as it was necessary to enter a long and not always easy dialogue with the awarding body, the Scottish Social Services Council (SSSC). Again some professional friends undertook to support Camphill in this by successfully lobbying the Scottish Parliament to include in the Regulation of Care (Scotland) Act 2001 an acceptance of the principle of diversity. Inclusion of this principle meant that official recognition could be accorded to different forms of professional training. Finally, in 2003 the SSSC included the BACE in the list of recognised qualifications for workers in the residential childcare sector, which opened up the possibility for graduates to be employed in non-Camphill care settings.

Many of our graduates have now found work outside the Camphill communities in the UK. However this is still a complicated process as laws and policies regarding required and/

or recognised professional qualifications and employment differ from country to country.

Despite the Bologna agreement, which aimed to make academic degree standards and quality assurance standards more comparable and compatible across Europe, there continue to be considerable variations. Given that our graduates are now applying to work and study abroad, the BACE is becoming more widely known and now is more frequently accepted as a recognised undergraduate degree, which enables graduates to apply for postgraduate study or to use the BACE as a professional qualification. For example, in Israel the government has accepted the BACE as a qualification for special needs teachers.

Our students and their future careers

Annelies Brüll from Camphill School Aberdeen (CSA) has recently researched the career paths of over 110 students who graduated between 1999–2009. Twenty-six graduates have progressed to further studies in the fields of social work, teaching, and music and art therapy. Seven have achieved Masters level qualifications and sixteen have obtained postgraduate Diplomas. Nine are currently enrolled on academic study programmes, ten involved in vocational studies and seven are considering further academic studies. The tables below reveal the occupations of the graduates.

Working in Camphill communities worldwide		
Profession	CSA	Others
Care managers or house co-ordinators	10	23
Teachers	7	5
Workshop and craft instructors	2	4
Therapists	4	4
Tutors and co-ordinators in BACE	6	1

Working in non-Camphill settings	
Anthroposophical care centres	26
Mainstream care centres	15
Fulltime students	2
Non-care related professions	2

Assessed practice

It also became necessary to demonstrate that the supervision, teaching and assessment of practice were transparent and objective. As a result criterion-referenced assessment of the students' practice was introduced and explicit learning outcomes, clear procedures and criteria for assessment were developed. This was not an easy task for those involved in assessing practice, especially when tutors, students and assessors live in the same community or even in the same house. More recently, in 2008, a formal two-day training for practice supervisors/assessors has been provided to support them in this role. This is now offered annually and is complemented by regular peer group meetings throughout the periods of assessed practice.

In 2003 in order to strengthen and improve practice teaching and learning opportunities for the students, the focus on education — a core feature in the second year of the first version of the BACE — was replaced by practice 'electives.' Students could choose from one of four areas of curative education: education, care, crafts or therapeutic activities, in order to deepen their understanding of relevant theories and their application in practice. This development meant that many senior co-workers had to learn how to act as a practice tutor and to guide, support and assess their students. Such developments allowed the BACE to stimulate and encourage a process of ongoing learning in many areas of the community and to further strengthen the quality of practice-based learning which had already been an essential element in the original Camphill Seminar.

However there was a growing realisation that the electives were leading students to specialise too early in just one aspect of curative education with a resulting loss of breadth of experience. Consequently when the BACE programme was revalidated by the University of Aberdeen in 2008 and the Honours programme developed, rather than continuing to encourage such early specialisation, it was decided that the electives should be withdrawn and the emphasis placed on the development of the generic curative educator.

Assessed practice, in generic curative education, is now included in each of the first three stages of the degree programme. The benefits of this continuation of assessed practice, in effect now over four years, is that it is supported by the development in the student of a critically reflective attitude and an ability to effectively integrate an ever expanding knowledge and understanding of a range of theories and approaches in their work as curative educators. This summer (2010) the first group of students to complete the full three stages of assessed practice will graduate. Our external examiners have commended the high standard of practice evidenced by this group and have been particularly complimentary regarding the use of their reflective abilities and the strength and breadth of the knowledge base they draw on to inform their work.

Personal development planning

The use of personal development planning in each stage of the programme ensures that a healthy dialogue is encouraged between student, personal and practice tutors and the wider community as the student progresses through the programme. In the later stages of the programme the students are expected to grow into independent learners and in consultation with tutors and communities to negotiate the content of their studies to accommodate their particular interests within the broad field of curative education/social pedagogy. In these latter two stages the students are introduced to research, both in terms of understanding and using research to inform practice and in developing the skills of the practitioner-researcher to undertake small-scale action research that will be of use to their community/organisation.

Some issues and responses: local and worldwide

At the beginning it was not always easy to convince colleagues in Camphill of the positive nature of these developments, as they placed such a heavy demand on all those involved. Students were seen to be taking too much time away from community life in order to pursue their studies, whilst the students often experienced a tension between the academic demands of the programme and the needs of the community. In the Camphill School Aberdeen, an increase in the overall number of co-workers was necessitated in order to provide students with the required study time. The advantages of having qualified, well-trained co-workers have now been clearly recognised.

A great deal of painstaking hard work has been involved in developing the structure, content and delivery of the BA programme, which was the first in the world to achieve academic and professional accreditation. This development was particularly significant in the wider context of international anthroposophic training in curative education and social therapy. Similar collaborative arrangements to those existing in Aberdeen can now be found in other countries (e.g. Germany, Russia and USA). Many colleagues from the international network continue to look towards Aberdeen, given its long pioneering record, and are impressed by what is seen to be a unique partnership between an anthroposophically inspired training and a long established and respected university. There continues to be a high measure of support and positive interest in the programme from Aberdeen University and over the years a relationship of mutual trust and respect has grown between Camphill and the university. This is greatly enhanced by the untiring and generous engagement of the University Programme Director, who not only carries much of the administrative responsibility for the programme but also teaches, assesses and supports students and teachers on the programme, as well as attending many meetings in Camphill.

Along our developmental path we have been fortunate to have received extremely helpful critical feedback and formative support from our external examiners. Our initial external examiner Professor Steve Baron encouraged the team to be ambitious in terms of creating a degree level qualification rather than a diploma, and supported tutors as they engaged in the initial painful birthing process and the challenges of marking and giving appropriate feedback within a university system. Professor Roy McConkey from the University of Ulster then supported our ongoing development of the electives and we also benefited from his extensive knowledge in the field of learning disabilities. Due to the expansion of student numbers we currently have two external examiners: Jan Göschel who lives and works in Beaver Run, a Camphill community in Pennsylvania, and is involved in the development of degree level training in curative education in the USA; and Mark Smith who is a lecturer in social work at the University of Edinburgh and teaches and writes extensively on the ethics of care, residential childcare and social pedagogy. Together they combine their different areas of knowledge and expertise to provide a critical review of the programme as it develops its courses to Honours level and begins to locate within the wider landscape of social pedagogy.

Throughout this journey questions have continued to be asked about the role of anthroposophy in the BACE. Initially these took the form of worries about 'giving up' and losing essential aspects and ideals of Camphill and a resistance to making the training too intellectual in order to conform to academic requirements. These reservations were gradually overcome when it became clear that: (1) most of the key objectives of the original Seminar could be retained; (2) anthroposophy was not threatened by a more critical academic approach; (3) a dialogue with other theories and understandings was essential in developing curative education and social therapy.

Change of title: BA (Honours) Social Pedagogy

More recently the question of the programme's title has arisen again. The term curative education is neither a familiar term nor one which is understood in the UK, where it is often interpreted as having a 'curing' connotation. There was growing unease with the use of the term because of its medical, diagnostic and school-based connotations which occasionally had resulted in misunderstandings regarding the nature of the training offered and the professional abilities acquired by the graduating student. The title was seen as misrepresenting both the academic content of the programme and the nature of the professional training provided. As a consequence, it restricted the potential contribution that this form of training could make to professional thinking and practice in care and education in the UK. Furthermore, the title was not conducive to recruiting UK students.

In 2006 the BACE was described by a researcher at the Thomas Coram Research Unit as 'effectively the first BA in social pedagogy on UK shores.' (Cameron, 2006: 58) It was recognised by Cameron as the only professional training in the UK that, since its beginning, had adopted a social pedagogical approach to education and care. The strong pedagogical character of the programme was revealed in its emphasis on life sharing and the use of creative, social, cultural and practical activities to support learning and development.

On many occasions over the years the programme team had considered the possibility of a name change. Eventually, during the 2008–9 academic session and following extensive discussions with students, tutors and all the Camphill communities involved with the programme, it was agreed that a proposal to change the title to BA (Honours) in Social Pedagogy should be put forward. This was accepted by the communities and was finally ratified by the University of Aberdeen in January 2010. The new title will be in place at the beginning of the 2010–11 academic session.

Although not a familiar concept in the UK, social pedagogy is now being regarded with greater interest (Petrie et al., 2006; Lorenz, 2008). An increasing number of childcare organisations and educational institutions in the UK are developing social pedagogical programmes of various kinds and at various levels. In 2007, for example, a charitable organisation funded a pilot programme of training and mentoring in two regions in England (Bengtsson et. al., 2008). In 2008 in Scotland another charitable body, the Aberlour Trust, developed a successful staff training pilot programme (Milligan, 2009). It was, therefore, an opportune moment to position our programme within this growing social pedagogical impulse.

It should be stressed that there is no one single social pedagogical paradigm. Interpretations of the concept vary from country to country. Neither is social pedagogy a new and unique approach. Social pedagogy is largely understood as a multidisciplinary field of knowledge, linked to education and social work (Gustavsson et al., 2003). Social pedagogy in practice covers holistic and personal approaches to work with individuals and their families, linking education and care and is recognised as congruent with the values and attitudes, philosophy, ideas, approaches and practices of curative education. As with curative education, the common aspect of all social pedagogical training is that students are trained to have authentic and mutual relationships with the individuals with whom they work, while using the relationship to work purposefully and therapeutically in the broadest sense.

Our existing model of practice in the BA is clearly based on and has evolved from a European pedagogic tradition (Cameron, 2006). There are many features in common with continental pedagogy; for example, Steiner emphasised that education had to attend to the whole person and encompass *thinking, feeling and willing* or *head, heart and hands* in the language of social pedagogy. Another example of the common ground is the focus on learning through doing. In common with existing social pedagogy programmes, our curriculum includes a range of disciplines which are taught in an interdisciplinary fashion: care, education, arts, crafts and personal development. Therefore the concept of social pedagogy can usefully be seen as an open concept which can be used in a creative way to reflect on and develop the existing practice of curative education. At the time of writing this new phase of pioneering work has now begun.

Questions and conclusion

The rich content of the programme combined with the ongoing challenge of community living continues to inspire and enable many individuals to take what they have learned into new situations, to build new Camphill communities and to further develop curative education. The inevitable changes ahead will challenge and enrich the programme as it adapts to the needs of training students for work with vulnerable individuals in Camphill settings, in other organisations and in the wider community in and beyond the UK.

Questions still remain about the role of anthroposophy in the BA in Social Pedagogy. Is it at the centre? Or is it seen as one approach among others? While the programme retains a close link with the philosophical and educational work of Rudolf Steiner, it draws on a wide range of theory and practice from the fields of care, education and therapy in working with individuals of all ages.

This approach seems to be very close to Steiner's vision of the task of anthroposophy:

> Anthroposophy is not intended to be an abstract, lifeless theory that caters only for people's curiosity; nor is it meant to be a means by which just a few people try, selfishly, to attain a higher level of self-development for themselves alone. What it can do is to collaborate on solving the most important tasks of contemporary humanity, and supporting developments which enhance human well-being.
> (Steiner, 2008: 4)

While the programme continues to incorporate the insights and practice wisdom gained by Camphill over more than sixty years, it is now designed to prepare the graduating student for work in any care context not just in Camphill communities. Recruitment of applicants from within the UK and even from the local areas within Scotland is one of our future challenges. This raises a major question as to whether the current delivery model is appropriate or indeed sustainable. In 2010 the vast majority of our students still come from outside the UK and live and work as volunteer co-workers in Camphill communities or related organisations. This mainly residential model of training, with students sharing their lives with the individuals they care for, is not easily replicable or adaptable to wider services. It also limits the possibility of opening the programme to applicants interested in social pedagogy but who are not seeking to join a Camphill or similar organisation. The programme design will need to undergo considerable change if we are to build up the numbers of applicants from outwith traditional Camphill settings.

Over four decades ago König provided, in broad terms, what can perhaps be seen as the central purpose of social pedagogy:

> This is the only answer we have today — inasmuch as we still want to be human beings — for a society dancing on the brink of disaster. No philosophical congresses, international conferences, religious gatherings and enormous scientific events will influence this dance of death in any way.
>
> Only support from person to person — the encounter of a self with another self — the awareness of another individuality without questioning the other's religion, convictions and political background — just the gaze from eye to eye between two personalities, creates the kind of curative education which can, in a healing way, counteract the threat to the core of humanity.
> (König, 2009: 42)

10. Camphill Village Communities in Norway

NILS CHRISTIE

Nils Christie is a Professor in Criminology at the University of Oslo who claims that the best teachers in his life have been Camphill villagers. Permission has been granted by the author and Norwegian University Press to include parts of Beyond Loneliness and Institutions: Communes for Extraordinary People (1989) *in this chapter.*

Power and influence

Camphill villages have no Directors, no King, and no Parliament. Who decides? Formally, it is simple enough. The villages hang together in one foundation with a formal constitution. At the top is the Board of Directors with members from the villages and outside, from Norway and abroad, from ordinary people and less ordinary. They meet twice a year. That is when they decide. But of course, that is only the theory.

A Board that used its power would soon be without villages. Decisions are the gasoline of social systems. Village life is based on humans who take an unusual amount of personal responsibility for their own acts, particularly vis-a-vis those close to them. Orders from above remove responsibility. The Boards are, therefore, extremely reluctant in deciding anything that has not been decided beforehand.

Before each meeting of the Board, representatives from the villages have their own one-day meeting, discussing all matters, forming an opinion on most. These ideas will be evaluated by the Board and mostly accepted. Sometimes doubt is raised, which nearly always results in a postponement until the next Board meeting. Doubts are mostly raised because ideas are not clear enough. This becomes particularly visible at Board meetings with foreign members, at present from Finland, France and Ireland. Their presence creates a situation where we all have to speak English, which is the only language we all have in common. It is a burden, but also a great advantage. Board members say less and with reduced eloquence. Problems cannot so easily be glossed over. Proposals sound considerably less convincing; the core of the problem appears. New ideas directly from the Boards might also be brought forward, but only ideas to be discussed in the villages. Decisions lie with those living with the consequences of them.

Local boards for each village operate in much the same fashion as the general Board. They meet four times a year, survey the local financial situation, and help to clarify matters about which the village inhabitants are in doubt. They operate as a link to the local community. But like the Board they will not decide what is not already decided.

So decisions grow out of the villages but from where? Authorities outside the villages wanted to have a formal structure with a director at the top within each village. They have got it — on paper. I think, however, that very few in any village know who is in charge at any time; I am only able to remember who the director of one of the five villages is.

Some would say power is in the village assembly. The village assembly is for all. It is a large meeting held every week for all living in the village. Guests often attend. They get a special greeting. So also do newcomers, villagers or co-workers. The assembly has a chairman who directs the discussion. Matters of concern can be taken up during the village meeting, or proposed to the chairman during the preceding week.

The meeting commences with a reading of the minutes of the last meeting. The audience pays exceptionally close attention during this reading. The repetition of last week's meeting brings it all back. Protests and comments are frequent from all attending. Complaints and proposals are many: the roads are icy, they need sand; strong protest from those who use 'sparkstotting' (a sort of sledge to be pushed on the ice); shops are not clean enough; people are too late for meals or for work; why have not the dancing classes reopened after vacation; who has taken my bike; what can we do to produce more candles this autumn? Very often people who by many would be classified as deeply disturbed or insufficient raise questions, good questions. Sometimes those asking for the floor might have a speech difficulty. The chairman seems to be able to understand and translate the most blurred of speeches. Except from A and B who have their own secret language, languages beautiful to listen to. They receive great applause. One of them, a girl, is completely worn out after her delivery: sweaty, breathing fast as after a marathon, and smiling happily. She gets the emotional message across.

Often there are confrontations between participants: harsh words. Sometimes someone cries or leaves the hall. At the last meeting I attended one villager had an epileptic fit. He was discreetly helped out and home, but without any intermission in the meeting. Epileptic fits are a part of life: important if given importance. Once a demonstration was staged outside where the assembly was to be held. There had been quarrels on the topic of radios. The demonstrators — led by a person with Down's syndrome — were in favour of private radios in private rooms. They got their way. The revolt against the unsuitable new rhythm of the day also took place here.

So matters *are* decided on in the village assembly — concrete topics of interest to those attending. Since those living in the villages are so interested in each other, it matters what is said there. There is a great turnout at the meetings. But some of the most important decisions are not easily handled between so many people: new villages to be established, new villagers to be let in, new houses to be built, and new types of relationships to the authorities.

To understand where these matters are decided, we have to turn to the more general base for power in these villages. There are no roles that carry formal power in the villages.

But certain categories provide possibilities for gaining more influence than other categories. *Seniority* is of importance. Also on this point the villages are in contrast to the ordinary society. The repetitive rhythm of village life makes experience an asset. Those with a long life have a store of the *relevant* knowledge. Limits on dangerous tools mean also a limit to the attraction of the young entrepreneur. Collective living likewise sets limits to fast exposures of material successes. The emphasis on learning is not put on learning 'the latest thing' but penetrating eternal problems. And there is no time for retirement in the villages. Participation ends when life ends. Old age becomes a condition, not a handicap. Because of all this, by and large those who have been there for the longest time gain the greatest influence. Formal leaders are also to some extent chosen among these but seniority is not a guarantee of influence. Three of the founders of the villages in Norway are still living in the villages. All are held in exceptionally high esteem but only one has strong power extending throughout the whole system.

Kinship might also have been a base for power. Two generations of adults are sometimes living within the systems of villages. A family with four generations present was for some years living in one of the villages. But it is difficult to see these relations as any base for power. Very old persons represent a need of care rather than authority. And there do not seem to have developed any particular alliances of power between those generations which are actively working in the villages. Dynastic systems have not evolved.

But *sex* is of importance. By and large, the Norwegian villages are female-dominated systems. Homes are of visible importance. Needs of the households are in the forefront of many discussions. Males participate but do not dominate. The traditional male territory, the arena of work and technical knowledge, is not gaining any monopoly. On the contrary, considerations of 'workers' welfare' are given high priority. Cultural life is filled with themes of equal relevance for males and females. The total result of all this is that these villages do not provide the usual breeding ground for male dominance. In this situation strong females come to the forefront when decisions are made.

My suggestion would be that influence in the village is based on the fulfilment of two demands. Firstly, as a general requirement, to get influence it is necessary to cope with the demand for general participation in all of the three general areas of life: housekeeping, work and cultural activities. To cope with it all, one needs experience. Young people are here handicapped. So also are males.

The second demand is much more difficult to describe in a modern society. It cannot be described as a role. It is a profile. And it has to do with knowledge. But it is not like the profile of a philosopher, or a scientist for that matter, found within usual academic settings. It is not a profile of a person who can concentrate most available time and energy on academic matters. On the contrary, power within the villages is to be found in those persons who combine the daily concrete demands of housekeeping and work with exceptional energy, in a lifelong search for knowledge from that type of literature and art seen as important within the village. One person in one of the villages had interests and a profile as a scholar but tended to be a dropout when the onions were to be harvested. He was initially highly regarded but then shrank and left the village for a role where he could specialise as a man of knowledge. Other persons in the villages are exceptionally able to cope with practical tasks in the households or within the workshops. They have great autonomy within these areas. They might install telephones, erect beautiful barns or factories against considerable opposition. They are obviously powerful. But if they are not particularly interested in cultural life, they will have limited possibilities of gaining general leadership.

The most influential person in the villages of Norway these days is a person who combines an earlier and successful performance in all the three major arenas. In particular, her life has been one long search for intellectual answers. She is a life-long student with deep knowledge of the literature regarded as the most important in the villages, particularly the writings of Rudolf Steiner. She is also a charismatic person. Not in the misunderstood meaning of one who can seduce listeners, carrying them away by her oratorical abilities. She can do so, but is often rather dry, with a vocabulary hardly accessible to most people. Her charisma is more in the literal meaning of revealing the message, telling what sort of decisions would be most acceptable to most people. She asks what Goethe or König or Steiner or one of their commentators including herself would have thought, and sticks to that; what the Ministry of Social Affairs thinks may be food for thought, but not necessarily the last word. Her anchorage in the world of general ideas makes her in many ways uncompromising vis-a-vis authorities outside the villages: kind but without sentimentality; without compromises but always willing to try really radical alternatives. A believer in God who would love to see a village built up around Buddhistic philosophy; a sceptic, full of beliefs. Such a character is the person who holds most power within the village movement of the country.

This type of power is one with built-in limits. Again, this is so because of the demands in the villages that all participants have to function in all major tasks. This demand hinders leaders developing who have not been exposed to all sorts of challenges. Some belief systems foster rather peculiar leaders: fanatics who take their believers from the USA to the Caribbean and there encourage them all to commit collective suicide; or leaders who abuse their followers, economically or sexually; or leaders who turn the whole thing into factions of political extremism. But leaders of that type need distance to develop, distance from their followers and distance from the trivialities of everyday life. Confronted with the demand to prove excellence also in the task of changing napkins, to treat the mad with respect, to pick vegetables, to perform as Maria or as a thief in the play, they just cannot make it. The leaders who do emerge in the villages come so close that the whole set of norms of the daily life is activated. If they were to forget the norms of care and tender concern, they would not be in a position of leadership. The chances are also great that they will not forget, being that close.

All participants have to function with all tasks. But with this restriction others follow. Particularly, this creates limits to the size of the total system of villages that can hang together. Changing of napkins takes time. To be tied to the daily tasks means limits to time used in governing others. With growth the system will fragment, which is all for the good. If the network of villages grew large under one coherent system of leadership, things would have to be organised in other ways. Power would be formalised, bureaucracies created, clear lines of command and hierarchical structures established. The rewards built into the present village life would not be there. Work would be labour. Decisions would be made far away. Demands for compensatory rewards would be raised and differentiated salaries reintroduced. Villages would be converted into institutions and it would all be lost.

Rewards

All formal organisations we know from the sphere of work have numerous rewards built in: a ladder of promotions, with differences in salaries, in titles, in office space, in equipment provided to do the job. Often people are seated according to rank around tables for lunch or for meetings. The most important member will often arrive last, when they are all ready, so that none of his important time is lost. When the meeting is over, he — it is nearly always a he — leaves before any other. The right to use power is often seen as a part of the reward system. Sometimes it is seen as such an important part that other rewards can be minimised.

The villages have next to nothing of the usual rewards built in. Promotions do not exist; there are no positions to be promoted to. Responsibilities for tasks do exist but no task is seen as more important than any others. And none are allowed to develop as more important. If anybody tends to put too great an emphasis on any particular task within the village that person is often encouraged to leave the area and move into other tasks. The accounting system was to some extent centralised and brought to perfection by one person with a talent for computers. He was gently, and sometimes not so gently, encouraged to go into farm work instead. The bakery increased its production steadily. This is going too well was the verdict; so large a production of bread indicates that other values are given too little attention.

To counteract production, key personnel were given important challenges in the area of cultural life.

The closest one could come to a position of formal rank was probably to be a member of a team of experienced villagers who moved around in other villages to give advice. During the last weeks of writing this book I learned that the team has been dissolved. It was felt that it lessened the importance of the Board of Directors. To be a member of that Board is also an indication of trust. But the Board tries to minimise this by inviting everybody who is interested to attend most of the Board meetings. What is free for all cannot be used as rewards for a few.

An analogy to village life is family life but then in a special form, a form that combines old-fashioned families and modern ones. Village life resembles *old-fashioned families* in containing many members with common ties. All households are large and the village as a whole can be seen as an even greater unit of extended kinship. Small celebrations take place in the individual houses but the large ones are for all living in the village. When a child is born, it is of general concern. The Christening is a public event, with a celebration open to everybody. So is marriage and so is death. Family life in the village is an open life with all attending.

The similarity to the *modern family* is in the authority structure. Paterfamilias (mostly in the form of the materfamilias) does exist within some households but with few visible signs of privileges connected with the position. In some cases mother or father figures can be observed who do not take their equal share of the menial tasks but usually they take more than their share of these tasks. It is also difficult to establish an authoritarian role in the house. New and mostly young co-workers will appear in the houses. They will come with standards from the surrounding society. They just do not accept the old style but complain or leave. The villages have had such cases. Many also have children of their own. It is striking, and a matter of surprise, how the ordinary child and youth culture of Norway has put its stamp on these children. The villages have no television, very little of the values of the consumer society and great emphasis on spiritual life. But the children are of the usual sort; often noisy, rebellious and representing a common culture where any display of old-fashioned authority is flatly rejected. To bring up a child is a soft matter, to help a youngster into adulthood is like getting a salmon up from the river on so vulnerable a fishing rod that it can break at any moment. Authority is of limited use. In addition there is the fact that house parents are continuously short of time. They have their work and their cultural life. The problem in most households is lack of time and will to take responsibility for decisions and necessary work, rather than any overdose of authoritarianism.

Rewards in the villages are, therefore, more like rewards in ordinary families of a relatively democratic type, which means there are none, except respect and love and no hope of anything more. No ceremony for the mother of the year, no particular attention for the father, the aunt, the obedient son — just ordinary life, led according to ordinary standards. In contrast to formal organisations, there is no specification of goals, nor are there rules for how these goals ought to be reached. The lack of specifications for goal attainments means that performance cannot be measured. No winners can be found. *She was a good mother.* But why? If children were to sum up during the funeral, they might have trouble in finding an exact explanation of why and how. It was probably something of the atmosphere, the flow of daily events, myriads of encounters, hopefully a majority of them good. Within organisations ladders are to be climbed, goals to be reached. Family life is its own purpose. The process is the goal.

In the villages all life resembles family life. This creates one particular problem: What to do with those who get tired of the multi-task existence and think they deserve some special attention and rewards? What to do with status seekers where status is no commodity? Within other types of social organisation two solutions are used. Such people get honorary positions of some sort or they are forced to leave the organisation. But neither of these solutions is easy to apply within the villages particularly not the expulsive one. Villages are not easy to leave. It is a unique world with so many attractions that ordinary society will seem meagre fare both for those contemplating leaving, and for those who might wish them to do so. And after years in the villages nobody has money to start a new life. All needs have been cared for but all surplus money has been ploughed back into the village. It is also felt as a breach of one of the most basic rules to push people out if they have been in for a long time. Villages are for the whole life cycle. This is what the graveyard in the village tells us.

Honorary positions are equally impossible to distribute. No formal rulers exist. This takes the meaning away from honorary appointments. And there is no increase in privileges with increasing age or with particularly good deeds performed. The burden of physical age is so small compared to other burdens visible in abundance within any village. Age is, therefore, an attribute of limited interest. Nobody pays attention to the legal pensionable age. Without usual salaries and with an abundance of tasks in need of attention, people work with these tasks until they literally cannot function any more. This is all for the good compared to the consequences of age outside the villages but it is bad if one wishes to use age as a criterion for obtaining privileges.

Those not satisfied with just being decent are thus in trouble, and the village with them. This is the cost of such a system. Honorary positions are not available and cannot be without a breach with the basic demands of general participation and equality in the importance of all tasks.

Villages do not offer possibilities of vertical mobility, but the horizontal one remains open. Both villagers and co-workers move around to a considerable extent. They move inside the village or between villages both in Norway and internationally. Only a minority will have remained in the same house for more than three or four years. Most often individuals or couples move, but sometimes great parts of households. Shifting of place of work also happens. These possibilities for moving seem to function as a sort of safety valve. A household might get sour. A person might be felt as intolerable, or feel that the others are. But a house or a whole village might also be in need of a new member. The same is the case with places of work. The moves thus have the advantages of a lack of clarity. They might be the result of a push but also of a pull; they might be the result of strongly felt needs in the mover to leave or they might be the result of needs in the old household to get rid of the mover, or in the new household to get just her or him. An irritant in one setting might prove a resource in another. An extremely noisy extrovert might be a problem among equals, but a blessing in a very docile household. And here comes the advantage in the fact that all households as well as all villages are organised according to the same basic pattern. A move means new people and new social constellations but not new forms and rhythms. Many villagers go abroad. They visit foreign villages for days or years. Often they do not speak the language and are classified by authorities as retarded. But the rhythm and system of the village they come to is not unfamiliar. A few days after arrival they function in the new system.

One other route of escape or reward is open to those in the village: it goes into inner depths, meditatively or intellectually. Villages are places for reflection. The small moments of silence before meals and before meetings help participants again and again to correct the course. Village life is a life in turmoil with an abundance of tasks with a fight to get it all done in time. Nonetheless it has at the very same time qualities of tranquillity which give room for moves towards inner resources.

Are villages institutions?

The kind doctor was fond of Vidarasen, as an excellent institution, open for experiments, with lots of human contact. But still, for him, it was an institution. It was not real life. It would therefore as a matter of course be an improvement if humans moved out of the village and into real life. Those close to the villages have another view. They look at the villages as the real life, maybe extraordinarily real. They agree that life in institutions might often have less satisfying aspects, but claim that the villages are very far from being one. Are they right?

Four attributes are typical of most institutions. Firstly, most of the time is spent within a limited geographical area. Work, leisure, sleep — all take place within the same building and with the same people around all the time. This is typical of institutions. And it fits the villages. Here there is communal living, day and night. It is a life in deep contrast to the life led by the ordinary family members in ordinary life where most members leave both home and neighbourhood for work and leisure, and then often associate with several sets of people who do not know the other sets. So, on this account, villages are similar to institutions.

The second characteristic of institutions is the strong differentiation between staff and non-staff. Important staff members claim to be experts. They often have received a specialised education. There is the army in white, the doctors and nurses; or the army with keys locking up people; or those with the power of age: the old ones in boarding schools or the young ones in old folks home. There are those with access to private offices, to staff meetings, to special canteens, or to separate tables in the common canteen. Most often all these staff members have authority over all non-staff.

It is all basic for institutions but not for the villages. As we saw, various features of village life minimise the difference between us and them: the system of roads and tracks as a functional alternative to staff meetings, the sharing of all tasks and the belief in the dignified soul. And above all, guards and nurses go home; they also have a life outside the institution: house, family, leisure. Their time in the institution is labour for money. In the village they all remain, some forever: living close, acting together, working together, and relaxing close to each other. It is a totality but then a total community, not a total institution. In a paradoxical way the villages are more total than most total institutions described by Goffman in his book, *Asylums: Essays on the Social Situation of Mental Patients and Other Inmates* (1961). If anything, they are more similar to ships than hospitals.

A third attribute of institutions is that life there goes on according to a master plan. It is a life with a common, specified purpose. Prisons and hospitals are prime examples as are special homes for children, for students living at the school, for old folks or for various categories of handicapped persons. Punishment, treatment, education or care becomes the central purpose.

That villages have not the purpose of punishment goes without saying. Nor are they places for incarceration or isolation in any form. None are prevented from leaving if they so wish. People come there, first for some weeks. If they like it and the village accepts them, they can stay on. The question of treatment is more complex. Another word for treatment is healing, which means to make people whole again. In that sense the villages are places for healing. But this healing is not a temporary activity; it is a continuous and everlasting process. And it is a healing for all living there, not only for those supposed by authorities to be deficient. The village people do not regard their villages as places for a temporary stay but as places for life. As to the conventional meaning of treatment, the villages are clearly not places for that activity. There is no treatment for having Down's syndrome. Through early tests and abortions one can prevent the very existence of such persons. Through facial operations one can to some extent make people with Down's syndrome look like ordinary people. The village people are against both 'solutions.' Instead they believe in creating communal forms which are good to live in for extraordinary people. Treatment goes on in the villages when people get sick but not treatment against being different. Education is also given at Vidarasen and in the other villages. Some people learn to read and write, or knit, or play the flute or to practise eurhythmics. Most people listen to lectures or music several times a week. But that is part of life, of everybody's life. Education is not in any way the specific purpose of the stay.

And what about care: the answer would be the same. Villages are full of care. And again it relates to everybody: care as a part of life. But the purpose is not care. The purpose is life. On this point, however, it is more difficult to draw a line. Particularly, institutions for old folks and for the permanently handicapped are similar to the villages in not necessarily being temporary arrangements.

Then to a last point: institutions have *many of the same sorts of people* around: prisoners, patients, pupils, old people, handicapped. Is that also the case in the villages? The answer depends on whose perspective is applied. From a conventional point of view there is generally more of one particular sort within the limited space of the village than are found in the usual society outside the village. There are more with pensions for disabilities and many who receive financial benefits. From this point of view, therefore, villages are similar to most institutions. They have — as institutions — relatively more persons of the same sort gathered within a limited area.

But seen from the perspective of the village, the matter becomes quite different. Villagers are characters, types, personalities. They are similar because of their difference from the majority, but at the same time individually different. Institutions often extinguish differences. Sometimes numbers take the place of names, uniforms or state provided clothes make everybody similar, and so also do compulsory haircuts and rooms or cells stripped of private belongings. In contrast to this, village life accentuates individuality and also to some extent eccentricity. From that perspective of the village the situation is therefore the opposite. It is in the external society that everybody is of the same sort, pale copies conforming to the basic demands of industrial society and its need for consumption of the products. The villages are a system where differences between individuals are allowed to develop and where individuality reigns.

To sum up: these villages are similar to institutions in having all aspects of life going on within the same limited area. Seen from *the state point of view* they are also *similar* in having many of the same sort living there. But seen from the perspective of the villagers this aspect of the situation is the opposite. They are also different from institutions in not being organised around a rational, specific purpose, and particularly in not accentuating any split between me and you, between us and them.

Is village life ordinary life?

Not in the statistical sense. Not if we use industrialised societies as examples of what is ordinary. People in the villages know each other — nearly all by their first name. And the first name is used. People meet continuously. They are important to each other. They hate each other, love each other and go out of their way to make both known. They help and hurt and care. Villages are vividly alive. They are typical tightly knit communities.

The contrast is striking when we move from villages and back to ordinary urban life. These societies are large and they are based on specialisation. This creates conditions for inequality and for segregation. Also within these large types of system there exists a mutual dependence but that is between roles played by easily exchangeable persons. The complex system of technical and social tools must function but that does not depend on one person. Roles have to be filled but performers are exchangeable. It is also in the interests of smooth functioning to make large categories similar, exchangeable. But at the same time these systems will easily consist of people foreign to each other. Most people are linked up in some sort of network. Nonetheless, the majority of those physically close to us are people we do not know.

Aliens have always existed, on the periphery of the hunter's district, outside the village, outside the small town, creating fear and anxiety. With the growth of the city a completely new situation occurred for most people. The trademark of the modern city is the close alien. The unknown ones came close, crept into the same building but remained distant.

Compared to this type of society, the villages are different. They are tightly knit. Villagers are dependent on each other, not only as roles open to everybody but as persons. If anything, the villages are closer to medieval small towns than to any modern settlement. But even this does not quite fit. Seen from the outside — particularly from the state's point of view — these villages contain an extraordinary number of humans who would not be able to cope with life in ordinary society. They have in their midst an extraordinary number of those with a right to a pension, or who are in need of some sort of extraordinary assistance. Here they also differ from the prototype of the medieval town. Old-fashioned towns had a more even distribution of people — some of all sorts. A concentration of one sort was only found within some quarters of some towns. Such quarters were often called ghettos.

The village as a ghetto

In one interpretation of history the word 'ghetto' stems from the Italian word *bourghetto* — a castle for protection or for expulsion. The old prisons grew out of the castles — some rooms deep down underground or up in a tower, a lonely view for the princess fallen from grace. Ghetto life has two aspects: persons are brought there against their will or they gather there for protection.

In more recent times ghettos are most closely associated with ethnicity: Italian or Chinese communities in New York, Turkish in Berlin, Scandinavian settlements for pensioners in Spain. But behind this easy use of words lingers another image, the one of shame for Europe and death for Jews. Ghettos were those parts of cities where Jews were restricted to live. It was where they had their synagogues, schools and centres of learning; it was where they worked and lived. And it was where they again and again were victims of massacres, in olden times as in recent. Killed inside the ghetto or deported to the gas chambers from the ghetto. There are not exactly good vibrations from that concept.

Nonetheless we do not change realities by shying away from words. There are people who compare the villages to ghettos and rightly so. There are similarities and we have to investigate. But here a dilemma comes up. If it is true that Camphill villages come close to ghettos but ghettos give everybody bad vibrations should we not then immediately try to dissociate the villages from that terrible word? But that would be to give Hitler and Himmler a triple victory. Then it was not only the Jews who were exterminated. Then it was not only the ghettos as physical structures, houses, shops, synagogues which were burned. It would also mean the extermination of ghettos as a linguistic symbol for an *idea* of an important form of social life. The national socialists — and their predecessors through centuries — could kill and burn. But if we lose concepts each time evil forces overwhelm their realities, we lose more than the battle. We lose the heritage; we lose the links to what was fine in the old idea and eventually the ability to learn how to preserve the species. We would also desecrate the memory of those living in these forms. We have instead to rescue the idea of ghettos, find out what was their essence, see if they contain values and a framework for life which are also of importance in modern societies.

But compared to ghettos, we find a fundamental difference when we come to the villages. Those living in Camphill villages might be seen as similar to other villagers by the state and by outsiders but this is not the villagers' own perception. They see differences between themselves and similarities with people in the external society. What gives villagers an identity is pride in the village as a social form, not pride due to ethnicity or any belief in being God's particular favourites.

The village as a collective

In the wake of drug problems in society, collectives for drug users have developed. Many of them have a social form rather similar to the villages. People with drug problems and their helpers often share basic life conditions; they live together in the same households, they work together and they take part in the same cultural activities. But there are also important differences. Collectives have important differences between us and them. Life in the collectives is also a planned life. Life goes on according to a treatment plan or an educational plan. Life has an explicit purpose. Those with drug problems are to reach a position where they can cope with the problem. And life in the collective has to come to an end. The goal is to be able to live outside the collectivity. Life in the collective is supposed to be a life in progress: first year, second year, and then third year filled with trust and privileges, with clients supposed to be models for newcomers, and with persons nearly ripe for life in the ordinary society.

Only a minority actually stays on until the last stage. Some of those who stay and also some of those who run away earlier, sometimes declare that they actually would have wanted to stay on, maybe mostly using it as a base to come back to, but in some cases forever. These express a longing for the collective form, for the ideals, for the communal living. Some also make it; they come back as staff.

Seen from the perspective of the villages the major problem with the collectives is exactly what some of these youngsters express. Life in a good social system becomes somehow unreal when it is only for treatment or training, and with a definite end. From the good life, appealing to ideals and mobilising warm social relations, those living there are pushed back into forms of social life which are far from collective and with an emotional temperature on quite another level. From the village perspective it seems natural to suggest that collectives are a good thing, but that they should never come to a forced end. Those who want to stay on should do so forever.

Impossible, would be the answer from society and also from many workers in the collectives. Then the whole thing would choke, there would be no empty places for new drug addicts. But again, from the village perspective, one would suggest the obvious solution: let new people create new collectives. The old ones would probably be able slowly to earn more money and need slightly reduced support from the social welfare system. Generation after generation of new addicts might thus be able to move into new collective systems. Drugs would then really be a powerful factor in shaping the social fabric of a country.

But again, a statement as to the impossibility of the idea would come, this time from professional circles. If collectives were not for treatment, what then with the treaters? What about professional standards, case-loads, utility and knowledge of how to bring it all to an end? If the master plan, utility thinking and the clear goal collapsed, and if the role of client collapsed, then the professional role would also collapse. Then only ordinary standards for life would be left in the collectives. So, it will not happen. But if it had happened, the present collectives would have been social systems close to what the Camphill villages are today.

The village as a village

To understand what villages are, an attempt has been made — I hope with care and concern — to describe these tender species. Then, an attempt has been made to understand even more by comparing villages to other social arrangements. Total institutions have been one. We found some important similarities but also basic dissimilarities. Our villages are not institutions and therefore not total institutions either but they are more total than the ordinary society. More close to our villages were ghettos and collectives but here too fundamental differences remained.

What then is a village? The Camphill villages have something from all these other types of social systems but they are also different from them all. They are peculiar. So peculiar that we have no general concept for them, no word in common use which immediately tells people what they are. A communal life, with many of one sort together, without other goals than life and understanding, for such a life we are without immediately understood concepts ready for use. So, let us accept to call them just villages.

Villages are not part of the Norwegian heritage. In a land mostly filled with stone the distances between the fields were so large that households were forced to settle apart from each other. Also, when it comes to Central European villages today, it can be doubted if they belong to the same species as the villages described in this chapter. The old villages came closer, even if they had their class differences and their rulers within and from without. But they also had qualities of cultural life and cohesion, close to what is found within Vidarasen and the other places. Modern life has extinguished villages as a major form of social organisation. Maybe the extraordinary needs of extraordinary people will help to re-establish a model of a social form which is good for most people. Maybe the extraordinary ones might initiate a push towards an intellectual debate on how to convert parts of cities into conglomerates of more or less independent villages.

11. Camphill in South Africa: A Narrative

JULIAN SLEIGH

Julian Sleigh joined Camphill in 1953 and from 1958 has worked in South Africa. In 1965 he was ordained as a priest in the Christian Community.

Political background

In 1950 southern Africa consisted of the Union of South Africa (a British dominion), a central African federation of Southern Rhodesia, Northern Rhodesia and Nyasaland (that also enjoyed dominion status), the territory of South-West Africa (formerly a German colony, then administered by South Africa), and the two Portuguese colonies of Angola and Mozambique. In addition there were three British protectorates, Basutoland, Bechuanaland and Swaziland. In South Africa the trappings of British rule still applied. There was the royal coat of arms in any public building; the ceremonial head of state was the Governor-General, representing the monarchy. The government was in the hands of the National Party, General Smuts and his United Party having lost the election of 1948.

The National Party consisted of many determined Afrikaners who, in their early childhood, had experienced the concentration camps set up by the British at the end of the Anglo-Boer War. The white population of South Africa was divided down the middle: some three million were Afrikaners, speaking the young and growing language of Afrikaans, bonded together by their language, their religion (the Dutch Reformed Church), their party (die Nasionale Party) and their tradition that stemmed from the epic of the Voortrekkers. They had a folk-feeling that was galvanised mostly by resentment against the British and the Jewish 'Uitlanders.' The English-speaking population (also about three million) were the descendants of those who had come from England, mainly with the 1820-settlers, and with the establishment of British rule. Britain had originally annexed South Africa at the end of the eighteenth century, to prevent Napoleon from taking over this territory. Somewhat allied to the English-speaking South Africans were the Jewish people who had come, largely from Eastern Europe and also from Germany, in response to General Smuts' open-door policy; many came with nothing and courageously built up trading and manufacturing enterprises; they entered mining, and soon became the main financial power in the country. In addition, many immigrants from the Netherlands, Germany, Italy and Greece adopted English as their lingua franca.

The English- and the Afrikaans-speaking people lived alongside each other with varying degrees of uneasiness. Many Afrikaners had avoided involvement in the Second World War, as they sympathised with the Germans: they were drawn from Dutch, French (Huguenot) and German stock: most surnames among the Afrikaners were Dutch, French or even German. Afrikaners tended to be farmers: hence they were previously referred to as 'die Boere.' The Afrikaans language had grown out of the Dutch language: a simplified form of the language that could more easily be learned by the Malay servants brought in by the Dutch East India Company. They provided the workforce and often the companions of the Boers, and gradually evolved into the Coloured People, concentrated mainly in the Western Cape.

As the Dutch were establishing their settlements in the Cape, so the African tribes were moving down through Africa and penetrating South Africa: the Zulus, Xhosas, Sothos and Tswanas. They each had their areas where they settled, which later became the Native Reserves and subsequently the Homelands. In 1950 the government of the National Party was pursuing a policy of strict separation between people of European origin and those of colour: the latter included the so-called *Coloured* people, the so-called *Natives,* and the *Indian* population that had settled in Natal to work on the sugar plantations. The Prime Minister, D.F. Malan, coined the word 'apartheid' and in the course of the 1950s and early 1960s a battery of laws was passed that established apartheid in every sphere of life. The aim of the government was to ensure the ascendancy of the white people and within this the supremacy of the Afrikaner people. The government felt constrained to root out the English influence that predominated in the civil service; and the top posts in the Judiciary, the Executive and the military establishment were filled by members of the secret Broederbond.

In the 1950s the English-speaking population were mesmerised by all that was happening. They were politically weak and disunited, in spite of their so-called 'United Party,' the party of Smuts and Hofmeyer that now was led by Sir de Villiers Graaf. It was an ineffective opposition.

The country was affluent. The great scenic beauty of many areas encouraged tourism; natural resources were considerable, especially the gold and diamonds which sustained the mining industry; and cheap labour was readily available. Nevertheless the fact that the vast majority of South Africans were black — and had no political rights — gave rise to the ongoing 'Native question.' (In the fifties one spoke of the *Natives,* later of the *Bantu,* and then of the *Blacks.*) Throughout this time the government was terrified that either Soviet communism or the expansionist policies of Red China would work through such organisations as the African National Congress and the Pan-Africanist movement, and would foment revolution, whereby the white people would be driven into the sea and the country would be overrun by barbarian communism. The blatantly-organised and subtly divisive influence of apartheid created an atmosphere of insecurity that to some extent tended to unite the white people, despite their different origins and separate cultures, and to lead most of them to 'go along' with the system.

What was done for people with learning disabilities?

The social services in this South Africa were minimal, even for whites. The services for children with learning disabilities were pioneered by a few private welfare organisations that provided mainly custodial care, and the few over-populated mental institutions run by the government were primitive and unpleasant. Provision for people with learning disabilities was the Cinderella service coming last in the line of services that needed amenities and subsidies. But change was on its way.

May Redman was sixty; she and her husband Frank were living in retirement in the then quiet seaside town of Hermanus two hours drive eastward from Cape Town. They had one son, Robert, who was severely handicapped, both physically and intellectually. In 1950 there were no facilities for caring for him now that he was eighteen. By chance May found herself reading an article in the English magazine *Picture Post* all about a special residential school called Camphill near Aberdeen, precisely for children and adolescents like Robert. May then wrote to the doctor in charge. Could he accommodate Robert? Dr Karl König replied that the Scottish climate would be too demanding. But given her problem could she not find other parents similarly placed who could help her to bring about a venture like Camphill in South Africa? And he pledged his support.

May successfully rose to the challenge. A small farm just outside Hermanus was bought and an experienced co-worker arrived from Camphill. Children with a variety of special needs came from near and far. Whilst the team of co-workers and employed staff grew, May Redman saw to public relations and fundraising. In 1957, Dr König came to South Africa to see the children, meet parents and give lectures. He helped to form a bond between the centre at Hermanus and the growing Camphill Movement. In time the centre became a Camphill school both in name and in spirit.

Dr König's visit opened the possibility of a Camphill centre in Port Elizabeth, Johannesburg and Natal. Indeed when he returned in 1961 he inaugurated the Lake Farm Centre in Port Elizabeth and Cresset House between Johannesburg and Pretoria. A small centre in Natal came about later. Let us follow the narrative of these developments in greater detail.

The new dynamic

For Hermanus the historic moment of acceptance was already having its effect. The first sign of future development had been the engagement of Gabor Tallo, Camphill architect, to draw up plans for a second house which was completed the following year and named Robert's House. It took a while before the other seeds sown by Dr König's visit began to germinate. Heinz and Lieselotte Maurer pursued their intention of moving into Cape Town and opening a day centre, whilst Jack Walker and Ralph Kaplan, in Port Elizabeth, began to consolidate their mission to start a Camphill centre there. Harold Bayne, and a group of people around him, held fast to the aim of a centre near Johannesburg.

Renate and Margrit

Before Dr König's departure for South Africa, his daughter, Renate, a qualified nurse, had asked her father to look out for a job for her in that distant land. Soon after his return Renate and her friend Margrit announced that they would be going to work at Dawn Farm at Hermanus. At that time I was running the office at the Camphill School Aberdeen. Renate came to me and asked, 'Would you help us fill out the many forms that we have to submit in order to obtain permanent residence in South Africa?' Without really thinking I answered, 'Yes, of course — provided I can come too.' Whereupon Renate, in her direct way said, 'Well, why don't you?' With that there arose not only the picture of our working together but a good deal more.

With their arrival at Dawn Farm began a transformation from a home, in which eighteen boys and young men were gently cared for, into a much more vigorous curative educational centre. It had been a pampered place where the main cooking and cleaning and heavy work on the land had been done by the team of 'natives.' There was Cilliers, with his deep voice and noble bearing, who cleaned the house; he was a Xhosa. And then there was Joseph, the cook; an Ovambo. Finally, there was Ernest from Basutoland, who worked on the land. And then there were 'the boys' — all white persons, of course — who did a bit here and there, and had a long rest in the afternoon! All this began to change. Schooling was introduced in the mornings and craft training in the afternoons; various festivals were prepared with great energy; and the Bible Evening was established for the co-workers.

Robert's House

I arrived at Hermanus on February 22, 1958. A good friendship sprang up between us all. It was a harmonious time as we prepared for the opening of the new house, which was then nearing completion. In September of that year the house was ready, and to celebrate its opening we performed *A Midsummer Night's Dream* outdoors on the bank opposite the new house. With the move of the older boys into Robert's House, intensive activity began. Soon Christiane Hansen from The Hatch in England joined the team, and became the leader of Robert's House. It was not long after this that Michael Lauppe also came, from Camphill in Scotland. Whilst Heinz and Lieselotte went to Cape Town to found their day centre, Renate and I prepared for our nuptials. It wasn't easy to know how we should marry, as we wanted a Christian Community wedding and there was no priest anywhere in Africa. So we invited Peter Roth to come out from Botton to hold the service, which he duly did — on February 22, 1959, in the dining room of Robert's House. This visit saw the first celebrations of the renewed sacraments on African soil.

Port Elizabeth

In the meantime Jack and Theia Walker consolidated their intention to start a centre at Port Elizabeth. In the process an active correspondence developed between Jack and Dr König. They decided to go to Camphill to take part in the training course in curative education, and together with their children they left early in 1959. They returned after one year, in 1960. They had enthused four co-workers to join them. On their return Jack saw the opportunity of buying Lake Farm Hotel, in the Kraggakama on the outskirts of Port Elizabeth. This hotel, which was more like a guest farm, was where he and Theia had celebrated their honeymoon. Now it was for sale, and Jack's committee was able to buy it. Thus Lake Farm began very much as a family venture, until the first co-workers joined them. The four whom Jack had picked out in Britain were Ebba Gross (an all-round curative teacher, craftsperson, farmer and organiser — a cousin of Gisela Schlegel), Felicitas Fuss (a eurythmist), Karin Herms (who could turn her hand to anything from nursing to agriculture) and Walter Brecker (who had come originally from South Africa). This team was joined a little later by Inge Chambers and her son Edgar. And soon one of the local friends decided to leave his retail business and join the team; his name was Melville Segal.

Johannesburg

At the same time plans were going ahead in the Transvaal to establish a centre near Johannesburg. Harold Bayne was actively looking for a site where a school could be founded. And something remarkable happened. Dr König suggested that Hans and Susanne Müller-Wiedemann should come out to South Africa to take charge of this centre. In the course of 1959 they arrived, but because no place was ready for them in Johannesburg they came to Hermanus. This meant a considerable boost to the work there, and soon a seminar (i.e. a curative educational in-service training course) was established and the first group of students began to be trained. They included Wendy Tucker from the Transvaal, Margaret Blomkamp from Cape Town, Melville Segal (who had come from Lake Farm) and Desiree Abraham (from the town of Hermanus) — four real South Africans! Soon they were joined by Essie Stemmet, Adriaan Mocke, Fred Geel and Faith Ferron. As the years passed, more young co-workers came and passed through the training.

Time for a village

In 1960 it became clear that we would have to consider the establishment of a village for the adults, as many of the inhabitants of Robert's house were already over 21. However, in order to prepare for this new venture, it was decided to build a house that would be suitable as a training place for young adults or older adolescents. The idea for this new house was to give maximum independence to the trainees, as well as fostering their interdependence, and to form a new kind of working community in which there would be workshops and an active social life. It was a seedling for the coming village.

The house was designed like a cloister, with the social part at one end, the workshops at the other, and in between the bedrooms, like monks' cells. Cloister House began to be built in the course of 1960. During this year we actively prepared for a second visit of Dr König, which took place in March and April of 1961. This would be a very different visit: it would not consist so much of public lectures but would give Dr König a chance to consolidate the three centres of the Movement in Hermanus, Port Elizabeth and Johannesburg.

A house had been found on the northern outskirts of Johannesburg, in an area called Halfway House (because it lies halfway between Johannesburg and Pretoria). This beautiful house stood on twenty acres of land. It had been built by a millionaire, who then did not wish to live in it, and so was for sale. The committee in Johannesburg, led by Mr Bayne, secured the property and named it Cresset House, after the quarterly review of the Camphill Movement called *The Cresset* (a cresset is a vessel containing fire to kindle torches). Christiane Hansen, Michael Lauppe and Magda Lissau formed the team that went up to take over this property and found the school.

The visit of 1961

Dr König arrived on March 4, 1961, the anniversary of the death of Ita Wegman. It was also on March 4 that he had arrived in 1957. But in 1957 the ship had reached Cape Town on time; in 1961 it had been due to dock on March 2 but was unexpectedly delayed. It had been planned that a foundation stone would be laid in the Cloister House; Dr König and Alix Roth arrived just in time for the beginning of the festivities. The copper pentagon-dodecahedron had been made by our friend Ky Kotzuba of Cape Town, and we placed in it a dedication and a prayer to the spiritual world to guard the building and to strengthen the impulse of service and love that would fill its rooms and fill the hearts of all those who would live in it. Renate placed the foundation stone in a deep hole in the centre of the main room of the house, and a large stone was cemented over it by one of our employees and myself, demonstrating the working together of black and white.

This visit of Dr König was not as spectacular as the one of 1957 but in each of our places there were special ceremonies. In Hermanus there was the laying of the foundation stone. In Lake Farm, Dr König opened the Rudolf Steiner Centre. In Johannesburg, on April 8, he inaugurated Cresset House. Rain had threatened to wash out the event as it had been raining all around us but at Cresset House the sun shone.

The presence of Dr König was central in the lives of all co-workers and in the development of each of our places. He experienced this on all his travels: it helped sustain him. Having renewed his connection to all that was happening in South Africa, through his visit in 1961, he was able all the more to involve himself in the details as well as the broader issues that each of us had to face.

It was during this visit that a major political development took place in the country. The National Party, driven by its longing for total self-determination, conducted a referendum (only for white voters) which led to the turning of the Union of South Africa into a republic. Very soon afterwards Dr Verwoerd, who was then Prime Minister, announced at the Commonwealth meeting in London that South Africa would leave the Commonwealth. If he had not taken this step South Africa would undoubtedly have been banished from the Commonwealth, because of the apartheid policy and the vigour with which it was pursued. For Camphill this had a good effect: we found straightaway that many more Afrikaans parents applied for places for their children in our schools. The predominance of the English element had come to an end and the country was now far more balanced: the Afrikaner had asserted his right to what he considered to be his own country. One could see that apartheid was an evil policy, though there was as yet no thought of its total destruction. This was still a far-off prospect, and much suffering would have to be endured before it could be realised.

Consolidation of new ventures

The second half of 1961 was a time of steady work in Hermanus. The training course was getting under way, guided by Hans and Susi Müller-Wiedemann, with occasional visits from Hans van der Stok. There was the new programme for the older residents now centred in Cloister House, under the energetic guidance of Renate and myself. Hans Müller-Wiedemann began to work on his thesis on the post-encephalitic child, with the Professor of Psychology at the University of Cape Town (Dr Vera Grover) as his mentor. He presented his thesis and achieved a Ph.D. in the course of 1965.

The establishment of Cloister House brought about a new impulse within Dawn Farm. There were the upper houses (Dawn and Roberts and the School House), which were orientated towards curative education. The school began to take in girls as well as boys. And there was the impulse of Cloister House, which was clearly to prepare the young adults for life in a village: in fact to be the pioneers of a village in South Africa. Cloister House became responsible for the development of the farm and fields, as well as for clearing the bush and cultivating the vegetable garden. A very fine training in weaving was developed by Ruth Ecker in the large workshop of the house, and the other workshop was devoted to woodwork. The area around the house was developed as a park with facilities for various sports; there were many excursions to Cape Town for concerts or up into the hills for long walks. The guideline was 'work hard and play hard.' And through this there came about an insight into the requirements of village life as being a balance between 'Form, Freedom and Fun.'

Meanwhile the seminar, conducted by Hans and Susi, was of a high order. Few people were as gifted as Susi in the realm of lyre-playing, eurythmy and general knowledge about anthroposophy. She expected a high standard of performance and a striving for self-development and made great demands on everyone including herself. In spite of the challenges involved, the quality of her guidance was highly respected.

Hans's contribution was also of a high order both as a medical doctor and a philosopher with a deep devotion to anthroposophy. The constellation of children present provided the full spectrum of learning disability. The social life was demonstrably therapeutic, as well as having a spiritual orientation. Though separated in the activities of daily life, the two streams worked together for the preparation of festivals.

Cresset also had a very good run after the visit. It settled into its existence as a Camphill school, and was helped by the coming, first for a visit and then to stay, of Hans van der Stok. His wide knowledge of anthroposophy and his gifts and skills in the arts (especially modelling) made him a popular lecturer and participator in the anthroposophical groups in Johannesburg and Pretoria, as well as in Cresset House: in no time he had a very full schedule of lectures. He also linked up with Mrs Hubrechtse, a Waldorf teacher who was in Johannesburg, and with a group that wanted to form a Waldorf school. It was clear that he would be joined before long by Ella Snoek from Camphill in Scotland, an experienced teacher; and so preparations were made, guided mainly by Hans, for the founding of the Waldorf school in Johannesburg. This has since developed into the highly successful Michael Mount School in Bryanston.

The high time of Lake Farm (mid-1962) began to crumble after Michaelmas. In November 1962 Jack wrote to Dr König expressing concern about his wife Theia. He indicated in plaintive terms that the other co-workers were turning her life into that of a drudge. The other co-workers were all Germans apart from Melville Segal. Jack wrote full of doubts about whether he had been right to impose on Theia the life that they now had to lead, and there was a subtle implication that what made it difficult was the European mentality that could not accept the true and genuine South African way of life. Dr König replied, reminding Jack that Lake Farm was *his* enterprise, *his* choice, and that he could not now blame the wider Camphill for his present difficulties with the co-workers who had come to support his venture. With this the long-standing correspondence between Dr König and Jack Walker was fractured. The sad consequence of this was the loss of Lake Farm to the Camphill Movement.

Then I was prompted to take a trip to Europe. This was to discuss my personal calling to become a priest in the Christian Community, so as to be able to serve the new village — wherever and whenever it would come about — in a pastoral capacity. The first sounding of this calling had taken place just before our wedding, during a conversation with Peter Roth. Then, just after Easter 1960, I had a serious illness: it was a form of meningitis, or maybe encephalitis, and it had the effect of rendering me incapable of undertaking the strenuous physical work that I had been doing on the land with our trainees. Also I had had two dreams which related to becoming a priest.

Then, in the course of 1962, I met Mrs Evelyn Derry (later Capel) when she came to South Africa, and she began to formulate a plan whereby Heinz Maurer and I could go to the Priests Seminar in Stuttgart and be trained and ordained, so that we could bring the impulse of the Christian Community to South Africa. During my visit to Britain I had further talks with her, to clarify and consolidate this plan: whereby, by the end of 1963, Renate and I with our family would go over to

Britain. Renate would have a sabbatical year at Delrow House, where Mrs König was now living, and I would be free to go to Stuttgart. I could also talk this over more fully with Dr König.

In 1963 South Africa had already shown itself to be a year of change. The second house at Cresset was being built — and also an ingenious house, basically a rondavel (a traditional round or oval African house with thatched roof) was built especially for Hans van der Stok and Ella. They married in 1963, whilst Ella was teaching at the newly-born Waldorf school in Johannesburg. At Hermanus, Margrit Metraux took over Cloister House, and was soon joined by Mark and Rosalind Gartner who had come out from Botton Village, where they had worked for a number of years, having spent many years at the Central Training Workshops at Newton Dee. They were sent out by Dr König to be the torch-bearers of the village impulse and to take care of this idea during the absence of Renate and myself. Before they sailed for South Africa it was possible for the four of us, together with Dr König, to discuss how far things had gone with respect to the forming of the Camphill Village Trust in South Africa, and what seemed to be the most likely and appropriate way ahead. Mark took up this impulse with great enthusiasm and determination: he became part of the community of Cloister House and could see how urgent it was for the young people in that house to move out into the wider setting of a village. He also fostered the idea that the village should be near Cape Town rather than Johannesburg, an idea with which I fully concurred. He set up, together with Walter Goldberg, the South African Camphill Village Trust as a Section-21 Company (i.e. non-profit-making) and he drew up a fund-raising brochure to appeal for support for this project.

Mark, together with the early group of directors of the Camphill Village Trust (particularly Mr Walter Goldberg), began to search for a farm for the future village. This led to finding Alpha, a tract of undeveloped land, mainly consisting of sand and Portjackson bush, fifty kilometres north of Cape Town. There was one small and primitive house, and some distance away a separate two-roomed cottage with a bathroom. No fences, no electricity, no roads; water from a well-point. Most of the land had never been cultivated; some fields near the house were planted with yellow lupins, which made a good impression.

Mark and Rosalind moved to Alpha on the October 10, 1964, together with Lindy de Klerk and her son Philip, Peter Townsend, Chris Rhynas and Jeanette Perceval. Financially they were still linked with Hermanus, but the initial step into the village had been taken. Everything now remained to be built up. The second small building was extended; Chris Wegerif drew up the plans and a larger house came about which was named Pine Close.

Fulfilment and return

In May 1965 Heinz Maurer and I were ordained in London, and a few weeks after this event Renate and I and our three children sailed back to Cape Town. With us to join our team were Renate's sister, Veronika König, and Henryk Binder. On our arrival in Cape Town at Ascension, Renate and I spent a number of weeks at Hermanus while the house at Alpha was completed, and then in July we went to Alpha, and Mark and Rosalind had a well-earned holiday. Then a piece of news burst upon us: Hans and Susi were called to Germany by Dr König, who wished to have Hans at his side in the development of the Middle European Region. It was clear that either Rosalind and Mark, or Renate and myself, would have to go to Hermanus. Finally the eagerly-awaited letters arrived: Dr König suggested that Mark and Rosalind should go to Hermanus. On December 16, 1965, the sacred public holiday of the Afrikaner folk called the Day of the Covenant, Mark and Rosalind left Alpha and returned to Dawn Farm.

So the end of 1965 saw Mark and Rosalind taking hold of the situation at Hermanus, and Renate and I and our team applying ourselves to the building of the village on the farm Alpha. Hans van der Stok, in his leading position at Cresset House, was supported mainly by Michael and Christiane Lauppe, who had married in August 1962. Hans took Hans Müller-Wiedemann's place on the Central Movement Council and as chairman of the Regional Movement in South Africa.

Camphill's venture into Natal

The Rotary Club of Richmond approached some members of the Committee of Friends who wanted to establish a centre in Natal, with the offer of a property near Peattie Lake. The property had been a guest farm, and had been built without much regard for durability or design. However, that whole area was scheduled to be flooded, as a result of the building of a dam, whereupon compensation would be paid to property owners, which would enable a new site to be bought and a new centre established. In view of this it seemed as if we could at least make a start with that property and build up our connection to Natal. Michael and Christiane Lauppe agreed to go there from Cresset House, and work began in June 1965. However, it was very difficult to build up a team of co-workers who wished to go there so the wisdom of getting involved in this area was put into question. After various quite difficult meetings and much consideration, our South African Movement Group decided to withdraw. After this no further attempt was made to establish a centre in Natal.

Camphill village takes shape

We were very busy at the village making roads, laying pipes for the water system and planning the further development. We were greatly helped by service organisations as well as by private donations. The Lions Club of Kirstenbosch took the lead and enabled us to build a much-needed complex of workshops. For several years the largest workshop had to become the chapel on Sundays, but then a private donation from Ruth Ecker, a co-worker in the village, enabled us to build a free-standing chapel. Moreover we had a breakthrough with the Departments of Welfare and Community Development, whereby we could obtain loans for building houses: and the first two permanent houses, as well as the chapel, were built in 1968.

We established a vegetable garden, which involved much composting, manuring and irrigation; also, with the welcome help of service organisations, two chicken houses and an implement shed. And thereafter we planned and built more houses and a community centre. The community centre became possible thanks to a legacy from an unknown well-wisher: the foundation stone was laid by Monica, the wife of Walter Goldberg, and the building was ceremonially opened by Mrs König in March 1974. For several years she had divided her time between Botton Village and Alpha, before settling down there for her final years in a cottage called Fairways that came about through the efforts of the Nomads Golf Club. All these buildings were designed by Chris Wegerif.

Gradually the work on the land developed, with the establishment of a herd of Jersey cows: later a dairy was built, as well as three further workshops. Numbers in the village grew steadily, and it became an active and many-sided community. Leisure time activities diversified with the building of the community centre: we became a branch of the Provincial Library; a well-designed stage with lighting facilities encouraged dramatic productions, whilst at other times the audience space could be used for indoor sports. Alongside the community centre was the newly-established swimming pool, with a shallow children's pool alongside, bearing witness to the village's concern for its growing number of staff children. Thanks to the dedicated work of Ruth Ecker, Bill Chambers and Doug Willmott, numerous trees gradually transformed a desert into a sheltering landscape.

Hermanus unfolds

In the meantime Lawrence Adler joined the school at Hermanus. Lawrence had a deep knowledge of art and had run the first professional art gallery in Johannesburg. His parents were interested in biodynamic agriculture, and had come out with him as refugees from Germany to settle in the Johannesburg area. Lawrence later returned to Germany to train as a Waldorf teacher (1964–66) and came back to join the young and growing Waldorf School in Constantia, Cape Town. After some years it became clear that his gifts lay more in the direction of curative education, and so he joined Camphill in Hermanus. There he met Ingrid Roder, who had come to Hermanus from Newton Dee village in Scotland, and they married in 1972. Sometime later his parents also settled in Hermanus, where their biodynamic interest was warmly welcomed.

The village had been growing rapidly and absorbing the trainees that came out of Hermanus, as well as taking in applicants from elsewhere. But it now became clear that the rapid expansion would have to ease off. This meant that Hermanus faced the problem of what to do with those who graduated from their training centre. Lawrence then took a very courageous step. He had the vision that the school should buy the two adjacent farms belonging to the Le Roux family, and that there a new village should be founded. This was indeed achieved, and the Camphill Farm Community came into existence on the newly-acquired farms in 1976. Lawrence then masterminded the building of a fine complex of workshops and a living unit surrounding a magnificent oak tree. He achieved great success in fund-raising and in public relations, and won the support of the Department of Welfare, which then approved a scheme for erecting five houses and a large complex of buildings for agriculture. It became very important for us to safeguard our schools, to ensure that we could practise curative education and give children with special needs a chance to benefit from the Camphill methods and residential care.

1970: a year of crises

Thomas Weihs had expressed the strong opinion, at the Central Movement Council, that work in South Africa should cease because the rule of law was not upheld by the apartheid regime. Indeed in that year, mainly through ill-health, Hans van der Stok decided to return to Europe, leaving us without our chairman and representative on the Central Movement Council. Also

Michael and Christiane Lauppe decided to return to Europe. Mark and Rosalind Gartner had already left for Europe in 1968. The remaining co-workers, however, resolved to continue the work in South Africa, as they had taken on the destinies of many souls, also undertakings had been made to parents, and progress had been made with the authorities. In spite of the power of the apartheid regime, progressive forces were gathering strength to bring about change. A younger group of co-workers, meeting in Camphill Scotland resolved to support the continued work in South Africa, and Karin von Schilling decided to come out to join Cresset House. One can understand Thomas's reasoning, as South Africa was a nation in disgrace. But it is noteworthy that Thomas did nothing to counter the resolve of those who wished to remain in South Africa to continue the work, nor did he try to influence Karin's decision.

The National Council for Mental Health

In October 1970 a meeting of the Division for Mental Handicap of the National Council for Mental Health took place in Johannesburg. This was the first meeting of its kind since we had begun to work in South Africa. Relations with the National Council had not been very positive since the time of Dr König's first visit: the then Director (Mr T. J. Stander) had strange ideas about us, and was in fact very surprised, but one could also say gratified, when I turned up at the meeting. I greeted him in an open and friendly way, and he made me welcome. The chairman of the division was the redoubtable Dr Vera Grover (Professor of Psychology at Cape Town University), with whom we had already had some contact when she attended a conference in Hermanus led by Dr König in 1961. At one stage of the gathering, I was asked to give a description of our village. It was my birthday, and maybe I was feeling a certain exhilaration, anyway my presentation was well received. Very soon after the conference I was informed that I had been appointed a member of the executive of the division, as one of the nominees of the National Council: this meant that in future my attendance at such meetings would be covered by the payment of my fare and an allowance. This was the beginning of my intensive involvement with the National Council for Mental Health and its Division for Mental Handicap. This led to my open connection to Mr Stander and his assistant, Lage Vitus, and my collaboration and friendship with Dr Vera Grover.

On my return home I felt that it would be very good if all the centres that served the people with learning disability in the Western Cape area would meet together from time to time, so as to be able to speak to the National Council with a united voice: and so I called a meeting which took place early in 1971 at the Oasis Centre in Cape Town, and was voted into the chair. This was the founding of the Western Cape Forum, and I remained convener of it for fourteen years. This without doubt was a very positive development. We called in Dr Grover as our mentor. We examined every area of learning disability and the provision of services. We realised the dearth of services for the coloured community in the Western Cape area, and set up a task force to address this need.

In all of this I took an active part, as a convener of the Western Cape Forum and as a member of the executive of the national division. The core group of the forum became a very strong team. Judy Cooke was appointed Coordinator, with a salary provided by the National Council, for they recognised the value of the forum. She worked for many years and then was succeeded by others who also rendered wonderful service. All of this eventually led to my succeeding Dr Grover when she retired as Chairman of the division in 1980. Pressure of other commitments limited my chairmanship to four years, but Camphill's standing in the country gained substantially as a result of this front-stage involvement.

Atlantis and Orion

The forum was not only a kind of talk-shop. We instituted in-service training courses under the auspices of the Extra-Mural Department of the University of Cape Town. Moreover, through the task force that had been set up, plans were made and new centres were established for the coloured people — by the Oasis Centre, by the Cerebral Palsy Association, and especially by the Cape Mental Health Society. Day centres came about in the various residential areas: and because there was a very big development plan to take place in Atlantis, in the vicinity of Camphill village. In 1982 I took on to spearhead the founding of a centre for the handicapped in that area.

With the help primarily of Veronica Jackson, a village co-worker, we called meetings of social workers, health visitors and ministers of religion in the nascent town of Atlantis: and the outcome of this was the founding of the Orion organisation. This was later in 1985 taken over by Melville Segal. We called him to become the Executive Director of Orion, a post which he filled with great distinction and success for twelve years, until illness forced him into early retirement in 1997. Fortunately a very capable director was appointed to take his place, namely Lizelle van Wyk, and this has safeguarded the future of this now major organisation.

In 1990 Melville received the Rotary Award of Excellence for his services to Orion from the Bloubergstrand Club, and in 1996 Melville, Vera Grover, Renate and myself were among those who received the award of the Hamlet Foundation for outstanding achievement in the service of persons with learning disability.

With the arrival of the new millennium, South Africa rejoiced at the peaceful overcoming of apartheid and the endeavour to build a truly human democracy in the spirit of *Ubuntu* — respectful togetherness. Our places now welcome all races. This constitutes a challenge, a new agenda and a deeply rewarding human task.

12. Healing and Transformation in Vietnam: The Peaceful Bamboo Family, Tinh Truc Gia

Ha Vinh Tho

Ha Vinh Tho is Head of Learning and Development, International Committee of the Red Cross. He has lived in a Camphill community in Switzerland for over twenty years.

Background

In 1982, some time after the end of the war in Vietnam, I had the opportunity to go back to Vietnam where my father lived. Since 1977 I had been working and living in a Camphill community (Perceval, Switzerland) with my wife Lisi and our two children. I felt deeply concerned by the situation in Vietnam and, more specifically, the fate of the children with disabilities. At that time, the country was barely recovering from the consequences of the war, and the situation of the children living with disabilities and their families was very difficult. As there were hardly enough schools and teachers for regular primary education, it was understandable why special education was not a priority.

To understand the situation in Vietnam, it is necessary to recall some aspects of the country's recent history. What happened soon after the French departure from Vietnam in 1954 became what the Vietnamese call the 'American war' but known in the West simply as the Vietnam War. This war constantly escalated during the 1960s and ended with the withdrawal of the American troops in 1973. This was soon followed by the collapse of South Vietnam and the reunification of the country under a communist regime in April 1975. The war had lasted over thirty years and had left the country utterly destroyed; most of the infrastructure had been bombed; 58,159 US soldiers, and an estimated three million Vietnamese had lost their lives. This does not take account of the physical and psychological scars and wounds the war left behind.

Early in the American military campaign it was decided that since the enemy were hiding their activities under triple-canopy jungle, a useful first step might be to defoliate certain areas. The defoliants were distributed in drums marked with colour-coded bands, including most notoriously Agent Orange, which contained dioxin. About twelve million gallons (45 million litres) of Agent Orange were sprayed over Southeast Asia during the American involvement. The Vietnamese government estimates that there are over four million victims of dioxin poisoning in Vietnam. These chemicals continue to change the landscape, cause diseases and birth defects, and poison the food chain. Although there are no independent scientific research statistics available, it seems reasonable to assume that the high proportion of children with birth defects and other disabilities was, and still is, related to this problem.

Eurasia

The Eurasia Association — later Foundation Eurasia — was created by my wife and I, out of a desire to contribute to solving this difficult situation. Its objectives are:

- To foster the development and social integration of mentally and physically disabled individuals and children living in Vietnam
- To strive for the recognition of, and respect for, their dignity and rights

What began as modest financial support for children and their families has gradually evolved into training teachers in curative education, creating special classes in regular primary schools and building special schools. The list of the activities of Eurasia is a long and varied one:

- Building eight classes for special education in regular primary schools
- Building two special schools for children with severe disabilities
- Building four vocational training workshops for both underprivileged and disabled youths
- Setting up a one year postgraduate training in special education in Hue University
- Organising, sponsoring and teaching each year training workshops in special education and social therapy
- Financing scholarships for orphans and disabled children
- Launching an environmental project 'Thousand trees for Vietnam' that involved Swiss schoolchildren sponsoring the planting of trees in order to reforest devastated areas in the Vietnamese hills and building a nursery for trees and a forestry school for hill-tribe children
- Translating and publishing literature on curative education
- Financing surgery programmes for children with physical disabilities: clubfoot, harelip, heart defect
- Developing home-based programmes to support families with children living with disabilities
- Building a centre for elderly ladies who have lost their relatives in the war
- Organising and sponsoring two festivals for and by the disabled children and youths in Hue: three days of exhibitions, performances, games

Foundation Eurasia has also sponsored seven Vietnamese students to attend full training at Camphill Perceval, Switzerland. All of them are now back in Vietnam, and four of them work directly with Foundation Eurasia.

A *challenging context*

Even though we have developed many activities over the years, when coming to a country like Vietnam with an anthroposophical impulse, we need to do so in a very subtle and careful way. Whilst we don't necessarily use the word anthroposophy, it has nevertheless been an impulse that has been nourished by what we have learned by working and living in a Camphill community.

We have come to a country that belongs to the Buddhist tradition, is under the political rule of the communist party, and has been colonised for many decades. Understandably there is a certain sensitivity on the part of our Vietnamese partners. We do not want to come to Vietnam with any kind of missionary attitude, trying to convert people or impose foreign ideas and values.

But how does one do that in a skilful way, so that it can really be helpful for the people to find themselves and is not seen as seeking to impose yet another ideology from the outside? The Vietnamese certainly do not need or want more foreigners telling them what is right and wrong for them, what to do and what not to do. Therefore we work in close cooperation with our Vietnamese partners: local authorities, schools, universities, Buddhist and Christian religious groups, parents, teachers, medical doctors (both traditional and western trained), psychologists and other professionals. Our strategy is to respond to needs and demands formulated by our partners and not to impose our views or our ideas.

Although the teacher training offered is based on our experience and work in Camphill, anthroposophy and Camphill principles and practice were not, until recently, explicitly part of that training. We wanted to address the local social, cultural, spiritual, economic and political needs arising from the specific requirements of the Vietnamese situation.

Building on local culture

To give one example of our effort to build on the local culture, I would like to look at a fundamental teaching of the Buddha that helps to create a spiritual basis for curative education and social therapy in a Buddhist country. There is a teaching by the Buddha called 'the teaching of the four kinds of nutriment.' The Buddha said, 'Nothing in the universe can live without food.' Whoever wants to practise the spiritual path, has to be attentive to four kinds of nutriments.

THE FIRST KIND OF NUTRIMENT

The first kind of nutriment is physical food, whatever we eat and whatever we produce to eat. The quality of the food we ingest not only has an effect on our physical body but it also affects our consciousness and our spiritual development. So the food that we consume has an overall effect on us. It also has a direct effect on the earth in which we grow this food and on the environment.

The word agriculture means etymologically 'cultivation of the field' which implies the activity to transform nature into culture; it is about the humanisation of nature. Food has a direct relationship between how we heal the earth and how we heal the human being and how these two aspects are interrelated. So when creating a community for social therapy in Vietnam, we can easily explain not only the importance of organic agriculture and of ecology but also of an appropriate diet for both residents and educators, all building on this teaching of the Buddha.

THE SECOND KIND OF NUTRIMENT

The Buddha describes sense perceptions as the second kind of nutriment. Whatever we perceive is food for our senses and for our soul. And in the same way that the food that we eat can be nourishing and healing or poisoning, perceptions — what we see, what we hear, what we smell, what we taste and so on — can be either nourishing or poisoning. The environment that we create determines the quality of our sense perceptions. This consciousness of the spiritual dimension of sense perception as a nutriment, as a nourishing factor or poisoning factor, is crucial to our pedagogical and social therapeutic work.

Here again, when we try to emphasise the importance of landscaping, of architecture, of using natural and beautiful material in the houses to create an environment conducive to curative education and social therapy, we can build on this teaching of the Buddha to convey these values to Asian students.

THE THIRD KIND OF NUTRIMENT

The third kind of nutriment is described by the Buddha as consciousness — what in Buddhism are called 'mental formations.' This describes whatever lives in our consciousness: thoughts, emotions, pictures and memories. Whatever appears in our consciousness is a 'mental formation.' In Buddhist psychology, there is the analogy which represents human consciousness in terms of a field. In this field there are all the different kinds of seed that exist in the universe. Depending on which seeds one waters and cultivates, consciousness will develop accordingly. In the same way that a gardener or a farmer decides which seeds he will plant and water in his garden, one needs to decide which seeds one wants to cultivate in one's consciousness. We need to observe and decide which seeds we are cultivating in our mind. From that will follow what manifests itself in our consciousness and in our life. So, from this point of view, spiritual work is a form of inner gardening, it is about choosing the right seeds, watering the right seeds and pulling out the weeds. The French writer Saint-Exupéry describes this in a wonderful way in his book, *The Little Prince*:

Now there were some terrible seeds on the planet that was the home of the little Prince; and these were the seeds of the baobab. The soil of that planet was infested with them. A baobab is something you will never, never be able to get rid of if you attend to it too late. It spreads over the entire planet. It bores clear through it with its roots. And if the planet is too small, and the baobabs are too many, they split it in pieces ...

'It is a question of discipline,' the little Prince said to me later on. 'When you've finished your own toilet in the morning, then it is time to attend to the toilet of your planet, just so, with the greatest care. You must see to it that you pull up regularly all the baobabs, at the very first moment when they can be distinguished from the rosebushes which they resemble so closely in their earliest youth. It is very tedious work,' the little Prince added, 'but very easy.'

This story presents a very good picture of this process of inner work and spiritual development. If we weed out the negative seeds that are in our consciousness while they are very small, it is quite easy to overcome them. A seed of anger or of violence, when it is still very small, is easy to remove. If we let it grow, it can turn into a conflict that will harm the community or the family and, ultimately, even escalate into a war where people will die.

We can see that the small seed and the powerful tree are of the same nature. The small seed of anger, the small seed of intolerance, the small seed of violence, as long as they are small they are easy to weed out. If I let them grow and multiply, it could create a disaster.

So consciousness is a field and we have to be the gardeners of our own consciousness. We have to keep our consciousness clean, we have to weed it and we have to carefully water and cultivate those seeds that can carry beautiful flowers and fruits for the well-being of mankind and for our own well-being. From this point of view, meditation can be seen as gardening our own soul, our own consciousness.

When we work with our Vietnamese colleagues, we can easily build on what the Buddha has said, to explain to them why as an educator, teacher, special teacher, gardener, we need to undertake this kind of inner work, for without it, without self education, it is not possible to educate and to heal others.

THE FOURTH KIND OF NUTRIMENT

The Buddha describes the fourth kind of nutriment as karma. The word 'karma' means 'action' in Sanskrit. We should become aware of the influence on our own destiny of the deeds that we do and do not do. Because karma is not only determined by what we do, it is also affected by what we have not done. It can be positive, like avoiding harm to others, or negative, like not assisting someone in need.

Actions have to do with moral responsibility, and there is a great need in our time to raise an awareness of our global responsibility. We have, as individuals, a broader responsibility. Each of our deeds determines the direction that mankind and the evolution of our planet and of the universe will take. It is in our hands. Therefore through our actions, we have the possibility of transforming the world but at the same time our actions help shape our consciousness and our destiny. So each action that we take helps transform the world and by doing so, transforms us at the same time.

So a very fundamental question here is to know if we can develop a global ethic: a kind of ethic that is not just Western or Asian, Christian, Buddhist, Hindu or Muslim or belonging to any specific ethnicity, nationality or group; but is a universal human ethic based on an awareness that every single deed that we do, every single deed that we refrain from doing has a creative power in the world. This creative power shapes my own destiny and also co-creates the world's destiny.

This is one example of how we have tried to develop our work in the field of social therapy which builds not only on local traditions, on Buddhist spirituality and on Vietnamese culture, but also encompasses values that are universally human and that build on the understanding and wisdom gained through the study of anthroposophy. In this way we can develop a common understanding, together with our Vietnamese friends and colleagues. We are not trying to convert anyone, we don't ask them to change their beliefs, but we do try to do what I believe anthroposophy is meant to do which is to provide the means to deepen our understanding of our own tradition in a more spiritual way.

The Peaceful Bamboo Family

Until recently, we felt that the time was not right to create a living and working community that would be directly inspired by the Camphill model. But three years ago, the situation changed. We realised how difficult it was to find suitable vocational training and also an appropriate place to live for the youngsters from our schools once they finished their primary education.

Our Vietnamese co-workers expressed the wish to create a community based on the same values and principles they had experienced when training and visiting various Camphill communities. This intention came at the same time as demands from parents and families who were desperate to find a way to ensure the future for their children. Out of the needs of the youngsters, the wishes of the parents and the will of our Vietnamese co-workers, the vision that led to the creation of the Peaceful Bamboo Family was born.

The Peaceful Bamboo Family is a life community located on the outskirts of Hue, in Central Vietnam, where youngsters and young adults living with disabilities live, train and work, very much in accordance with the 'village model' developed within Camphill. In line with the teaching on the four nutriments, our first effort was to create an environment and architectural forms that would manifest the ideals of the community, and that would have a healing quality. We worked with a Vietnamese architect living in Switzerland but who was originally a native of Hue. We tried to put our vision into words in such a way that the architect would be able to help us to transform our ideas into concrete architectural forms.

The outcome was a design based on the yin/yang polarity formed by two buildings. It also reflected our wish to unite in an harmonious way both Western and Eastern culture and spirituality, hence the name Foundation Eurasia. In the first building called The Lotus Pond, there are living quarters for the youngsters and their educators, workshops, the kitchen and the dining room. In the second building called The Sunflower, there are training rooms, the office, a showroom and guestrooms. The buildings are both L-shaped which creates an inner open courtyard that is the heart of the centre.

We also planted many trees, bushes and flowers, adding to the many bamboos that surround the property and that gave the name to our community. It is our aim to raise environmental and ecological awareness, but also to show how a beautiful, harmonious environment is part of the healing effort of a social therapeutic community.

The process of creating the centre was in itself a community effort. With our small core team, we worked simultaneously on the buildings, the surroundings, the complex administrative issues, the equipment, the pedagogical and social therapeutic concept, the recruitment of the staff and, not least, the fund-raising, because when we originally conceived of the project, Eurasia did not own any capital worth speaking of.

THE INAUGURATION

The first youngsters coming to live and start their vocational training in the Peaceful Bamboo Family arrived in February 2009. In the beginning everything was new to everyone. The construction had not yet been finished, and the daily activities, the household tasks, the educational activities, but also the events for the inauguration, all had to be thought about and prepared. About thirty members of Foundation Eurasia came from Switzerland and they joined in the festivities at the inauguration as well as many officials, friends and local partners. Thanks to that common effort all was ready for the wonderful three days of festivities. It was an auspicious beginning for this new community.

SATURDAY APRIL 11, 2009

On Saturday evening, we welcomed the Swiss delegation comprising almost thirty friends, most of them professionals in the field of special education and social therapy. After a festive dinner in the inner courtyard, the guests shared their experiences of working and living with disabled children and adults, and spoke about the Camphill Movement as an international organisation that has been a pioneer in this field. It was an inspiring evening for our team from the Peaceful Bamboo Family.

EASTER SUNDAY APRIL 12, 2009

Our team worked late and got up early to prepare everything for the ceremony that began at 7.30 a.m. It was a lovely morning with the sun shining bright and hot. The Swiss delegation had arrived by bus at Tu Hieu Monastery, the root temple of Zen Master Thich Nhat Hanh, and they walked for ten minutes through fields and bamboo groves from the temple to the centre.

The altar was covered with fruit, flowers and other traditional offerings, and a delegation of monks from Tu Hieu monastery, supported by three head nuns from other local temples, recited sutras and prayers to bless the centre. A deceased friend had donated the funds to buy the vegetable garden and we had engraved a stone to commemorate her, the monks blessed the stone to honour her memory. I gave a talk on behalf of the team; the Swiss friends performed eurythmy and sang. Everyone shared a tasty breakfast with traditional Hue cakes and homemade jam from the youngsters' workshop. Then we all went for a walking meditation to Tu Hieu monastery.

This is only a summary of some of the visible activities of this wonderful morning. The most important event was the creation of relationships between people, cultures and traditions, all meeting in a spirit of respect, mutual tolerance and appreciation. This set the tone for the spirit of our community.

MONDAY APRIL 13, 2009

We organised a first curative education and social therapy conference, as a starting point for the ongoing training facility that the centre wants to develop. About eighty participants had come together: special teachers from the seven schools that Eurasia had created, professors from the department of education of the Hue University, educators and therapists from Switzerland and the team from the Peaceful Bamboo Family.

The participants divided into several workshops and explored various pedagogical and therapeutic activities: painting, music, eurythmy, physical therapy, special education and the Padovan method (form of neurological re-organisation therapy). After these practical experiences, several round table conversations provided an opportunity to share and exchange questions and challenges facing a special educator. This first conference confirmed the needs of educators to have more opportunities to learn together, and to be offered continuing training in their field.

TUESDAY APRIL 14, 2009

The day of the official inauguration had arrived. From the Monday afternoon, the whole team, supported by many volunteers, worked hard to prepare everything for this event. A tent was put up in the courtyard; there were so many colourful flowers everywhere, and large banners to announce the event. Teachers dressed in traditional Ao Dai welcomed the guests and showed them to their seats under the tent. More than two hundred people came for the opening ceremony including the Swiss Ambassador who had come from Hanoi.

The youngsters from the centre opened the ceremony with

a Vietnamese and a French song. Some officials gave speeches, including the Swiss Ambassador and the deputy chairman of the province, there was a symbolic cutting of the ribbon and the Swiss delegation provided some choral singing. We then visited the centre and had an informal time socialising around a delicious buffet. The weather had been perfect for us during these days with sunshine in the morning and refreshing rain in the afternoon.

CURRENT SITUATION AND FURTHER PROJECTS

THE RESIDENTS IN THE PEACEFUL BAMBOO FAMILY

There are now twenty residents and three day students: seven girls and sixteen boys. The youngest is fourteen and the oldest 32. The progress they have achieved in such a short time is impressive. Their behaviour, social and practical skills, self-confidence and openness have all improved in a visible way. Community life is now well established and real friendships are developing among the youngsters. Of course, there are occasional conflict situations but overall they have a sense of belonging and have become a tightly knit group which gives each member help and support. One of the residents, a young woman with Down's syndrome in her early thirties, had never been to school before. She is slowly learning to read and write and it was deeply moving to witness how happy she was when she recognised her name for the first time. There are also three deaf-mute young people with well-developed intellectual abilities. The team is committed to improving their programme, so that opportunities can be offered to them to meet their needs and fulfil their potential. The team has created individual pedagogical programmes so that each resident has clear learning objectives in all areas including social and life skills.

This effort has also provided a training opportunity for the staff. Every Friday afternoon and Saturday morning, co-workers meet to discuss all aspects of their work and life. During the Friday afternoon meeting, a special teacher from another school created by Eurasia gives lessons to all residents with more academic skills. A good rhythm has now been achieved between vocational training, boarding and cultural activities.

THE PEDAGOGICAL TEAM

The Vietnamese pedagogical team is well trained and very motivated. Here again, it is impressive to observe how in a relatively short time, the team has grown into their task and learned through practice. We have had the first yearly appraisal conversations with each co-worker and the opportunity to listen to them. We have been impressed by the level of commitment and enthusiasm displayed by the team, although there is a lot of work to be done in this pioneer phase.

THE VOCATIONAL TRAINING WORKSHOPS

The vocational training and production in the workshops have developed better and faster than expected. First of all, there is the vocational training which has been of a high professional standard in a wide variety of fields: jam and ice-cream production, embroidery, lacquer painting, gardening, household work. As a result of the quality of the work, the products sell well. The jam is so popular that the production team has a hard time to meet the demand. The lacquer paintings have been a great success, especially in Switzerland. While the financial income generated is still modest, it nevertheless represents a real contribution to the running costs of the workshops. As the painting teacher is also a trained potter, we plan to open a pottery workshop in the near future. We also want to develop further biodynamic gardening, not only for our students and our own consumption, but also as an ecological pilot project for the province. A next phase will include the development of the guest-rooms, which will provide an opportunity to train our youngsters in this field.

An important challenge is to develop our economic activity so that progressively the centre becomes more financially independent and less dependent on foreign support. On the other hand, the educational mission should not be undermined by financial imperatives; it is therefore a constant effort to find the right balance in the workshops between economic productivity and vocational training.

ONGOING TRAINING IN CURATIVE EDUCATION AND SOCIAL THERAPY

It is the intention of the Peaceful Bamboo Family to become an educational resource centre and an ongoing training facility not only for our own staff, but also for the city, the province and even for the region. In November 2009, the centre organised a week-long training course in child development and developmental disorders. Fifty teachers, educators from all the special schools in Hue, as well as lecturers from the Hue University attended the course.

In April 2010, the Peaceful Bamboo Family hosted a regional conference on curative education and social therapy on the theme, 'Educating the head, the heart and the hand.' Eighty participants attended including several professors from the Hue University and some of their students; there were also contributors from Switzerland, Holland, Thailand, Brazil, France and Vietnam. We plan to strengthen cooperation with other training institutes and universities, both locally and internationally.

CAMPHILL

Not being affiliated to the government or any religious institution, the Peaceful Bamboo Family needs not only friends but to feel 'part of a community.' There is a genuine wish from our Vietnamese co-workers to be part of the Camphill Movement and to belong to something bigger than their daily work in Hue. Many questions still remain: how can Camphill manifest itself in a totally different surrounding? How can Vietnamese culture — its spirituality, history, social, economic and political context, be taken into account — without diluting the fundamental values and principles of Camphill? These questions offer an opportunity to explore ways of manifesting the Camphill ethos in different cultural contexts and in challenging and changing times.

13. Eco-communities: An Eco-history of Camphill

JAN MARTIN BANG

Jan Bang was a kibbutz member in Israel for sixteen years and a Camphill co-worker in Norway for seven years, and now co-edits Landsbyliv, *the Norwegian Camphill magazine.*

When Camphill was founded in 1940 ecology and the environment were not current issues, indeed they were hardly thought of as subjects for discussion. Both the biodynamic and the organic agricultural movements were still in relative infancy, and it was survival through a world war which was uppermost in people's minds. However, even right at the beginning, certain decisions were made which set the course for future developments. The original founders had neither the resources nor the inclination to employ staff to take care of the physical task of looking after the land belonging to the school. In a rural setting, and surrounded by the natural beauty of the landscape, working the land fell quite easily into the pattern of school life.

> At the same time, we had to learn to care for the grounds and the garden, to look after the house, to do the cooking and all the other domestic work, because from the very beginning we had decided not to employ any staff or servants but to do all the work with our own hands. (König, 1993: 15)

When König later came to frame the ideals of the Camphill community he included the surroundings, the natural context, and invited all who did their work to do so out of love for the children, the sick, the suffering; and out of love for the soil, the gardens, fields and woods (König, 1954).

In the late 1940s and early 1950s there were very few people aware of the ecological consequences of modern industrial farming. Rachel Carson had not yet written *Silent Spring* and the organic and biodynamic movements were tiny and relatively unknown (Carson, 1962). Yet König was aware of the dangers that the environment faced:

> There are, however, other aims ahead of us. One
> of the foremost tasks will be the care of the land.
> Gardens and farms today are ruined and exploited by
> mechanised work and chemical fertilisers. The soil
> all over the world is like someone who suffers and
> cries out for help and healing. It is to be hoped that
> the Movement will find the right helpers to create
> remedial work in this field.
> (König, 1993: 34)

König was of course greatly inspired by Rudolf Steiner in many fields of endeavour, not least in agriculture. Not only in agriculture as such, but he discovered an esoteric connection between farming and curative education. In a lecture in 1964 he described how after Steiner had given the 'Agriculture Course' at Koberwitz over Whitsun 1924, he had travelled on to Jena where he opened the Lauenstein — the first curative educational institute. After that he carried on to Dornach where he gave the course on curative education. König noted that:

> Where these two streams — flowing from a renewed
> agriculture and from an all-embracing curative education
> — meet, there arose the village impulse as a new, third
> element. These will be villages where the farmer will
> be responsible for the land, the livestock and the plants.

> Around him tradesmen, artists and craftsmen will gather
> in order to be creatively active out of a new spiritual joy.
> (König, 1964: 475)

Steiner regarded the farm not as an isolated cog in a vast agribusiness economy, but as a self-sufficient cell which produced a surplus. Indeed, one of the basic ideas in biodynamic farming is to see the farm as a single organism, creating an internal ecology where the animals are fed by the land, which again is nourished by the manure generated by the animals. The farmer's skill lies in managing this cycle in such a way that it produces a surplus. Steiner's view was endorsed by Barton (2008: 171) who observed that: '... a farm comes closest to its own essence when it can be conceived as a kind of independent individuality, a self-contained entity. In reality, every farm ought to aspire to this state of being a self-contained individuality.'

With the establishment of Botton Village in 1956 a more holistic human community could be developed. König envisaged the Camphill village of Botton to be quite different from the previously established schools. Instead of teaching children, the focus was to be on working alongside adults who needed help, in a variety of work situations, farms, gardens, houses and workshops. Instead of a school, we had a microcosm of society: a microcosm which was to have a wide-reaching influence over the rest of society. In an address entitled The Three Great Errors which was given by König on May 27, 1956, he said, 'The Camphill village could be a vital experiment for future social needs.' (Farrants, 1988: 15)

König was clearly anticipating the needs of the future when establishing the shape of the Camphill villages. His vision went far beyond the needs of the handicapped and anticipated the ideals of the ecovillages which were to be formulated clearly only decades later. As we saw earlier, he was already well aware of the erosive results of chemical agriculture leading to the loss of good farmland. He also knew how air and water were declining in quality due to a mixture of pollution and over use. Farrants has noted that:

> The resources of the earth are gigantic and mankind has taken them for granted as unquestioned conditions of existence to which there was no thinkable limit. But in recent decades, the results of man's insatiable use of the elements have begun to loom threateningly all over the world.
> (Farrants, 1988: 9)

During the 1960s, 1970s and 1980s the establishment of a network of alternative communal living arrangements occurred both in Britain and worldwide. Their focus was social rather than environmental, though care for the environment in an organic way was largely taken for granted. There was not a great deal of overlap between these alternative communities and the Camphill villages. Andrew Rigby (1974) in his book *Communes in Britain* mentions Camphill communities as religious and/or therapeutic communities basing their worldview upon anthroposophy. Clem Gorman, writing a year later in the book *People Together*, a good straightforward account of communes in England from the early 1970s, does not mention them at all (Gorman, 1975). Nick Saunders published his *Alternative England and Wales* the same year, and does not mention Camphill as a movement, but has this to say about Botton Village: '... [this] Rudolf Steiner village is involved with organic growing. They welcome visitors to help and learn.' (Saunders, 1975) Sarah Eno and Dave Treanor (1982) who by the early 1980s had acquired over a decade of communal living experience published a helpful handbook which made no mention of any contact with Camphill. In 1978 and again in 1983 The Teachers Community, based in North Wales, published directories of alternative communities in the British Isles but again without any mention of Camphill. However, the situation was about to change.

I was personally involved in arranging a series of three gatherings in Britain between 1978 and 1983 on the theme of Cooperative Villages. Throughout the early 1970s I was active in the alternative commune network, visiting communities, and attending occasional gatherings. I did not come across Camphill at any of these events. At the first Cooperative Village conference in 1978, held at Lifespan, a small commune in the Pennines, two people turned up in the middle unannounced, spent some time listening, and then broke into the discussion by saying, 'We live in a village like that!' They were from Botton, and the excitement caused by their descriptions of Botton life led to the next conference being held there in 1980 in order to create a link between the Camphill network and the wider alternative network. However, despite the fact that many people involved in alternative communities attended and were shown around Botton, there was very little follow up. But at least Camphill was beginning to be known.

The Teachers' Community disappeared from the scene after 1984, but a loose constellation of alternative communes — Diggers and Dreamers — began to publish regular directories of British communes, and Camphill was mentioned from the 1990 edition onwards (Communes Network, 1991, 1995, 1997). There was no mention of the Camphill Movement as a network, but only individual Camphill places; Botton, Ochil Tower, Pennine, Glencraig, Camphill Rudolf Steiner School near Aberdeen and The Sheiling, all had entries during those years. This does not mean that the Diggers and Dreamers did not know about other Camphill communities. They were sending out over four hundred questionnaires before every edition, but were getting back a good deal less than one hundred replies. It may well be imagined that in the busy day-to-day life of a Camphill village few co-workers had the time or energy to reply.

In the autumn of 1995 the Findhorn community in Scotland organised a conference on the theme 'Ecovillages and Sustainable Communities.' On the way there, I travelled with one of the founders of the Global Ecovillage Network (GEN), Albert Bates, and together we visited Botton Village and several other Camphill communities, including Camphill School and Newton Dee. While at Botton he gave a presentation about GEN to a packed village hall. Albert Bates wrote the entry for ecovillages in the *Encyclopaedia of Community* and mentions Rudolf Steiner as one of the influences guiding ecovillage development (Christensen & Levinson, 2003). At the conference the Global Ecovillage Network was formally founded and a definition of what an ecovillage might be was considered. This was no simple task, as the network was created in order to be inclusive, and the aim was to stimulate and encourage positive environmental projects of a wide variety of types.

Diane and Robert Gilman (1991) had been asked to write a report on ecovillages, and it was this that had created the thinking that eventually led to the creation of GEN. The Gilmans had defined an ecovillage under five main headings:

- Human scale
- A full featured settlement, in which the major functions of life are all present in balanced proportions
- Human activities harmlessly integrated into the natural world
- Supportive of healthy human development
- Successfully able to continue into the indefinite future

Most Camphill co-workers would feel comfortable with these aspects as part of their village life, though they would probably want to add in social and spiritual aims, and extend healthy human development into the areas of care for people who need help in their lives. Although the Camphill Movement played no part in this new initiative, it was clear that the Camphill communities would fit well into any definition of an ecovillage.

The connection had been built, and though the Camphill network did not enthusiastically join the growing network of ecovillages, key figures in GEN were very aware of Camphill's existence. In the GEN *Directory of Ecovillages in Europe*, published in 1998, a few Camphill and curative education places were mentioned: Camphill Vallersund in Norway, Mourne Grange in Northern Ireland, and Solheimar in Iceland (Brinkheim & Kennedy, 1998). Four years later Hildur Jackson, one of the founding members of GEN published *Ecovillage Living* together with Karen Svensson, which had three articles about Camphill initiatives, (Jackson & Svensson, 2002). Anyone reading about ecovillages would now be aware of the Camphill Movement.

While this exciting development in the world of social and environmental alternatives was taking place, Camphill was not standing still and resting on its laurels. If we go back through the magazine *Camphill Correspondence* over the last two decades, we find an increasing number of references to how Camphill co-workers were responding to the challenge of industrial society's growing destructive effect upon the ecology of our planet. These initiatives are exactly what GEN was attempting to inspire by its creation; local action growing out of a global perspective.

In 1989 Fiona Wessels wrote in response to the question 'How can Camphill respond to the needs of our time?'

> What is Camphill's contribution towards healing the pollution of the earth? Pollution makes the earth and her spheres into an ill body. It is the healing impulse within Camphill that can contribute to her healing ... in responding to the needs of the world there will always be a true meaning behind the existence of Camphill. (Wessels, 1989: 4)

Four years later Deborah Hudson (1992) reports on the cooperation between Camphill Larchfield and the newly opened Botanic Centre in Middlesbrough: '... the board of the Botanic Centre is full of potential for mutual sharing. It encompasses members from Camphill and Emerson, as well as individuals representing both local industry and government.' This is a good example of Camphill building ties with local environmental activists. In 1995 an example of outreach came up again with Karen Hems from the Camphill Devon Community reporting on the activities of a biodynamic seed saving and exchange group: '... our work is in developing methods which allow the plant to find its rightful connection to the environment, the local physical conditions and the cosmos.' (Hems, 1995)

In 1993 Peter Bateson gave an address at the official opening of Watch Oak Farm and summed up wonderfully why Camphill was concerned with environmental issues:

> ... in agriculture, by using the biodynamic method we try to bring about the same kind of healing–in–balance

and balance-in-healing with our relationship to the land
itself — to create in the life of a farm a complete and
complex organism of mineral, plant and animal processes in
one whole, husbanded by man. The fundamental principle
is that in caring for the land, by maintaining the health
of the soil, we can not only receive ever more richly the
fruits of the earth, but can help to maintain and improve
the environment itself. Care for the land, not exploitation.
Ecology is not a matter of mere self-preservation but a
moral duty for the well-being of the whole earth.
(Bateson, 1993: 18–20)

Another new Camphill initiative in Russia echoes a similar
aim a year later. Margit Engel writes under the title *A Camphill
village in Russia*?:

In regard to our specific Camphill impulse the main task
seems twofold: to receive villagers from the overcrowded
institution nearby but also from parents of the county
which has welcomed us so warmly. A second task is to
start biodynamic (ecological) farming. This meets with
great interest in the surroundings.
(Engel, 1994: 10)

In 1995, *Camphill Correspondence* published an article by Will
Browne, who has worked in Botton and with Iris Water (and
now has building and planning responsibilities at Vidaråsen
in Norway) (Browne, 1995). The article was originally printed
in *Resurgence* magazine and describes in great detail the waste-
water treatment systems pioneered by Ove Burke using Flowform
cascades developed by John Wilkes at Emerson College. These
have now become standard in many Camphill villages; indeed the
one installed at Camphill Solborg in Norway was the subject of
a thorough study by the Agricultural University and led to these
systems being accepted as rural waste-water solutions in Norway.
     In 1996 Eric Hoyland from Camphill Tiphereth outside
Edinburgh described a new venture aimed at diversifying the
activities there:

> On the premises we have a small wood workshop, a
> reasonably sized garden and a composting scheme. We
> collect kitchen and garden waste from local houses (sixty
> at the moment) and make this into compost. We hope to
> transfer this composting scheme to an adjoining disused
> quarry, as soon as the council have made the quarry
> safe, using the compost to make a wildlife garden in the
> quarry, expanding our day activities there to include
> some gardeners who are confined to wheelchairs.
> (Hoyland, 1996: 10–11)

In 1998 Will Browne again writes in *Camphill Correspondence*,
this time turning his hand to ecological housing and describing
the new care and therapy house at Vidaråsen in Norway which
he helped design and build in collaboration with Joan de Ris
Allen of Camphill Architects.

> A special effort has been made to incorporate as many
> ecological building principles in the project as possible
> including the use of solar panels on the roof which
> should provide the energy for heating most of the hot
> water needed in the house. Other measures include
> 'breathing walls,' recycled newspaper insulation, natural
> ventilation, wood-fired heating and natural paints and
> finishes throughout the building.
> (Browne, 1998: 13–14)

These examples, from the ideological underpinnings,
outreach, farming and gardening, wastewater treatment and
now housing show how holistic and all encompassing Camphill
village design has become. This is exactly the way that GEN
conceived ecovillage design and shows how the developments
were running in parallel, even if there was relatively little cross-
fertilisation.

In 1998 Richard Phethean reflected on the Camphill Easter
Symposium and discovered the deeper parallels running between
social design and natural ecologies: '... leading a group in plant

observation, I was very aware of how many times during our deliberations, community processes were described using terminology taken from plant growth and forms.' (Phethean, 1998: 4–5) This again reflects some of the basic thinking in ecovillage design, where patterns are taken from nature and applied to creating systems that the ecovillage requires.

At the end of the twentieth century Patrick Lydon described a more ambitious project, combining agriculture and energy production at Camphill Ballytobin in Ireland: '... we are busy building a bio-gas digestion plant that will provide us with heat and electricity from fully renewable sources. Our partners are neighbouring farmers who will supply us with our essential raw material ... and together we will achieve a clear environmental benefit.' (Lydon, 1999: 2–5) Five years later Clanabogan hosted a Renewable Energy Conference which was covered by Hetty van Brandenburg and Patrick Lydon in *Camphill Correspondence*. He wrote then about their initial aims at Ballytobin which were:

- The establishment of fuel systems that were more eco-friendly
- The establishment of local economies in which we could participate with more sense of responsibility
- A sense of using our strength as a kind of local leadership in ecological and energy development
(Lydon, 2005: 6)

Hetty van Brandenburg went into more detail:

On September 29 the Renewable Energy Project in Camphill community Clanabogan was launched in partnership with the Omagh Environment and Energy Consortium — OEEC. This project is continuing with a particular focus on addressing the training needs of those pioneering the use of this renewable energy technology ... the wish arose to share findings and knowledge and to reflect on the question of what this new feature of life has to do with the Camphill ethos. Thus a Camphill

Conference was organised, where local specialists
involved in renewable energy projects across Northern
Ireland were invited to speak to Camphill participants
from all over Scotland, Ireland, England, Germany
and the Netherlands. The contributions included slide
presentations about technical aspects and practical
application of renewables in various localities. The
renewables presented were wood burners, solar panels,
photovoltaics, windmills and geothermal heat pumps and
hydro-energy.
(Brandenburg, 2005: 5–6)

Establishing personal connections and motivating young
people were taken up by Vivian Griffiths in 2000: '... there are
Camphill communities where land work is in association with
other local biodynamic initiatives: Oaklands and The Severn
Valley Training; the biodynamic experimental farm at Camphill
Hapstead. And there are Camphill places where people from
neighbouring towns can experience working on the land as
volunteers: Larchfield, Camphill Houses Stourbridge. These are
some of the ways forward where the land is not marginalized.'
(Griffiths, 2000: 10) Hartmut von Jeetze echoes the same
sentiment a couple of years later: 'I am convinced that to the
extent to which we begin to take the land into our midst ...
our Camphill places will also become attractive again for young
people who look for progressive motifs in communities.' (von
Jeetze, 2002: 5–6)

Wider aspects of land use planning and what impact new
thinking might have upon the locality that the Camphill
community finds itself in led Cherry How to reflect upon:
'our responsibility to be environmentally aware, in our farming
and gardening but equally towards landscape and nature in
general; to guard our places from increasing urbanisation and
dislocation from nature.' (How, 2002: 7–8) Andrew Plant takes
the logical next step: '... the Camphill Movement could have
a voice on issues such as community-supported agriculture,
ecological responsibility and sustainability, social enterprises,
and promoting community — both in its own right as the social

form of the future and also as a setting for the inclusion of people with learning difficulties.' (Plant, 2009: 1–3)

In 2006 the term 'sustainable community' had entered into mainstream thinking and Botton was given public recognition in that year. It was accorded Special Recognition in an awards scheme for sustainable communities run by the office of the Deputy Prime Minister (John Prescott). The following is an extract from the commendation of the awarding committee:

> Founded fifty years ago, Botton Village has demonstrated a long track record of working to realize the potential of all residents through living and working together in a largely self-sustaining environment. The community's culture focuses on tolerance, respect and developing individual strengths.
>
> Sustainability is core to the ethos behind the village as well as rearing livestock, growing crops and managing forestry, the community sells products made in their workshops on a not-for-profit basis; activities that also provide skills training. The Panel was impressed by the dedication to the ethos of sustainability and mutual respect shown by those involved in Botton Village.
>
> The Panel considers that this model offers both lessons and inspiration to the endeavour to create sustainable communities. The culture of respect that is evident in Botton is particularly relevant and is one to which every community would do well to aspire.
> (Office of the Deputy Prime Minister, 2005: 11)

Noel Bruder (2004), a co-worker in the small urban community Camphill Greenacres in Dublin, was very aware of the spreading ecovillage network, and began to apply some of the ecovillage criteria to his own community. In answer to the question: 'Are Camphill communities sustainable communities?' he attempted a definition which would encompass both Camphill and the ecovillage. He wrote: '... in the Camphill context a suitable definition of a sustainable community might be: an attempt to integrate the ecological, social, economic and spiritual aspects of life towards creating a harmonious and inclusive society in perpetuity.' (Bruder, 2004: 1–3) In the article he advocates that Camphill enters into a dialogue and a partnership with the growing ecovillage and sustainable community movement worldwide.

The Camphill Movement has managed to create communities which combine working with people who need help, pioneering environmentally friendly techniques and creating a new kind of society. That this has been achieved with such minimal cross-fertilisation between Camphill and the ecovillage network shows how Camphill is nonetheless responding to the needs of our time, and in a way which has meaning and relevance. The idea that small communities may create solutions to vast social and environmental problems was foreseen many years before by the founder, Karl König. Lecturing in 1964 he declared:

> The whole twentieth century will be drenched in blood and misery, and this will go on until the idea of the threefold social order gradually develops in small communities, and it will continue until this social ideal spreads over whole countries and continents.
> (König, 1990: 73)

What does Camphill have to offer for the future? Our mainstream western, capitalist, industrial civilisation has reached the end of the road based on materialism and reductionism. Recognising the spiritual dimension, and using holistic planning methods, Camphill can show a number of ways out of the dead-end we have reached.

• Camphill has built up a great number of working examples of micro societies where everyone is integrated, and where people with special needs are able to contribute meaningfully. In a Camphill village there is no unemployment.

• Camphill has developed integrated environmental designs that are applicable in many situations, like rootzone waste water treatment systems using flowforms, low impact

housing using local materials, producing energy from wind and biogas from farm slurry.
- Camphill has been in the forefront of biodynamic agriculture, producing healthy food with a lower carbon footprint than chemical industrial farming thus mitigating climate change.
- Camphill has pioneered new alternative economic systems, first with the economic fellowship where work and income were separated and everyone was given a secure economic support, and over the last decade by developing Community Supported Agriculture where farm and garden produce is distributed directly to a group of consumers, thus bypassing the enormous supermarket distribution models.

A Camphill village is an ecovillage but of a particular kind. As we have seen, in many ways Camphill has been an ecovillage well before the concept was originally thought of. It is my hope that we can create a dialogue between Camphill and other ecovillages, for while Camphill has a relatively long tradition, the ecovillage model can bring in new ideas and new people. Camphill can provide the maturity and the long-term experience, the spiritual and philosophical foundations, while the ecovillage network can tap into a vast surge of enthusiasm and motivation which we find gathering all across the planet.

14. Quality of Life: Dimensions, Perceptions and Practice

ROY BROWN

Roy Brown is Emeritus Professor of Educational Psychology at the University of Calgary. He has designed and developed research programmes around individual and family quality of life.

The Murtle campus of the Camphill School Aberdeen presents a delightful and restful atmosphere, an aspect that almost all parents commented upon quite spontaneously when I interviewed them on a research project in which I was engaged (Brown, 2006). These views were also shared by many of the co-workers and other personnel that I met. However I was confronted by a question which kept arising. Given this tranquil and natural environment, which appeared to have many qualities associated with human well-being, how could the situation be further enhanced by adopting a quality of life approach? The Camphill that I saw with its humanitarian and caring co-workers showed many of the social and psychological attributes of a quality of life approach which has been adopted in the field of learning disabilities. But many aspects of this approach were absent. Adopting such an approach would entail an examination of the values, concepts and principles and their application. The current environment has many features which meet some of the more serious challenges facing the field of learning disabilities where children with very severe and multiple disabilities are concerned and where adults with a variety of conditions require support and care. The attributes of this approach also have important implications for families.

Quality of Life

For the past thirty years quality of life has become an important and focusing approach involving support and intervention for people with learning disabilities. More recently there has been the development of the concept of family quality of life, which has gained its impetus from the approaches and models that have been consolidated within the quality of life field. Although a number of demonstration projects and conceptual studies have been developed in both areas, it is only in recent times that quality of life has been practised within services and agencies to any large extent. Unfortunately the concepts and principles involved in quality of life have often been misunderstood and have not been entirely supported by the education and training which have been provided to frontline personnel. There is often a gap between policy, management and frontline intervention and support, which has led to some rough patches in terms of the realistic development of quality of life. It is important at the outset to indicate that quality of life should not be regarded as a mission-oriented approach, but rather, as a sensitising concept, which enables practitioners to modify the approaches they make towards persons with disability (Taylor, 1994). In one sense, the quality of life model has followed but also has arisen out of other concepts and practices such as normalisation and inclusion. However, there are a number of very important differences which we shall see as the concepts are described.

What is quality of life?

Over the years a variety of definitions of quality of life have been put forward, along with a number of overarching concepts. The definitions of quality of life are many, but in the field of learning disabilities there are a number of commonly accepted ideas. Quality of life is:

- the social well-being enjoyed by people, communities and society (Bach & Rioux, 1996)
- both objective and subjective, involving material well-being, health, productivity, intimacy, safety, community and emotional well-being (Cummins, 1997)
- experienced when a person's basic needs are met and when he or she has the opportunity to pursue and achieve goals in major life settings (Goode, 1994)

Broadly speaking and at a very practical level, quality of life recognises the importance of individual thinking and learning, which requires passing much of the control within the developmental context to the person with a learning disability. The person with a disability has to be in the driving seat. There may be an instructor and passengers but, as far as possible, the driving has to be turned over to the person with a disability. Research and practice indicate that this is possible to a much greater extent than most people, including professionals and parents, think. Furthermore, it is recognised that quality of life needs to measured, but that it cannot always be measured entirely by objective and numerical procedures. Many authors (Schalock & Felce, 2004; Cummins, 1997) have referred to this other side of assessment as subjective, although I prefer to see this as the perceptual component of quality of life. In no way do objective and perceptual assessments necessarily match one another, nor is there a demand that they should do so. Objective measures are external and important but perceptual measures are internal and critical from a behavioural perspective. For example, feeling unwell may be very different from measurements of wellness by medical or other practitioners. How one feels nevertheless affects one's performance and the way one deals with challenges and situations in one's life.

Principles and concepts in quality of life

The following principles and concepts are fundamental to an understanding of a model of quality of life:

- Domains of well–being
- Holism
- Lifespan
- Choices
- Personal control
- Perception
- Self-image
- Empowerment
- Inter and intra personal variability
- Values

These have been expounded by Brown, Bayer and Brown as early as 1992 and for practitioners and managers of services by Brown and Brown (2003). Much of this and other material has been consolidated in the research and applied literature, (see Schalock, Brown, I., Brown, R., et al, 2002; Goode, 1994; Renwick, Brown, I. & Nagler, 1996). Unfortunately, much research and demonstration does not get into local service systems very quickly and the research to practice gap is extensive. An important issue involves life domains that represent functioning areas (e.g. physical, material, productive, social, emotional), which are experienced by most people but not all people with learning disabilities. The point is that in quality of life they are viewed in a holistic sense with the idea that success or failure in one domain significantly influences success or failure in other domains. This is very important, because it suggests that intervention and support can be carried out through a variety of these areas. For example, someone who has poor health may receive medical treatment in terms of pharmacological intervention that may improve physical health but also psychological well-being. However, we may also affect both physical health and mental well-being through leisure and physical recreation. If individuals have ability or interest in a particular area or domain, it is likely that they will more readily practise the skills required, resulting in improvement. Some data that we collected (Brown, Bayer and Brown, 1992) suggest that following such a route, (i.e. giving support in areas where individuals like to perform) results in improvement in a wide range of other activities, even those in which they do not receive support and practice. We wondered why? It may have resulted because improvement in an area which one enjoys raises one's self-image and a sense of self-worth, which can cause a rise in overall confidence and increased motivation.

Other principles are also important. Choice is important because it allows people to have control over what they do. At times this has been seen as providing freedom to everybody to do what they wish. As Brown and Brown (2009) have pointed out, it is important that choice is within a conceptual framework. Choice can only occur effectively when people have opportunities and experience. If they are not provided with choice, opportunities and experiences it is very unlikely that development will occur. Furthermore, mediation of choices can be offered at different levels and experienced in a way that growth is encouraged. For example, one can be given open-ended choice or somebody can enumerate the choices that are available. It may well be that people decide what is the best for the individuals concerned, because they believe they know what the individual thinks or needs. This is particularly the case with children and older adults. However, the evidence suggests that proxy interpretations of what a person would choose are different from those perceived by the individual (Cummins, 2002). Frequently the individual appears to have a clear understanding of what they want to do and what they wish to try and many have a good idea of their current limitations.

One of the important impacts of perception and choice is the effect that it has on self-image. Whether one feels positive about oneself is important because it can enable one to improve performance and become further involved. Note that these two different principles and others are interrelated. Once again it means that we can provide support in different areas in different ways, and it is the job of professionals and support personnel or co-workers to discover the best ways for particular individuals. This is best done through unbiased observation of behaviour, by taking note of what individuals say, and by observing carefully what they do (Brown and Brown, 2003). Obviously there is an issue of duty of care, and one should not provide opportunities for activities which have high risk without proper support and reasonable protection (Brown & Percy, 2007). However, it should be pointed out that individuals who do not have learning disabilities are often able to take risks and chances, which will often be considered dangerous and unwise. Some might argue society, particularly for very young people and older people, is moving to more control of the environment, which suggests we are limiting choice and therefore learning, thus making people more vulnerable and leading to greater institutional care rather than support. Along with this there is likely to be increased anxiety in unfamiliar situations, inhibiting behaviour and therefore additional learning. These are critical issues that need to be examined very carefully.

Family quality of life

The notion of family quality of life has developed out of the more general concept of quality of life. There has been much work done in relation to families where there are people with disabilities (Turnbull, Brown, I., & Turnbull, 2004; Zuna, Turnbull, & Summers, 2009) and although at times support is given to other family members, one of the major changes in our society is that people with intellectual disabilities are expected to be looked after by their parents, even when there are severe, multiple or extreme disabilities for the person involved. This gives rise to major challenges in terms of quality of life for each member of the family. For these reasons a number of researchers and practitioners have paid attention, particularly over the last ten years, to issues related to the family (Journal of Policy and Practice in Intellectual Disabilities, 2006). In other words, when supporting a person with developmental or learning disabilities, it is important to recognise the impact that this may have on the family, and the extent to which the issues are interactive, preventing the family members performing effectively. This has psychological, social and economic implications for all family members and society. From this comes the notion that services need to be very responsive to quality of life issues including those affecting the family. If this is not done we can be faced with further family deterioration and malfunctioning or, alternatively, the likelihood of the child being removed from the family permanently or for long periods of time. However, with support, families can often adapt effectively, though this may require, in some instances, the necessary removal of the child with severe disabilities from the home for periods of time, or daily attendance in a specially supportive environment with skilled and dedicated personnel. This view is critical to the future development of organisations like Camphill School Aberdeen which supports children who have extreme and often multiple disabilities. Two major questions need to be asked. What is the effect of the child on the family? What is the effect of the programme on the child and therefore the family?

MEASUREMENT

In the field of family quality of life a few instruments have been developed to measure and assess, both quantitatively and qualitatively, the effects on the family. One technique is the Family Quality of Life Survey (Brown et al., 2006) which seeks views of family in the following areas:

  Health of the family
  Financial well-being
  Family relationships
  Support from other people
  Support from disability related services
  Spiritual and cultural beliefs
  Careers and preparing for careers

Leisure and enjoyment of life
Community and Civic Involvement

One of the major influences on the quality of life for the whole family is the nature of the child's learning disability. The more severe the disability and the more behavioural issues involved, the more likely it is that there will be stresses on the family which cause disruption, making it very difficult for the family to function in the way it would wish to do so (i.e. a perceptual gap between the 'hoped for' and the 'current' life experience). This does not mean that some families do not get on very well, nor does it suggest that individuals do not work together as a family. But the overwhelming evidence is that the more severe the behavioural challenges the greater the efforts that have to be expended by the family. Some of these are worthy of comment. For example, it appears that in family quality of life surveys, regardless of country, there are impacts across domains of family quality of life and issues such as family health, support from neighbours and disability services and enjoyment and pleasure from life each interacting with the other. Very often we think and behave as if the nature of the learning disability is the same across the ages, but this is not true, neither in quantity nor in quality. It is important that we take this into account when we look at the impact of disability on the family (see Brown, Hong, Shearer, Wang & Wang, In press; Brown, Macadam Crisp, Wang & Iarocci, 2006).

There is also evidence that as children age and as parents become elderly, the rating of family quality of life improves (Jokinen and Brown, 2005). There may be many explanations for this. For example, there may be differences between age cohorts because people's values and experiences are different. It may be that the nature of disability is changing. For example, when I started work in the 1950s in the field of learning disability, most of the people had mild or moderate cognitive impairment. Fetal alcohol spectrum disorder was not known, although doubtless it occurred, but today there is a much larger number of such children. Furthermore, children with learning disabilities are living much longer and their life quality appears to be improving, particularly amongst individuals who are more mildly and moderately handicapped. Therefore the change in the nature of disability must be borne in mind. Further the unusual and disruptive behaviour in autism tends to ameliorate as the child moves into adulthood.

Impact of quality of life and family quality of life on policy and management

The foregoing account deals with the conceptual nature of quality of life and family quality of life and in terms of the principles involved. It has been indicated that measurement, including observation as well as objective and perceptual recording, are critical parts of the process. And these records are necessary, as is an examination of the principles involved, if there are going to be appropriate supports provided to the children or adults with learning disabilities, as well as support for family members (Brown et al. In press). Everyone involved in support of the child or adult should examine each of these concepts. This means that managers of agencies and policy makers need to take into account the nature of quality of life and family quality of life in determining how policy and the organisation of an agency or service are developed. If one accepts a quality of life approach the concepts and principles should be explicitly employed in the design of policy and management. This means that organisations which believe that quality of life and well-being of people are important will also need to consider how these principles impact their services and the organisations with whom they cooperate as well as the people they serve. This gives rise to the important notion of values, because quality of life is very much concerned with the values that people hold. It is necessary that organisations state their values in writing so that everybody can see what they are. This should include the principles to be used in running services. There needs to be a means by which these can be questioned openly and discussed amongst all personnel, so that a coherent structure can be developed. Beyond this it must be recognised that individual value systems and personal beliefs or perceptions of each individual who is within a service will often differ markedly from the values and approaches required professionally in order to run a coherent, integrated and personalised service. Personal and professional beliefs and values are not necessarily the same. One of the key questions that needs to be asked by each individual is: *How do my personal values differ from my professional values?* What I might think is reasonable to happen in my family, may be very different from the choices, images and actions of other parents and the individuals who have learning disabilities (see Brown & Percy, 2007). In summary the applications we are talking about relate to the following:

1. Assessment and measurement of quality of life and family quality of life
2. Intervention and support
3. The development of policy
4. The management of services
5. The education and training of personnel, including issues of ethical behaviour in the context of personal and professional perceptions and values

Camphill with particular reference to adult services

Organisations like Camphill often provide onsite employment and work that run in a supportive and integrated manner and may involve some inclusion within the outside community. Examples may include a café or restaurant and various stores which outsiders patronise. However, work needs to be meaningful for individuals. Questions like: What are the goals of employment? What is work leading towards? What effects does such work have on the development of the individual in terms of stimulation and cognitive and emotional development, including holistic activities such as social, recreational and physical involvement? There must be ongoing questions about who does the work, for although it may be appropriate that co-workers support and model for clients, it should always be an integrated process so that real employment takes place. Work needs to be meaningful and rewarding, and the choice of the individual. Opportunities to try things out should feature largely in the programme. One should ask the question: How is such work rewarding and does the individual perceive it that way? Who says it is rewarding? For some, working in a store will be productive and supportive. Working in the bakery or restaurant can be positive for many individuals. Carpentry, metal work and horticultural work may be suitable for individuals at different phases of their development. This leaves open the question of how one moves from internal work on the campus to work outside?

The history of Camphill is very relevant here. Camphill services in Aberdeen were set up in beautiful surroundings for both children and adults. It was principally a place of care, for Camphill was based on a particular approach involving methods devised by Rudolf Steiner including the adoption of a religiously oriented philosophy and approach towards people with learning disabilities. That basic structure and mission is still in place. The fact that it was set up in the 1940s, when the ethos then was one of institutionalisation and primarily care, appears to me to still be the basis of the current programmes. There seem to be a number of co-workers who believe that adults cannot survive outside. But the evidence from other programmes indicates that such individuals can often do so, with appropriate support (see Brown, Bayer & Brown, 1992).

The nature of work has always been a challenge for many of the adults with learning disabilities as noted by Camphill founder, Dr Karl König. Some get employment but the percentage in every western country is relatively poor. Despite this, changes have taken place in terms of contact with the outside community through a variety of processes, for example on the Murtle campus of Camphill School Aberdeen there is a holistically-oriented general medical practice which caters for people in the surrounding area. On a neighbouring Camphill campus there is a café and shop which a large number of people from the outside community can use. In these areas it is generally a busy, inclusive 'internal' environment. The argument here appears to be that inclusion is present because it brings the community in. But this does not lead to many people living and working outside on a permanent or semi-permanent basis. Aspects of support intervention and, for adults, employment in the outside community are not seen as values to be strongly promoted. This is a matter of concern because it is apparent that a number of adults would, if they had support, choose such a route. Discussions I had with residents support this view. Such wishes are, apparently, not readily explored. Has this to do with the value system of Camphill? There is little doubt that despite Camphill's caring and healing environment many outsiders misunderstand what Camphill does, and this appears partly to do with the fact that there is little recognition of the importance of an inclusive value system as part of living and growing. Care has to go on, but care supported by enlightened inclusive educational practice and up-to-date social approaches to rehabilitation.

The question for Camphill and other facilities is whether there is sufficient discussion of a value system and opportunities for those people who can or would like community inclusion. For example, do co-workers work in a somewhat secluded residential programme because they like the way of life for themselves, perhaps a slower or more sheltered way of life, protected from some aspects of the outside world? There is nothing wrong in such an outlook provided it does not prevent others in care from following their own interests, even if the co-workers would not make such choices for themselves. Such a value system may discourage people from exploring and trying the outside inclusive community. I had the opportunity of raising the issue of whether residents would like to go out and work in the community. When it was put with the proviso that support and help would be available, several stated that with such support they would like to try such a life at least on a stepwise basis. Further, it is not uncommon in such facilities to find opposing views amongst co-workers. A range of choices and opportunities for older clients is important because it opens up opportunities for growth and people's self-image can expand as a result. The evidence from the field is that many people with learning disabilities do much better than people expect. For example, there is now an increasing number of people with learning disabilities in various countries who go to colleges and on occasion to university (Hughson and Uditsky, 2007). We have an increasing number going into the work force, though there are still major challenges. More recently we have quality of life approaches involving local communities supporting people with disabilities (Schippers & van Boheemen, 2009).

Another example is the advances in community living for adults with Down's syndrome. We increasingly come across instances where people have partnered or married and support one another, living effectively in the community. The reports of many parent associations such as the Down's syndrome associations around the world, stress the extent to which individuals with Down syndrome have done much better than most professionals predicted they would do. It is now recognised that people with Autism Spectrum Disorder often improve as they age and many live effective lives through specific areas of interest and ability, such as art or music (e.g. MukiBaum Treatment Centres, Toronto with its extensive art programmes and art gallery).

Education of support personnel

There is also the issue of the education and training for support personnel. Because of different approaches and increasing knowledge, co-workers should for professional and ethical reasons update their practices. A variety of courses are available and their content should be used to consider how a programme or organisation could advance. Such courses as well as workshops may be run on site. Frequently one finds that personnel including managers and directors are not focused on incorporating change, such as reducing exclusion, building cooperative links between organisations and local communities or encouraging integrated policy and practice between different government departments (e.g. services for ageing and learning disabled should include common goals and joint practices).

What are the different aspects of exclusion and inclusion? Experience suggests that they are often minor things and relate to choices and affect self-image. It might be a useful exercise for all personnel to consider ways in which exclusion could be minimised and inclusion increased. Social role valorisation or normalisation in terms of the environment needs to be studied and updated. Many of the features of such residential services as Camphill aim to be sensitive and understanding of the needs of children and adults. However, such organisations can benefit from an examination of the ways in which modern knowledge about child and adult development, particularly that relating to those with learning disabilities, could be applied in their programmes. The effects of adults remaining in residential facilities for the remaining part of their life raise major issues. Given that people with learning disabilities are increasing their lifespan, very often approaching that of the rest of the population, even amongst such groups as those with Down's syndrome. The challenge here is that if only a care model is employed, it will become extremely expensive. If support and learning are applied more and more individuals can live on the outside, making room for individuals who in their late years require increasing personalised care. Many suggest it should be inclusive. How do residential facilities modernise their practice to deal with such changes? For example, how can dementia and deterioration be delayed? What are the factors that we know about which can enable this to occur? Facilities such as those provided by Camphill often have many assets such as the availability of the holistically-oriented general medical practice on the Murtle campus. This could focus on the processes of ageing and understanding of brain functioning, along with other modern approaches involving environmentally and therapeutically based programmes that can ameliorate or control certain aspects of ageing and disability.

It is important that the value systems expressed by co-workers should be clear and consistent in terms of the individual programmes for both children and adults. Co-workers frequently have differing views and personal value systems which sometimes seem to conflict with the existing organisational philosophy. Further, value systems change over time and it is essential to examine what changes are taking place. There is also the need for particular priorities and professional value systems to be clearly in place. This does not mean that personal value systems in family settings have to be of just one kind, but it does mean that they need to be suitable for the aims and directions which an organisation wishes to develop for its clients. It may be wise to consider who the clients are. Increasingly it is recognised that parents and siblings are as much clients as the person with the named disability. Such views may differ over time for every child and adult, and it may take a variety of forms. Clients' needs should be paramount and choices need to be open. At times there seems to be a view that it is better to protect individuals and keep them confined in terms of accommodation. The question is: If society as a whole does not explore or promote development, which we know is possible, then it is likely that dependency will be fostered, anxiety of the outside and unfamiliar will come to dominate, and thus become a self-fulfilling philosophy in terms of the organisation and development for the people involved.

Recommendations

Are opportunities designed, provided, and tested with people who would like to have the choice to take a more exploratory and self-supporting role in life? Could they and are they skilfully supported in doing this? This does mean that some people will not stay at Camphill, although Camphill itself needs to look at the issue of what happens if everybody stays there throughout their life. This, again, appears to be truer in the adult than children's services, where many parents seem prepared to welcome their children home as improvement and stabilisation occur.

Many of the following recommendations derive directly from discussions and observations in Camphill and other services.

1. Life-long care needs

The role of life-long care needs to be examined in the context of the values and policies agreed on by the organisation. It should be remembered that if life-long care is provided for each individual, then unless there is major expansion, the organisation will become locked into a long-term residency for all individuals, which is very expensive. There is a need for support of individuals who face ongoing issues (Courtenay, Jokinen, & Strydom, 2010). This is particularly true in the field of developmental and learning disability and needs not only to be discussed in the context of current data on ageing (Janicki & Ansello, 2000; Bigby, 2003) but also requires a plan for future action.

2. The nature of inclusion

The nature of inclusion, and importantly, exclusion warrant further examination. It might be valuable for all co-workers to examine the types of exclusion from normal life that occur and the kind of programmes and supports that can be offered and ways in which inclusion can be expanded. It would be useful to do this in the context of a supportive structure with the widest range of choices in order to encourage growth and development.

3. Choice

The wishes and choices of all individual clients, and particularly adolescents and adults, need to be considered in an open-ended manner as, in family homes and residential services where there is stress, these can be easily diminished. Limits should not be set by the personal values of co-workers and personnel, but as far as possible be the result of consultation consistent with the values of the supported individuals themselves.

4. Arts

Arts and fine arts programmes should be considered as part of a quality of life approach, as such activities, apart from enjoyment, often tap into the individuals' skills and represent a holistic process which can positively influence other activities and skills. Exploration and expansion of these activities is critically important, not only for people who suffer from extreme disabilities including emotional and multiple disabilities. This is not to negate the role of art for therapeutic purposes with people with disabilities (Baum, 2010).

5. Residential provision

In the case of children with extreme disabilities serious consideration should be given to removing children from home for periods of time, but this needs clear agreement and criteria for returning to the family home. This should be seen as an effective part of rehabilitation both for the individual and the family. It is not in the interest of the child, family or society to overlook such extreme needs for it is critical to stabilise nurturing family environments. This is particularly important for children as the results from Camphill show.

6. Family involvement

Families need to be more closely involved in the process of development, because disability is not just about the person with a disability, but it is also about the impact and interacting effects that go on amongst family members. They need support, guidance and opportunities to speak together on a regular basis. Indeed one of the findings in my investigation was the enthusiasm in which parents, meeting in focus groups, found support and help just in talking through issues of common concern. Several suggested that they would like to have such meetings more regularly. This will encourage them to develop more coherent views about the nature, purpose and value of family involvement in their children's development which, in turn, can lead to positive family development.

7. *Value systems*

Value systems need to be published so that everybody who considers becoming involved with the organisation can read about the approaches on offer. The range of supports and programmes and the extent that they are intended to match individual needs on an ongoing basis should be indicated. This is important because without it, there is room for misinterpretation by all parties, including government agencies and services, who may not have understood the role that the organisation plays in the life and development of children and adults and their families.

15. The Challenges Facing Camphill: An Internal Perspective

ANDREW PLANT

Andrew Plant has been a co-worker in Camphill for over thirty years as a house co-ordinator and has been involved in farming, management and community development.

I have lived in Camphill for nearly thirty years, both in Northern Ireland and Scotland. Over that time, I have become aware of the many changes that there have been at work, especially over the past few years. I have tried to understand what lies behind these changes and where they are leading us. As the first part of this process, I carried out research by visiting all the Camphill communities in Scotland, as well as some of the Garvald centres and one of the L'Arche communities. My questions were about how people experienced and understood change in their community and how they experienced 'the sense of community.' What I found was a series of paradoxes. The first was that the older co-workers said that they felt that the experience of community was on the decline; that there was less commitment to the traditional forms of Camphill — the Bible Evenings, the Sunday services, the festival celebrations and the study groups. They felt that there was less sense of self-sacrifice and less willingness to serve the community. Yet the newer and younger co-workers and the employed co-workers felt that things had got better; there was less sense of duty and expectation and there were more possibilities and opportunities;

there was more room for the individual and more attention given to professional development.

The second paradox was that people said that they wanted more time and space for themselves and their families and yet they also wanted more community events and time to socialise. The third paradox was that there was a very obvious trend in the communities towards professionalisation and increasing regulation. At the same time there were fewer people joining the communities as residential and unsalaried co-workers and therefore more people working in the communities — in a variety of central roles — on an employed basis. Yet despite this, many co-workers had been — and some remain — wary of the need for professional organisation, training, qualifications; inspections and standards; and the engagement of employed staff.

Following upon this initial research, I then embarked on a more extensive piece of work, which was to try and understand the phenomena of change in Camphill when set in the context of other community movements and in terms of other forms of societal and organisational development. As a result I was able to highlight the archetypal trends and patterns in the ways that communities have developed over time.

My research has been based on my experiences in Scotland and what I was hearing from other regions. Whilst my experience of the English communities is rather limited, I have no reason to believe that the situation in Scotland is so different from that south of the border. I propose to look at some of the changes taking place in Camphill communities and to explore the reasons behind these changes. I will then look at some of the challenges facing Camphill today and some of the responses to these challenges that have emerged in various communities. Finally, I will look at the possible future development of Camphill communities as new models of community health, resilience and sustainability are tried and developed.

I will start by looking at some changes as they affect the families of pupils and residents in Camphill communities. I think that it is true to say that in earlier times the parents of children and adults in Camphill communities had a strong feeling of respect for the founders of Camphill and for all those they encountered in Camphill — whether teachers, doctors, therapists, houseparents or co-workers. There is no doubt that they formed close connections to the co-workers, which lasted over many years. They witnessed the beautiful and ordered surroundings; the devoted work of the co-workers; the inclusive and holistic education offered; the purposeful work activities; the rich cultural and social life; and the dignity and respect accorded to the pupils and villagers. As a result they were no doubt glad that their son or daughter had found a place in Camphill.

However, there is another side to this picture — a side that I remember from my own experience as a Camphill houseparent some years ago. It is one that has emerged again from recent research into the Camphill archives (Brennan-Krohn, 2009). There was an attitude — deeply engrained into our consciousness — that was somewhat ambivalent with respect to the role of the families and their involvement with their children and siblings. It was an attitude of paternalistic benevolence that discouraged parental involvement. More accurately, I should call it *maternalistic* benevolence, as it was often the Housemother who was the most significant presence. In a way Camphill co-workers became surrogate parents; they spoke of 'our children' and 'our villagers.' The Camphill model of care created a sense of ambivalence in the respective roles of co-workers and families. The role titles of those days are illuminating, all of which speak of authority. There were superintendents, matrons, workshop *masters* and house*mothers*, and house*parents*. There was an assumption that the co-workers knew better than the parents what was good for the pupils and residents. It must also be said that this attitude — of Camphill knowing best — also extended to Camphill's early relationships with the state, with placing and funding authorities. This attitude meant that the initial response to state intervention and regulation tended to be wary, defensive and rather dismissive.

Of course, attitudes have now changed, as has the experience of parents and families. While some parents today might wonder what is going on in Camphill, the relationship between Camphill and families has now more to do with cooperation, collaboration and partnership. There is a shared and equal interest in the welfare of children and adults in Camphill. More than this, experience from Scotland demonstrates that parents are now increasingly aware of their rights and are prepared to contest decisions taken by placing authorities concerning their sons and daughters. They argue that the needs of their children can only be met by a placement in a Camphill community and, on a number of occasions, have pursued their challenge to a successful outcome through the courts.

There has been a significant shift in the outlook of society and the state towards people with learning disabilities: a shift from a medical model of pathology — which claims that there is something wrong with the person — to a social model of disability, which argues that there is something wrong with society. As a result, perceptions and attitudes towards people with learning disabilities have changed from shame and marginalisation to dignity and inclusion.

The state has done a lot in terms of introducing legislation and increasing funding, all of which reflect these societal changes. Much has been done to professionalise and objectify the nature of the role of care provider in relation to the service-user and to put control more firmly in hands of the service-user. This has been a major factor in the shift within Camphill communities towards enabling and encouraging pupils and residents to have more control of their lives, to have more choices and to develop more individualised programmes of care and support.

Many Camphill people would agree that these moves towards promoting rights and fostering empowerment would not have happened — or at least would not have happened so soon — had it not been for the pressure from the regulatory bodies. The important thing here is to preserve a balance between the rights of the individual and the responsibilities that come with living in a community. It is also critical to maintain and foster the 'mutuality of relationships', the experience of learning from each other, of sharing our lives with each other, of active interest in the other person — all of which are characteristic and defining features of Camphill communities.

All of this serves to highlight some of the fundamental shifts in attitudes, outlook and experience in Camphill communities in recent years. Through speaking to many people in Scottish communities as part of my research, I have been made aware of a wide range of changes.

- In general, the house units are smaller and there are more of them. Whilst most residents have single rooms within houses, many co-workers live separately from residents in flats or in rooms outside the house units, or in flats and houses outside the community.
- There are more offices which points to an increase in administrative work. More space is dedicated to carparks which reflects the increase in the number of employees and day attenders.
- There is less evidence of people willingly participating in the cultural life of their community. Whilst there used to be an expectation that most co-workers would go to all the cultural events in the community, it is now left to the individual co-worker to choose whether or not to attend.
- No longer is it the case that every co-worker is engaged 'hands-on' with the core tasks of running houses and workshops. There is a greater measure of role specialisation. This is due in large part to the fact that some areas of work require high levels of expertise and not everybody is equipped or willing to take on such a responsibility.
- Co-workers increasingly take responsibility for one particular area of work and not responsibility for the whole community (e.g., running a house or a workshop or becoming involved in training or administration).
- There is more regulation from external bodies (e.g., Care Commission; Scottish Social Services Council; Her Majesty's Inspectorate of Education) and the necessity for contract compliance (e.g., Health and Safety; Environmental Health; Fire Regulations; etc). However there is less internal regulation within the communities themselves; there are fewer rules about what one can and cannot do (e.g., use of radios and TVs; alcohol consumption; dress code for formal occasions).

Community life is now more liberal, flexible and adaptable and less narrow and fundamentalist in character.

- There have been significant demographic changes: there are more employed people, especially in key roles such as house co-ordinator, manager and administrator; and the residential population of communities is ageing — both villagers and co-workers.
- Communities are not so self-absorbed and introspective and are increasingly turning outwards to engage in the wider community. There has been an increase in the amount of traffic — both literally in terms of the number of people coming in and out of communities — but also in the continuous flow of external demands and expectations and the responses made to these by the communities. But, of particular importance, has been an increasing exchange of information and ideas.

What are the reasons for these trends? When people are asked this question, they point out that these are the same changes that are happening elsewhere in society. And that, of course, is true. Camphill is not exempt from these changes. But in order to understand this better and to come to terms with these changes and to engage in a proactive, positive and forward-looking manner, we need to see that there are certain inherent patterns in the development of civilisations, societies, organisations — in fact all social groupings, including Camphill communities. This is not the same as saying that these trends are inevitable and there is nothing that we can do to affect them. It is more about having an insight into the ways that organisations and communities evolve so as to be in tune with what is happening and develop the most appropriate social forms, organisational structures, attitudes and outlooks that lead communities forward.

From my reading and research, it would appear that Camphill communities are moving through a series of recognisable and archetypal phases. The first phase is when a community is founded, when it is in what we could call the Pioneer phase. At this time the community is very intense, idealistic, cohesive and rather fundamentalist in outlook. It demands conformity from its members and expects its members to serve it even above their own interests. The community members are inspired by the visionary and charismatic leadership of the founder. The community has a belief system that is at variance with the mainstream culture and a utopian conviction that it can create a new and better social order through living its beliefs, practices, ethos and values. Thus it turns its back on society, enjoys a strong sense of identity and maintains high and defining boundaries that are physical, psychological and ideological.

In subsequent phases the community becomes less radical, less idealistic, less visionary and less marginal and becomes more settled, stable and better organised. Leadership and responsibility now rest in mandated responsibility groups. The community has come to terms with the demands of organisational management, professional development, service standards, policies and procedures, internal and external accountability and models of governance. In the process many people are employed, not just to replace co-workers who have left or retired, but also to fill new posts that have had to be created — posts requiring specialist knowledge, skills and expertise. The community is now more diverse, people are more specialised and everything is more complex.

At the same time the community members begin to express their needs for more time and space for themselves and their families and for more financial security. And the community realises that it has reached a phase in its development which should ensure that each person — pupil, resident, co-worker or employee — is able to develop to their full potential. The need for conformity and control has been replaced by a recognition of the importance of individualisation, inclusion and empowerment.

This has not always been a straightforward journey. Communities have had to face a succession of major challenges and to adapt to new ways of doing things. The responses have varied from person to person, from community to community and from issue to issue. Whilst there has been resistance and disengagement, there has also been positive engagement and optimism. There have been stories of community failure but also stories of communities successfully transforming themselves.

Celebrations for the seventieth anniversary of the founding of the first Camphill community occurred in 2010. And there is much to celebrate. Camphill has powerfully influenced the lives of many people over the years. It has lasted far longer than most other community movements and it is one of the most experienced and successful voluntary care movements in the world. There are 10,000 people living and working in over 100 communities in 23 countries throughout the Movement. Although the days of expansion appear to be over in the West, several new communities have formed recently in Eastern Europe and there are currently new initiatives seeking Camphill membership in Asia.

Throughout their history Camphill communities have been very resilient, integrating a wide range of major changes and adapting to a variety of challenges, both internal and external. I would now like to list some of the more immediate challenges facing Camphill along with some of the positive responses that are emerging.

What are some of the internal challenges?

POOR COMMUNITY PRACTICES, CONFLICT AND SOCIAL DISINTEGRATION

In most communities there are several fault lines that lead to conflict. The causes of conflict can be interpersonal, structural or ideological. There has been conflict between people and between groups of people and between reformers and traditionalists. What is clear is that conflict in its manifold manifestations is a major force for community destabilisation. For a time it jeopardised the future of three communities in Scotland — one of which subsequently closed and the other two had to start again with new people. It has caused a crisis at various times in some communities in Northern Ireland and it has recently led to questions of succession and sustainability in some Irish communities.

POOR MANAGEMENT

This has been an issue in some communities. Most co-workers did not join Camphill in order to become managers and administrators. Some rose to the challenge nevertheless and some did not. There has been a degree of reluctance in some quarters to engage with the need to acquire the skills required to lead communities through this developmental phase. In some situations expertise, authority and leadership have ended up in the hands of just one or a few individuals. Such a model is likely to face problems of long-term stability and sustainability. There are worrying signs that when too much authority is vested in too few individuals, there is a danger of individuals experiencing 'burn out' or having to stand down which creates instability and crisis. In such situations too few people really feel empowered and involved and develop the skills needed to share the overall responsibility for all aspects of their community and to lead it forward.

DEMOGRAPHICS

There are two concerns here. Firstly, there was a wave of young people which joined Camphill as part of the alternative movement of the 1960s and 1970s. Many of us are now coming up to the point of standing back and standing down and are wondering where the next generation is going to come from. In Scotland some co-worker children and some graduates of the Aberdeen-based BACE degree course are staying on but there are not enough new residential co-workers to take the communities forward. Secondly, the group of co-workers who joined some years ago are growing older — along with the residents in the adult communities. All of these people are going to need care and support and somewhere to live. This is going to need both money and other resources.

INDIVIDUALISATION, DIVERSITY AND SPECIALISATION

As we have seen, there has been a trend towards individualisation in the communities. There are many very positive aspects to this but the question remains of how to achieve a balance between personal autonomy and choice on the one hand and a sense of community on the other. In addition, many people are taking up work in the communities who have little background or interest either in community or in Camphill principles and values. At the same time there is less commitment to traditional social and cultural forms and activities, and all those things that give a sense of community solidarity, cohesion and identity.

What are some of the external challenges?

STATE MODELS OF CARE PROVISION

The move towards inclusion and normalisation, towards supported living and 'care in the community' and away from what is termed 'congregate placements' has led to the situation in which Camphill has to argue the case for community as an appropriate setting for education and care in the face of the charge of not being 'strategically relevant.'

REGULATIONS, INSPECTIONS AND COMPLIANCE

Some co-workers cite these factors as the major problem facing Camphill in recent years. They talk of an inappropriate and unnecessary regulatory regime that has undermined community and mutuality, and diverted energy and resources away from other community activities. However, others see this in a different light and have welcomed the professionalisation, objectivity and the promotion of individual rights of residents as a force for good and as a result of which the communities have improved their practice. Seen from either perspective, regulations, recording, assessments, paperwork, training courses and professional development have meant that the communities have had to allocate time, money and human resources and employ extra specialist staff. No one can doubt that the consequences have been considerable.

FUNDING

Several factors indicate that funding will not always continue to be as secure as previously. These include the recession and poor financial management at the level of local authorities, both of which have led to the need for savings and cutbacks; strategic planning priorities; threats from placing authorities not to fund placements out of the local authority area. Very worrying in terms of funding elderly care in Camphill is the fact that adults with learning disabilities lose their disability funding at the age of 65. In addition, communities are obliged to increase their fees as they create a more person-centred service, employ more staff and accumulate funds for retiring co-workers.

How have Camphill communities responded to these challenges?

POOR MANAGEMENT

Camphill communities are not just alternative intentional communities grounded on social care. They are also registered charities, limited companies, special schools and registered providers of housing, care and support. All of these require a high level of governance and compliance with regulatory standards. It is no longer enough to run communities on good will alone. Some communities have managed the transition to this new climate of governance remarkably well. Others have been through a process of structural reorganisation; some have bought in expertise by employing managers and consultants.

Camphill Scotland, which is an association of the Councils

of Management of all the Scottish communities, has recently focused on the theme of accountability and governance and rolled out good practice guidelines throughout the region. Altogether the roles of Management Councils — or Boards of Trustees — have been greatly enhanced, partly in response to the need for higher levels of governance and partly as a response to crisis in some communities. Unfortunately, however, the more that the tasks, duties and responsibilities of council members are emphasised, the more difficult it is to recruit new external council members.

POOR COMMUNITY PRACTICES, CONFLICT AND SOCIAL DISINTEGRATION

It is clear that we need to improve our community-building skills — skills that will promote healthy and sustainable communities for the future — skills such as personal development and moral responsibility; consensus decision-making; conflict avoidance and resolution; and responsible and empowering leadership. It strikes me as strange that there are so many training courses for everything imaginable but not for living well in community. We are making a start with this in the Scottish region with Community Development Workshops.

DEMOGRAPHICS

It is clear that the workforce of the future is going to be a mix of residential and unsalaried co-workers, salaried co-workers, employed managers, administrators, teachers, house co-ordinators and workshop co-ordinators, and one-year volunteer co-workers from abroad. The challenge inherent in changing demographics has been about finding the right people to join communities and help take them forward. Many co-workers join Scottish communities in order to take part in the BA in Social Pedagogy course at Aberdeen University and many graduates stay on in Camphill. This course now attracts students from communities in Ireland, Northern Ireland and England.

It is also about offering the right opportunities to suit a diverse range of people. Corbenic Community in Scotland, for example, has salaried co-workers who live outside the community as is normal practice elsewhere, but also salaried co-workers who live in the community — some on a full salary and others who have free board and lodging and reduced salaries and, others again, who are moving to an unsalaried, needs-met basis. And having attracted the right people, communities need to integrate the necessary skills in order to build a team out of diversity and also to promote a process of 'enculturation' or 'socialisation' to introduce newcomers to the Camphill way of life. Coleg Elidyr in Wales, for example, is running an introductory course for all of its employees. Several communities in Scotland and England have adopted the Ways to Quality system as a means of creating a shared common vision and to develop and integrate healthy community and organisational processes.

The other aspect of demographics concerns ageing. Many people are now aware that it is a pressing challenge to provide resources for ageing residents and co-workers but not enough is being done to address it. Simeon — the Camphill community for the elderly in Aberdeen and the only one of its kind so far — is spearheading what is called the Harbour Project — looking at a range of possibilities involving creating mixed communities that include houses and facilities for the elderly. Simeon has recently hosted the first UK-wide workshop on creating age-friendly communities, in an attempt to share experiences among all the Camphill centres. This issue is going to need a lot of work put into it over the next few years.

EXTERNAL CHALLENGES

I would like to address the external challenges of state intervention, regulations and funding all together, since the responses that have been developed in Scotland relate to all three. Firstly, the work of Camphill Scotland has been critical in all of this in two ways. It has opened up channels of communication with a variety of state bodies and has become a part of the process that informs proposed legislation. At the same time it has served to lead and guide the communities through the process of adapting to and integrating new social care and organisational practices which are required in order to comply with new regulations and standards. Through alliances with other voluntary organisations, Camphill Scotland has been in the forefront of the argument for choice and the benefits of Camphill provision.

The Camphill communities in Scotland and the Garvald communities have worked together over a number of years to bring about a series of biennial conferences focusing on inclusive community-building at New Lanark — where Robert Owen began his pioneering social reform work. These conferences have attracted international Camphill participation and the involvement of other community initiatives such as the Iona Community and L'Arche communities. Camphill and Garvald also run an ongoing series of one-day conferences for residents and people attending on a day basis. All of these initiatives serve to heighten the public profile of Camphill and public and political awareness of the work that Camphill is doing.

There are many other innovative new projects taking shape in Scotland that serve to show that Camphill is developing creative responses to new challenges and needs. I have already mentioned the degree course developed in conjunction with the University of Aberdeen. This award is recognised by the Scottish Social Services Council as a professional qualification for social care work in Scotland. There have been other significant developments.

- In England, the Crossfields Institute, in collaboration with the University of West of England, is developing a wide range of accredited Camphill courses.
- The Camphill School Aberdeen has collaborated in the development of two new SVQ units (the same as NVQ in England) in spirituality and disability and also in autism.
- The school has pioneered a nature-nurture kindergarten for pre-school children with disabilities and an outreach project to support children in their homes in some of the more deprived areas of Aberdeen.

- Ochil Tower School is going for the Green Flag award
  for Eco-school status.

All these developments are attracting a great deal of interest in
government circles and a high level of funding. These innovative
and forward-looking responses to challenges are on top of the
constant work in the communities to develop and improve their
workforce, training programmes, facilities and professional care
practice.

We have seen positive and practical examples of resilience and
creativity. If we put these together with what we know of the
principles of community development, we can begin to see what
kind of activities are going to ensure the future sustainability of
the Camphill communities. New social forms are developing
within the communities that are empowering and inclusive and
new ways of creating community in diversity are being explored.
These new social forms will have to create a better balance
between the competing demands of the people living in the
communities and of those people working in the communities
— organisational forms that are better able to deal with conflict
and better able to promote community health.

We have seen the development of new forms of personalised
education, care and support and the development of a trained
workforce. New organisational structures are also developing
and along with this is the question of developing moral authority,
individual and community responsibility and initiative and also
appropriate forms of leadership. This is about the personal and
professional development of both residential and employed
co-workers. The principles of organisational development show
that in the future large centralised organisational structures
will give way to fluid and responsive networks that exchange
information and ideas.

The strength of the communities has always been the power
of the relationship between its members — how people speak
and listen to each other; how people trust and respect each
other; how people work together co-operatively, share ideas,
resources and support each other. But there are also shadow

sides to this and it is this shadow side that needs to be overcome through self-development, through learning new skills and through a new commitment to community-building. It is these qualities, combined with good governance and a strong sense of community that will continue to take Camphill forward. The communities are also realising that their boundaries are becoming more porous and diffuse. It is less a matter now about defence and protection and more about the exchange of information that will lead to growth and engagement; to a confident dialogue and collaboration with both society and the state.

We are in a stage of transition from one phase of development to another — from the phase of organisation and individualisation to something new. The old ways of doing things no longer seem to work so effectively and yet the new answers have not yet fully emerged. There are no clear answers to all of this and we will have to live with uncertainty for a while and to continue to explore new ways of doing things.

Yet in this uncertainty we can have the confidence that all that we are experiencing — whether it seems like it or not, and whether we welcome it or not — are signs that the communities are progressing to higher levels of complexity and also higher levels of consciousness, awareness and of responsibility to, and engagement with, the world, as they seek to bring about the Camphill ideals of personal transformation and social renewal.

16. Camphill: Further Notes from the Boundary

KATE SKINNER AND STEPHEN BARON

Kate Skinner has worked in England and Scotland as a social worker, manager and academic. She now works independently as researcher and consultant in social services. She has been Chair of Camphill Scotland since 2006.

Professor Stephen Baron has worked with the Camphill communities since 1971. He held a variety of academic posts in Education, Sociology and Research Capacity Building.

Introduction

In 1991 Stephen Baron and Douglas Haldane published a paper in *The British Journal of Special Education* which sought, in a modest way, to give an assessment of where the Camphill communities stood both in the then constellation of services and in terms of internal community dynamics. The intention of this chapter is to provide an analogous perspective some twenty years on. Firstly, we will give a brief résumé of the arguments of 1991; secondly we will specify the major changes in the external environment over the past twenty years which have impacted on the communities. Thirdly, we will then assess the permeability of the boundaries of Camphill; and fourthly, the significant developments in Camphill training provision. Fifthly, we will then analyse challenges to Camphill's identity before turning, sixthly, to Camphill's place in current policy and commissioning systems. We conclude by considering the ongoing issues of power and authority in the communities' work and the current state of the communities in terms of the oft repeated mission statement of 'serving the Image of Man where it is most threatened.' Our analysis is based primarily on the Scottish experience but we believe that the trends identified will have resonances across the UK and beyond.

The 1991 assessment

The 1991 paper was structured by an over stark division between 'positive aspects' of Camphill and its 'negative aspects.' Three positive aspects were highlighted: firstly, Camphill works with a positive concept of disability in which the impairment is seen as a developmental challenge to the individual spirit on its journey through different incarnations (Baron & Haldane 1991: 75–77). Such a metaphysical perspective generates both a relentless optimism about the possibility and significance of progress and an organic respect for the dignity and validity of the person 'behind the veil of handicap.'

Secondly, and perhaps necessarily entailed by the former, Camphill views the individual with impairments as an existential challenge both to the 'normal' engaged in the 'encounter of ego with ego' and to the society as a whole. The 'normal' is challenged to recognise in the exaggerated characteristics of the impaired those elements in themselves (and the blockages which these may cause). The societal challenge lies in the mirror which impairment holds up to what is valued as normal or desirable. The third positive aspect of Camphill outlined in 1991 was its innovatory work in providing education, further education and community based care for people with special needs some decades ahead of wider British social policy. We hold the first two positive aspects of Camphill's work still to be true (and are not further discussed) while we turn to the question of Camphill's continuing innovatory influence in the Conclusion.

Three negative aspects of Camphill were posited in 1991: Baron and Haldane suggested that there was a 'separatist image' (while carefully avoiding the key question of whether this had a real base) but that: 'Here in the past the Camphill communities often defensively turned inwards, they are now increasingly actively engaging with the issues, persons or organisations experienced as challenging or confronting.' (1991: 77) We will turn to this question in the section below on the boundaries of Camphill.

Similarly Baron and Haldane argued that Camphill training took place in an enclosed system and that 'the balances remain to be struck between preserving identity and seeking formal recognition of the training.' (1991: 77) We will address the issues of identity and training in the respective sections below. The third negative aspect in 1991 was that of hierarchical structures and unresolved conflicts which, it was suggested, were 'a significant source of unresolved division and conflict.' (1991: 77) We turn to this in the Conclusion.

A changing social policy environment

Since Baron and Haldane wrote in 1991 the social policy environment in which the communities operate has changed radically. In education the 'Standards' discourse has evacuated the field of debate about primary questions with education (effectively) being reduced to comparative examination results. In this children with special needs are, inevitably, a threat to the standing of a school and the pressure is to remove them if possible. This organisational pressure is, of course, directly contrary to the avowed rhetoric of inclusion and mainstreaming but has resulted in the rate of growth of expenditure on special education being double that of mainstream provision. Given the financial pressure on local authorities, placement in a Camphill community appears to be an extra, rather than marginal, cost. This has resulted in referrals to the Camphill schools increasingly being of older, more challenging pupils often with a disturbing history of failed local authority provision.

The National Health Service and Community Care Act (1990) was a landmark piece of legislation that set out new arrangements for health and social care. It divided the role of health authorities and local authorities by changing their structures, so that local authorities assess the needs of the local population and then purchase services from 'providers.' The intention was to ensure people needing long-term care live either in their own home, with adequate support, or in a residential home setting.

Other important legislation shifted responsibility for regulation and inspection of social care services from local authorities to national inspection agencies — the Care Commission in Scotland and the Commission for Social Care Inspection in England, Wales and Northern Ireland — working from national standards. Social care agencies are now inspected more often and more rigorously than in the past, requiring greater effort from service providers than previously. The transparency of the new inspection regime has led to more informed decisions about placements and greater involvement of service users and carers in evaluating services. With the advent of direct payments the range of those commissioning services has expanded radically to include people with learning disability themselves and their carers.

Together these trends in social policy have created a demanding external environment for the Camphill communities.

The permeability of boundaries

The increasing permeability of boundaries has been perhaps the most striking feature of the Camphill communities since 1991 with the communities engaging in public discourses in a manner that was unimaginable a decade previously. The creation of Camphill Scotland in 1996 drew on a sense, particularly among some external members of the Councils of Camphill communities, that the communities needed to become more visible and assertive as the external environment became more fluid and challenging.

Since its inception Camphill Scotland has been responsible for a significant (and positive) enhancement of the public profile and understanding of the communities, not least within the Scottish

government. For example, Camphill Scotland was a member
of the Stakeholders' Reference Group, which helped formulate
the current Scottish policy framework *The Same as You* in
2001   (www.scotland.gov.uk/Resource/Doc/1095/0001661.
pdf). It has played a central role in the voluntary sector
umbrella organisation Community Care Providers Scotland
and, as part of this, has been a member of numerous working
groups established by the Scottish government such as the
Adult Support and Protection (Scotland) Act Implementation
Group, the Adult Support and Protection (Scotland) Act Code
of Practice Working Group, and the Learning Disability and
Co-morbidity Working Group. Similarly Camphill Scotland
has worked with the Scottish government in initiating major
conferences on Transitions for People with Learning Disability
and on Social Pedagogy. Such activities represent a step change
in the bi-directional engagement of the communities with wider
public discourses.

The work of forming a 'community of communities'
and making its boundaries more permeable has not been
unproblematic. A major public issue for Camphill throughout
the period has been the proposed Aberdeen Western Peripheral
Road whose Murtle route threatened to split Newton Dee and
the Murtle Estate, running so close to the Murtle Estate that its
work would no longer be tenable. Opinion within and between
communities was divided over whether to accept the route and
bargain for the best amelioration package (relocation of the
work of the school) or whether to oppose the route entirely
and risk diminishing the chances of proper amelioration if (as
was almost universally expected) the Murtle route was chosen.
The Save Camphill campaign was formed to pursue the latter
course of action and was remarkable not only for its success
in defeating the Murtle route but for the breadth and depth of
support fostered locally, nationally and internationally, noted in
the national press as a rare example of what a community group
can do if well organised and well supported.

One of the key features of the Save Camphill campaign
was its commissioning of research to analyse the effects of the
proposed route on the communities and to counter the academic

opinion commissioned (on the basis of two half-day visits) by the roads team. Professor Roy Brown of the University of Victoria assessed the quality of life in the Aberdeen communities in the context of a pan-national study, while Professor John Swinton of the University of Aberdeen was commissioned to study how the communities provide for the spiritual needs of residents. Simultaneously, Professor Pamela Cushing of the University of Western Ontario spent a year conducting an ethnographic study of the Camphill School Aberdeen, while Zoe Brennan-Krohn completed a brilliant undergraduate dissertation on re-imagining disability and society. These (and other pieces of research) are reported elsewhere in this book.

The value of this participation in the research arena has led the communities to engage more systematically with research. There are two contemporary initiatives: as part of the Anthroposophic Health and Social Care Movement, Camphill co-workers are prominent in generating a proposal to establish a Centre and Chair in Anthroposophic Medicine and Integrative Care in a British university. The intention of this proposal is to 'mainstream' anthroposophic medicine and care and to act as a node in the English-speaking world for high quality research. The Centre and Chair would have the following objectives:

- To develop strategic research in anthroposophic medicine and integrative care gaining funding from research councils and relevant charities.
- To subject anthroposophic medicine and integrative care practices to critical evaluation using contemporary research methods, elaborating innovative methods as appropriate.
- To make a distinctive contribution to current developments in medical policy, practice and education especially in terms of integrative care, the personalisation of medicine and the role of spirituality in health.
- To offer postgraduate degrees and diplomas specialising in anthroposophic medicine and integrative care, contributing to other postgraduate and undergraduate degrees as appropriate.

Concurrently Camphill Scotland has launched a research development programme which is seeking to form networks of co-workers interested in common topics to develop into research for peer review and public consumption. As part of this process 'horizon scanning' the challenges facing Camphill over the next five to ten years is being undertaken with a view both to conducting 'in-house' research and to commissioning further research from external academics.

This radically increased openness of the communities collectively has manifested itself in individual communities. More flexible forms of provision have been developed with a more diverse population in communities for varying parts of the week. Full time, un-waged resident co-workers have been joined by salaried non-resident workers, often not sharing the anthroposophical belief system but committed to the values and ethos of the communities. Community cultural life has continued strongly but has been complemented by increased participation in cultural events outwith the community. Religious observance through the Christian Community still plays a central role for many but attendance at other religious services is facilitated and there is an increased recognition of the variety of spiritual experience. The co-worker-led household has been complemented by more independent forms of supported living. Relatively isolated rural communities have been complemented by communities which are urban in both location and ethos. Perhaps the most significant single development in increasing the permeability of the boundaries of Camphill has been the collaboration with the University of Aberdeen in mounting the BA in Curative Education degree, recently renamed as the BA in Social Pedagogy. It is to this which we now turn.

Camphill's training provision

In 1949 Karl König instituted the Seminar in Curative Education to provide resources for the increasing numbers of people joining the rapidly expanding community who had not participated in the initial elaboration of the Camphill approach. The provision of such training was, as is many aspects of Camphill's work, decades ahead of the mainstream of British policy. This internally-run Seminar continued into the 1990s but had been under pressure for some time. Internally the Seminar was not recruiting, nor retaining, the numbers of co-workers needed to provide the backbone of the increased number of communities and it was felt not to be meeting the needs of those communities not working with children (with other internal training courses developed to fill the gap). In external terms the Seminar had no place in the increasingly credentialist education and care systems and its internal focus and unmoderated assessment processes made gaining such a place unlikely. Given the emerging registration discourse, there were real threats to the ability of communities to continue their work.

In the early 1990s a new Camphill organisation was formed, The Camphill Education Trust, which consisted of senior co-workers involved in training in different aspects of Camphill life across the UK, together with a small group of very senior academics supportive of the communities. The remit of the trust was to develop strategies by which the training (and thus work) of the communities in Britain could be recognised. The trust met only for one year before the external members put the trust into abeyance until the communities could agree amongst themselves about strategies for training. The trust never reconvened.

Simultaneously in Scotland a working party of Camphill co-workers and academic supporters met over a two-year period and drafted a proposal for a Higher National Diploma course, with over fifty modules fully specified, which would encapsulate both the content of the Seminar and selected other perspectives on learning disability. SCOTVEC, the then awarding body, appointed an engineer as the liaison officer and found the idea of a vocational course based on the idea of re-incarnation altogether too challenging. The proposal was declined on the grounds that the Camphill communities (unlike, for example, the Guide Dogs for the Blind Association) were too small and specialised to justify an award.

While these formal attempts to establish a place for Camphill's training in the national system were failing, an informal conversation between a co-worker and a member of staff of Northern College of Education (now the School of Education of the University of Aberdeen) led to a proposal for a general BA in Curative Education which started in 1996, with an Honours strand and an advanced entry route being developed later. From an initial student population concerned with work with school-age children the scope of the BACE has expanded to provide for students working with people across the life course so that now there are some eighty co-workers studying different parts of the degree. In recognition of this expansion, the content and process of the degree and the increasing policy recognition of the value of such an approach, the degree was renamed in August 2010 as the BA in Social Pedagogy (to which we turn below). Perhaps the most significant moment in the development of the BA in Social Pedagogy was its recognition by the Scottish Social Services Council as an appropriate qualification for managers of the full range of relevant residential care services.

Establishing and nurturing the BA in Social Pedagogy has been a steep learning curve for all involved, whether Camphill co-worker or academic (although it is on the former which we focus). Taking the Seminar with its stamp of reproducing the ethos of an enclosed system into the public realm of a university degree has necessitated fundamental developments in terms of curriculum, assessment, staffing and community organisation. The degree programme now draws on a wide range of theoretical perspectives on the person, learning disability and care other than anthroposophy. Assessment which had strong *ad personam* elements has had to develop public quality criteria and be subject to external moderation. Co-workers, often without the benefit of higher education, have had to learn how to tutor at degree level while communities have had to meet the heavy financial and logistical demands of supporting the large numbers of both tutors and students.

A different approach to developing training in anthroposophic endeavours has emerged in England where the Crossfields Institute has formed a partnership with a multinational company (Pearson plc) which claims to be:

> ... the world's leading education company. We provide
> learning materials, technologies, assessments and services
> to teachers and students of all ages and in more than sixty
> countries.
> (www.pearson.com/, accessed June 1, 2010)

Crossfields has also formed partnerships with Alanus University (a recently incorporated university in Germany oriented to anthroposophy) and the Rudolf Steiner University College, Oslo. Crossfields can design and award qualifications up to foundation degree level through the partnership with Pearson (trading as Edexcel). Crossfields acts as the UK office of Alanus University in order to enable British providers to offer the Alanus range of degrees in the Arts, Education and Business up to Ph.D. level. With the Rudolf Steiner University College in Oslo, Crossfields offers a three-year, experience based MA in Educational Research.

In these contrasting approaches to education the issue of how permeable boundaries for Camphill should be are neatly encapsulated: should the communities open themselves to the general British higher education and professional discourses, gaining insights from outwith the anthroposophic movement but at the expense of diminishing the exclusivity of the anthroposophic approach? Should the communities work with a purely process and profit-oriented company and with Steiner-oriented institutions internationally, thus maintaining the anthroposophic focus but at the costs of perpetuating training in an enclosed system? Here the question of the identity of Camphill is central and it is to this which we now turn.

Camphill's identity

Camphill communities have, and will continue to have, a strong reputation for high quality care. Based on Steiner's vision of personal liberty, economic cooperation and shared cultural life, communities work through co-workers and people with special needs sharing life-space. At its heart is a positive concept of disability and reciprocity. These notions are a significant feature of Camphill life and make the difference when considering what communities offer. Co-workers literally live in the same house as residents, so they sleep, eat and spend leisure time in the same house. Many co-workers have other Camphill responsibilities during the working day, so are teachers, workshop leaders, architects, doctors etc. It is one of Camphill's strengths but it may be seen as its weakness in a social care world where policies have shifted towards a business-like style of service delivery. As others have moved away from live-in residential staff with a unionised workforce and formalised conditions of service, an approach based on a daily life together, with all its irregularities, may appear old-fashioned and unregulated. There is no 'us and them.'

There are good reasons why Camphill works this way, but these are rarely explicitly articulated. Stemming from his Christian beliefs, Steiner proposed that inside those of us with special needs is a whole person in 'search of growth through ... experience.' (Baron and Haldane, 1991) Pestalozzi (1894) talked of education through learning for 'head, heart and hands' as the key to long-lasting physical, emotional and social well-being and this is deeply embedded within the Camphill approach. This theoretical basis supports this way of working and should be in the forefront of how Camphill represents itself in its relationship with the wider world.

Since the late 1980s social care policy for people with disabilities has centred on integration and normalisation. Sometimes this has been pursued without proper thought: for some integration has meant isolation — people with disabilities living in a property in a geographical community that has not accepted them or where their disabilities are such that they are confined to their homes seeing no one but paid carers for long stretches of time. Camphill community life can offer so much more than this. The flow of people, especially young people, through Camphill for one or three years makes for a refreshing group of workers who bring energy, commitment and, often, a new culture. This makes for a rich background against which to learn and develop. Fraser (in Baron and Haldane, 1992: 34) talks of Camphill creating 'ecocultural niches' or econiches — collective action to accommodate persons with special needs, originally in families and then consciously cultivated within Camphill. Attention is paid to individuals' abilities and all are found work. Those with an aptitude for household tasks are given such work but in another house, not their own, so that it becomes *real* work. Abilities are harnessed for the benefits of the whole community. But Camphill life is not for everyone, and one useful step that communities can take is to be clear about whom it does not suit. Camphill's identity as providing care for people for whom they hold and demonstrate positive regard is a real strength, and making clear its approach and where communities can and cannot help is part of that strength.

Holding on to the best of what Camphill provides while assuring others that its boundaries are appropriately permeable is not an easy task, but is one that needs to be successfully tackled. Openness and willingness to share are principles that Camphill communities use very effectively in their internal work, and this has been seen in examples such as Camphill residents attending local churches, open days etc. In Scotland the BA in Social Pedagogy recruits students from other services enabling sharing across organisational boundaries. Camphill communities need now to build on and develop their external relationships to ensure that openness further characterises their outward-facing work, especially with local and central government.

A further issue in relation to Camphill communities is that of introspection. Reflection and analysis are everyday occurrences and are part of the Camphill way. However, it is not difficult to see how communities could become exclusive and introspective and steps need to be taken to avoid this very real danger. In the same way that isolation for people with disabilities within geographical communities is undesirable, so would existence within an enclosed system be, however benign or therapeutic the system. Camphill people need to guard against this by taking their place in the wider world, carrying ideas both ways across the boundaries. It may not mean having televisions in every house, but it might mean finding other explicit ways of helping community members keep up to date with current affairs.

The Camphill Movement has demonstrated its ability to adapt and grow with external developments. There are communities that have responded to the needs of different groups of people from those that König thought of. Newer services have been built around people suffering from mental illness and substance misuse and for older people. These are excellent examples of a flexible, organic and adaptive organisational response to an emerging need, and follows Camphill's oft-repeated mission of 'serving the Image of Man where it is most threatened.' Scanning the horizons of social care for new opportunities is an important role for Camphill and ensuring this happens. We return to the importance of this in the Conclusion.

In the UK there is growing interest in social pedagogy whose main tenets are closely allied to the way in which Camphill works. These are often described as elements of the diamond model (Thempra, 2009). The diamond represents the diamond that is believed to be inside all of us. The model incorporates well-being and happiness, (pedagogic) relationship, empowerment, positive experiences and holistic learning into a rights-based approach. Central to social pedagogy is a part professional, part personal relationship that supports social skills and the ability to build strong, positive, trusting and authentic relationships with others. Social pedagogy calls on research, theories and concepts from philosophy, sociology, psychology and education. Petrie et al. (2006: 22) suggest that social pedagogues:

- Focus on the whole person and support for her/his development
- See her/himself as a person in relationship (to service users)
- Inhabit the same life-space as service users
- Reflect on their practice and apply theory and self-knowledge to demands with which they are confronted
- See associative life as a resource
- Fully understand and build on service users' rights
- Emphasise teamwork, valuing contributions from others (professionals, family, community etc.)
- Place relationship centrally and recognise the importance of listening

Much of the UK development in social pedagogy has been concerned with children — particularly, though not solely, in early years and residential care. While this is to be welcomed, social pedagogy has much to offer people across the whole of their life course, which fits very well with Camphill's mission. This is another opportunity on which Camphill could usefully capitalise by stating more explicitly how much of the social pedagogical approach is built into the Camphill way, and engaging with national debates on how social pedagogy could be used more widely.

Commissioning and policy systems

The development of and increase in regulation and inspection of social services over the last decade have impacted on Camphill communities as much as they have on other social care enterprises. Accompanying these shifts has been the proliferation of private provision in all aspects of group social care. The result has been an increasingly competitive field, often likened to a market place, in which Camphill communities have needed to find not only their place, but also a way of organising themselves so that they are able to compete and present their unique selling points to potential purchasers of services. Baldly put, this may be about 'survival of the fittest' (Baron & Haldane, 1992), where only organisations that explicitly address the needs of service users will survive, as competition forces out those who are not able to adapt to changing requirements. With the advent of self-directed support systems in the UK, purchasers will, from now on, include service users, or their carers, in addition to placing local authorities.

These drivers have become the imperatives which have both encouraged and supported Camphill communities to stay alive to the need for change and to respond positively to it. In 1991 Baron and Haldane wrote that:

> Those within the movement often experience the increasing definition of standards and the extension of

both central and local government regulations to all
aspects of the communities' lives as inimical to their
work, as restrictive and disabling … However, where in
the past Camphill communities often defensively turned
inwards, they are now increasingly actively engaging
with the issues, persons or organisations experienced as
challenging and confrontational.
(Baron & Haldane, 1991: 77)

Today there is little evidence of this defensiveness. While it is
crucial that Camphill communities are clear about their purpose,
the way in which they carry out their work and about what it
is that differentiates them from other social care organisations,
this is now generally done in a positive and open way. One of
Camphill's important strengths is that it works through the
relationships built with service users through learning, living
and growing together. In Camphill communities mutuality and
reciprocity are emphasised and service users are perceived as
giving as well as receiving. There is still little understanding of
these principles in the wider field of social care.

Significantly, there are many influential people in regulating and
commissioning bodies who do not understand how Camphill
works and who perceive it through lenses shaped by the more
bureaucratic and hierarchical styles of social care that influence so
much of current public sector provision, even in the voluntary sector.

A crucial factor here is that the blame for any misunderstandings
or gaps in understandings cannot be laid at the door of
commissioners or regulatory bodies. It must be up to Camphill
communities to lay out their stall in such a way that their approach
to their work is clear. Equally, the supporting or underpinning
philosophy needs to be spelled out. These need to be articulated
in a way that explains not only *what* Camphill does but *why*
it does what it does in this way. Paramount here is that these
expositions need to be made in a way that can be understood by
professionals in the field and increasingly by parents, carers and
potential service users themselves, as we move towards a position
where placements may be chosen by those more closely involved
than the system has permitted in the past.

In most social care environments, over the last decade, there has been growing interest in quality management. Many organisations have used service standards as a way into this arena, and while this is a reasonable place to start, it must be remembered that service standards are minimum standards, not necessarily goals to be striven for. Some Camphill communities have signed up with the Ways to Quality approach to quality management and service development. The process explores the formation, governance and sustainable development of working groups (Wege Zur Qualitaet, 2009). This framework is seen as having the capacity to take on board the fundamental principles behind the Camphill approach, and to acknowledge the very particular way in which communities work. Its implementation has been relatively slow to take off as the capacity to undertake Ways to Quality audits and support subsequent development work has been gradually built up and disseminated. Again, the merits of the Ways to Quality approach are not immediately obvious to those not involved: Camphill communities could usefully capitalise on the use of such a thorough and far-reaching approach to quality management and development in their relationships with commissioners of services.

Conclusions

This chapter has focused on the 'negatives' which Baron and Haldane posited in 1991 and has suggested that the Camphill communities have changed beyond recognition in terms of their separatism and provision of training. These arguments do not need summarising here. The increased permeability of the boundaries of Camphill poses challenges to the communities in striking the balance between the need to maintain the cohesion and identity of the anthroposophical project and the need, from within that project as well as from external demands, to engage more fully with external agencies, individuals and communities. In managing this tension we suggest that attention be given to two features of Camphill which are strategically important.

Yet to be undertaken in our view, is addressing issues of

community power and authority in a more comprehensive and transparent manner. A stark, but helpful, way of posing this comes from the work of Manuela Costa of the Camphill School Aberdeen where she explores the gap between 'myth' and 'reality' in the communities (2008: 56). She produces the binary chart which is illustrated in the following table.

Aspiration	Reality
Love-based	Law-based
Compassionate	Punitive
Forgiving	Vengeful
Forward-looking	Retrospective
Extrospective	Introspective
Democratic	Hierarchical
Participative	Authoritarian
Exoteric	Esoteric
Intuitive	Calculated
Conciliatory	Uncompromising
Pragmatic	Idealistic
Inclusive	Exclusive
Attitudinally open	Attitudinally closed
Psychologically open	Psychologically closed
Challenging	Complacent
Creative	Uncreative

While the focus of this work is largely historical, and the polar oppositions should not be read as a choice between two lists, Costa's work points to the incomplete transition of the communities from the charismatic authority of König and Weihs to more routinised forms of power and authority consonant with the more open and dialogic communities which have emerged since Baron and Haldane wrote in 1991.

We finish where we started with the oft-repeated mission statement of 'serving the Image of Man where it is most threatened.' In the Aberdeenshire Manse in 1940, with the technology and systems of the Holocaust already developed on German people with learning difficulty, the threat was understood in a particular way. Camphill has since addressed new threats in an ad hoc manner but, seventy years on, we suggest that a systematic consideration of the major contemporary threats would be productive both for community renewal and the wider social good.

References

Abberley, P. (1987) 'The concept of oppression and the development of a social model of disability', *Disability, Handicap and Society*, 2(1): 5-19.

Abrams, L. (1998) *The Orphan Country: Children of Scotland's broken homes from 1845 to the present day.* Edinburgh: John Donald.

Adams, S. (2005) Interview by author. Camphill Special School, Beaver Run, Pennsylvania, 4 May.

Aims and Purposes of the Catholic Worker Movement. (1940) *The Catholic Worker*, February.

Alma, G. (2005) Interview by author. Camphill Special School, Beaver Run, Pennsylvania, 2 May.

Anderson, P. (2006) *The Lord of the Ring: A journey in search of Count Zinzendorf.* Eastbourne: Kingsway Communications.

Anonymous. (2002) Interview by author. Camphill Village Minnesota, Sauk Centre, Minnesota, June 29.

Bach, M. & Rioux, M. (1996) 'Social well-being: A framework for quality of life research' In R. Renwick, I. Brown, & M. Nagler, (eds.) *Quality of Life in Health Promotion and Rehabilitation.* Thousand Oaks: Sage. (pp. 63-74)

Bang, J. (2010) *A Portrait of Camphill: From founding seed to worldwide movement.* Edinburgh: Floris Books.

Baron, S. & Haldane, D. (1991) 'Approaching Camphill: From the boundary', *British Journal of Special Education,* 18(2): 75-78.

— (1992) *Community, Normality and Difference.* Aberdeen: Aberdeen University Press.

Barton, M. (ed.) (2008) *Spiritual Ecology.* Forest Row: Rudolf Steiner Press.

Bateson, P. (1993) 'Address at the official opening of Watch Oak Farm', *Camphill Correspondence,* (September/October), 18-20.

Baum, J. (2004) 'The youth group in Vienna', In F. Bock

(ed.) *The Builders of Camphill: Lives and destinies of the founders.* Edinburgh: Floris Books. (pp. 10–38)

Baum, N. (ed.) (2009) *Come to Your Senses. Third International Come To Your Senses Conference: 'Creating Supportive Environments to Nurture Sensory Capital Within'.* Proceedings. Toronto: MukiBaum Treatment Services.

Bausman, S. (2002) Interview by author. Camphill Village, Copake, New York, 9 August.

Beck, U. (1992) *Risk Society: Towards a new modernity.* London: Sage.

Beecher, J. (1986) *Charles Fourier: The visionary and his world.* Berkeley: University of California Press.

Bendle, M. (2002) 'The crisis of "identity" in high modernity', *British Journal of Sociology,* 53(1): 1–18.

Bengtsson, E., Chamberlain, C., Crimmens, D. & Stanley, J. (2008) *Introducing Social Pedagogy into Residential Childcare in England: An evaluation of a project commissioned by the Social Education Trust.* London: NCB/NCERCC.

Bickham, W. (2000) Interview by author. Viva House Catholic Worker, Baltimore, Maryland, 25 May.

Biestek, F. (1961) *The Casework Relationship.* London: Unwin University Books.

Bigby, C. (2003) *Ageing with a Lifelong Disability: A guide to practice, programme and policy issues for human service professionals.* London: Jessica Kingsley Publishers.

Blatt, B. & Kaplan, F. (1966) *Christmas in Purgatory: A photographic essay on mental retardation.* Boston: Allyn & Bacon, Inc.

Bock, F. (ed.) (2004) *The Builders of Camphill: Lives and destinies of the founders.* Edinburgh: Floris Books.

Boddy, J. & Statham, J. (2009) *European Perspectives on Social Work: Models of education and professional roles: A Briefing Paper.* Thomas Coram Research Unit, Institute of Education, University of London.

Bowles, M. (1989) 'Myth, meaning and work organisation', *Organisation Studies,* 10(3): 405–421.

Boyce, E. M. (1996) 'Organisational story and storytelling: a critical review', *Journal of Organisational Change Management,* 9(5): 5–26.

Brandenburg, H. (2005) 'Of biomass and biogas', *Camphill Correspondence* (July/August), 5-6.

Brennan-Krohn, Z. (2009) *In the Nearness of our Striving: Camphill communities re-imagining disability and society.* Unpublished dissertation: Department of History, Brown University.

Brett, L. (2002) Interview by author. Lukas Community, Temple, New Hampshire, 7 January.

Briggs, L. & B. (2000) Interview by author. Camphill Village Minnesota, Sauk Centre, Minnesota, 30 July.

Brinkheim, B. & Kennedy, D. (eds.) (1998) *Directory of Ecovillages in Europe.* Steyerberg: Global Ecovillage Network (GEN)

Brown, I. & Brown, R. (2003) *Quality of Life and Disability: An approach for community practitioners.* London: Jessica Kingsley.

Brown, I., Brown, R., Baum, N., Isaacs, B., Myerscough, T., Neikrug, S., Roth, D., Shearer, J. & Wang, M. (2006) *Family Quality of Life Survey: Main caregivers of people with intellectual or developmental disabilities.* Toronto: Surrey Place Centre.

Brown, I. & Brown R. (2009) 'Choice as an aspect of quality of life for people with intellectual disabilities', *Journal of Policy and Practice in Intellectual Disabilities,* 6(1): 11-18.

Brown, I. & Percy, M. (2007) *A Comprehensive Guide to Intellectual and Developmental Disabilities.* Baltimore: Paul Brookes.

Brown, R. (Updated 2006) *Examination of the Effects of the Proposed Aberdeen Western Peripheral Route on the Camphill Rudolf Steiner Schools: Quality of life: Children and families.* Consultant's Report on behalf of the Camphill communities.

Brown, R., Bayer, M. & Brown, P. (1992*) Empowerment and Developmental Handicaps: Choices and quality of life.* Toronto: Captus.

Brown, R., Bayer, M. & MacFarlane, C. (1989) *Rehabilitation Programmes: Performance and quality of life of adults with developmental handicaps.* Toronto: Lugus Productions Ltd.

Brown, R., Hong, K., Shearer, J., Wang, M. & Wang, S. (In press) 'Family Quality of Life in Several Countries: Results and discussion of satisfaction in families where there is a child with a disability.' In R. Kober (ed.) *Enhancing the Quality of Life of People with Intellectual Disability: From theory to practice.* Dordrecht: Springer Science+Business Media.

Brown, R., Macadam Crisp, J., Wang, M. & Iarocci, G. (2006) 'Family quality of life where there is a child with a developmental disability', *Journal of Policy and Practice in Intellectual Disabilities,* 3(4), 238-245.

Brown, S., Denning, S., Groh, K. & Prusak, L. (2005) *Storytelling in Organisations: Why storytelling is transforming 21st century organisations and management.* Oxford: Elsevier Butterworth-Heinemann.

Browne, W. (1995) 'From waste to wealth', *Camphill Correspondence* (January/February), 13-15.

— (1998) 'The new care and therapy house at Vidaråsen in Norway', *Camphill Correspondence* (July/August), 13-14.

Bruder, N. (2004) 'Are Camphill communities sustainable communities?', *Camphill Correspondence* (September/October), 1-3.

Brüll, A. (2008) Personal interview. 30 June.

Bucknall, M. (1968) Editorial. *The Cresset* (Easter): 4.

Burman, E. (2008) *Deconstructing Developmental Psychology.* (Second edition) London: Routledge.

Butler, I & Drakeford, M. (eds.) (2005) *Scandal, Social Policy and Social Welfare.* Bristol: BASW/The Policy Press.

Calder, P. (2006) Personal communication.

Cameron, C. (2003) 'An historical perspective on changing childcare policy', In J. Brannan & P. Moss (eds.) *Rethinking Children's Care.* Buckingham: Open University Press.

— (2006) *New Ways of Educating: Pedagogy and children's services.* Thomas Coram Research Unit, Institute of Education, University of London.

Cameron, C. & Petrie, P. (2007) *Implementing the Social Pedagogic Approach for Workforce Training and Education in England.* Unpublished report to DCSF.

Cameron, C., Kleipoedszus, S., Wigfall, V., Petrie, P. & Jasper, A. (2010) *Implementing the DCSF Pilot Programme: The work of the first year.* Thomas Coram Research Unit, Institute of Education, University of London. Unpublished report.

Campling, P. (2001) 'Therapeutic communities', *Advances in Advances in Psychiatric Treatment* 7, 365–372.

Carson, R. (1962) *The Silent Spring*. New York: Houghton Mifflin.

Cash, M. (1997) 'Stories within a story: parables from "The New Zealand Experiment"', *The Learning Organisation*, 4(4): 159-167.

Chase, W. (1857) *The Life-Line of the Lone One; or, Autobiography of the World's Child*. Boston: Bela Marsh.

Checkland, O. (1980) *Philanthropy in Victorian Scotland: Social welfare and the voluntary principle*. Edinburgh: John Donald.

Children's Workforce Development Council. (2009) *Social Pedagogy and its Implications for the Youth Workforce*.

Christensen, K. & Levinson, D. (eds.) (2003) *Encyclopaedia of Community: From the village to the virtual world*. London: Sage Publications.

Clyde, Lord. (1946) *Report of the Committee on Homeless Children*. Edinburgh: HMSO.

Communes Network. (1991) *Diggers and Dreamers 1990 – 1991*. London: Care of Edge of Time.

— (1995) *Diggers and Dreamers 1994 – 1995*

— (1997) *Diggers and Dreamers 1996 – 1997*

Costa, M. (2008) *Camphill: An Island of Promise — Myth or Reality*. Unpublished MSc dissertation: University of Strathclyde.

Costa, M. & Walter, C. (2006) 'Care: the art of living', In R. Jackson (ed.) *Holistic Special Education: Camphill principles and practice*. Edinburgh: Floris Books. (pp. 37-49)

Courtenay, K., Jokinen, N. & Strydom, A. (2010) 'Caregiving and adults with intellectual disabilities affected by dementia', *Journal of Policy and Practice in Intellectual Disabilities*, 7(1): 26-33.

Cownap, B. (2005) Interview by author. Camphill Village Kimberton Hills, Pennsylvania, 6 May.

Coy, P. (ed.) (1988) *A Revolution of the Heart: Essays on the Catholic Worker*. Philadelphia: Temple University Press.

Cresset. (1961) 'Camphill's first twenty-one years'. (Summer 1961).

Cummins, R. (1997) 'Assessing quality of life', In R. Brown, (ed.) *Quality of Life for People with Disabilities: Models, research and practice*. Cheltenham, UK: Stanley Thornes. (pp. 116-150)

— (2002) 'Proxy responding for subjective well-being: A review', *International Review of Research in Mental Retardation*, 25: 183-207.

Curtis, M. (1946) *Report of the Care of Children Committee*. London: HMSO.

Dahlberg, G. & Moss, P. (2005) *Ethics and Politics in Early Childhood Education*. London: RoutledgeFalmer.

Davie, G. (1991) *The Scottish Enlightenment and Other Essays*. Edinburgh: Polygon.

Davis, M. (2002) Interview by author. Camphill Village Minnesota, Sauk Centre, Minnesota, 29 June.

Day, D. (1963) *Loaves and Fishes*. New York: Orbis.

— (1997) *The Long Loneliness*. San Francisco: Harper.

de Saint-Exupéry, A. (1943) *The Little Prince*. Paris: Gallimard.

Dean, J. (2002) Interview by author. Lukas Community, Temple, New Hampshire, 7 January.

Delano, S. (2004) *Brook Farm: The Dark Side of Utopia*. Cambridge, Mass.: Belknap Press of Harvard University Press.

Department for Children, Schools and Families. (2007) *Sure Start Children's Centres: Phase 3 Planning and Delivery*. (Accessed 28 March 2010) http://publications.everychildmatters.gov.uk/eOrderingDownload/DCSF-00665-2007.pdf

— (2008) 2020 Children and Young People's Workforce Strategy   http://publications.everychildmatters.gov.uk/eOrderingDownload/CYP_Workforce-Strategy.pdf

Department for Education and Skills. (2003) *Every Child Matters*. London: HMSO.

—(2005) *Children's Workforce Strategy: Building a world-class workforce for children, young people and families*. London: DfES.

— (2006) *Children's Workforce Strategy: Building a world-class workforce for children, young people and families: The Government's response to the consultation*. London: DfES.

— (2007) *Care Matters: Time for Change*. Cmnd 7137.

Department of Health and Social Security. (1971) *Better Services for the Mentally Handicapped*. Cmnd. 4683. HMSO: London.

Diamond, J. (2009) *Meeting Children's Needs through Appropriate Placement: An exploration of the relationship between social pedagogy and therapeutic childcare*. Unpublished paper.

Douglas, R. & Payne, C. (1981) 'Alarm bells for the clock-on philosophy', *Social Work Today*, 12(23): 110-11.

Eichsteller, G. (2006) *Treasure Hunt: Searching for Pedagogic Ideas within Youth Work in Portsmouth*. Unpublished BA dissertation, University of Portsmouth.

Eliot, G. (1985) *The Mill on the Floss*. Oxford: Oxford University Press.

Elmquist, C. (2002) Interview by author. Community Homestead, Osceola, Wisconsin, 17 March.

Elmquist, R. (2002) Interview by author. Community Homestead, Osceola, Wisconsin, 16 March.

Engel, M. (1994) 'A Camphill Village in Russia?, '*Camphill Correspondence* (September/October), 10.

Eno, S. & Treanor, D. (1982) *The Collective Housing Handbook*. Dumfries: Laurieston Hall Publications.

Evans, W. (1982) *The Philosophical Analysis of the Contributions of Karl König to the Education of the Exceptional Child*. Doctoral dissertation, University of Southern California.

Farr, T. (2000) Interview by author. Camphill Village Minnesota, Sauk Centre, Minnesota, 22 July.

Farrants, W. (ed.) (1988) *Camphill Villages*. (Second edition) Botton: Camphill Press.

Ferguson, R. (2001) *George MacLeod: Founder of the Iona Community*. Glasgow: Wild Goose Publications.

Fewster, G. (1990) *Being in Childcare: A journey into self.* New York: Haworth Press.

Foucault, M. (1991) *Discipline and Punish: The birth of the prison*. London: Penguin Books.

— (2003) *Birth of the Clinic*. London: Routledge.

Frankl, V. (1969) *The Will to Meaning: Foundations and applications of logotherapy*. New York: New America Library.

Furnival, J., McQuarrie, A. & Smith, M. (2001) *A Review of Residential Childcare in Scotland*. University of Strathclyde.

Gabriel, Y. (2000) *Storytelling in Organisations: Facts, fictions, and fantasies*. Oxford: Oxford University Press.

Gardner, R. (1997) *Changing an organisational culture.* (Accessed 24 March 2006) www.cognitivebehavior.com/management/concepts/changing_org_culture.html

Garfat, T. (1998) 'The effective child and youth care intervention: A phenomenological inquiry', *Journal of Child and Youth Care,* 12(1-2): 1-178.

Garrett, P. (2008) 'Social work practices: silences and elisions in the plan to 'transform' the lives of children 'looked after' in England', *Child & Family Social Work,* 13(3): 311-18.

Geider, S. (2008) Personal interview. 13 June.

Gilman, R. & D. (1991) *Eco-villages and Sustainable Communities.* Bainbridge Island, USA: Context Institute.

Goeschel, J. (2005) Interview by author. Camphill Special School, Beaver Run, Pennsylvania, 4 May.

Goffman, E. (1961) *Asylums: Essays on the social situation of mental patients and of other inmates.* New York: Doubleday

—— (1963) *Stigma: Notes on the management of spoiled identity.* Englewood Cliffs, N.J: Prentice Hall Inc.

Goode, D. (1994) (ed.) *Quality of Life for Persons with Disabilities: International perspectives and issues.* Cambridge, MA: Brookline.

Goodman, P. & P. (1947) *Communitas: Means of livelihood and ways of life.* Chicago: University of Chicago Press.

Gorman, C. (1975) *People Together: a guide to communal living.* St Albans: Paladin.

Griffiths, V. (2000) 'The land question', *Camphill Correspondence* (July/August), 10.

Guarneri, C. (1991) *The Utopian Alternative: Fourierism in nineteenth-century America.* Ithaca, N.Y.: Cornell University Press.

Gustavsson, A., Hermansson, H. & Hämäläinen, J. (eds.) *Perspectives and Theory in Social Pedagogy.* Gothenburg: Daidalos.

Hansmann, H. (1992) *Education for Special Needs: Principles and practice in the Camphill Schools.* Edinburgh: Floris Books.

Harris, E. (2009) Kibble: Living Legacy series. (Accessed 26 June 2010) www.kibble.org

Hart, N. & Monteux, A. (2004) 'An introduction to Camphill communities and the BA in Curative Education', *Scottish Journal of Residential Childcare,* 3: 67-74.

Harvey, D. (2005) *A Brief History of Neoliberalism*. Oxford: Oxford University Press.

Heitzman, D. (2005) Interview by author. Camphill Village Kimberton Hills, Pennsylvania, 6 May.

Heller, S. (2006) *The Absence of Myth*. Albany: State University of New York Press.

Hems, K. (1995) 'Saving the seed', *Camphill Correspondence* (January/February).

Hendricks, C. (2002) 'Building 'villages of the Lord': the birth and development of the Moravian Congregation town', Paper presented to the Symposium *German Moravians in the Atlantic World*, Wake Forest University, Winston-Salem, North Carolina. 5 April 2002.

Heywood, J. (1959) *Children in Care*. London: Routledge and Kegan Paul.

Higham, P. (2001) 'Changing practice and an emerging social pedagogue paradigm in England: the role of the personal adviser', *Social Work in Europe* 8(1): 21–28.

— (2006) *Social Work: Introducing professional practice*. London: Sage.

HM Treasury and DfES. (2005) Support for parents: the best start for children. (Accessed 28 March 2010) http://publications.everychildmatters.gov.uk/eOrderingDownload/HMT-Support-parents.pdf

Hobson, M. (2002) Interview by author. Lukas Community, Temple, New Hampshire, 7 January.

Hobson, N. (2002) Interview by author. Lukas Community, Temple, New Hampshire, 7 January.

Hockey, J. & James, A. (2003) *Social Identities across the Life Course*. London: Palgrave.

Holtoff, S. & Eichsteller, G. (2009) *The Implementation of Social Pedagogy from the Perspectives of Practitioners*. (Accessed 28 March 2010) http://www.socialpedagogy.co.uk/downloads/Social%20Pedagogy%20from%20the%20Perspectives%20of%20Practitioners.pdf

How, C. (2002) 'New Year's Forum for the Scottish, English, Welsh and Irish Regions', *Camphill Correspondence* (May/June), 7–8.

— (2004) 'Barbara Lipsker' In F. Bock (ed.) *The Builders of Camphill: Lives and destinies of the founders.* Edinburgh: Floris Books. (pp. 63-84)

Hoyland, E. (1996) 'Tiphereth — diversifying to survive', *Camphill Correspondence* (July/August), 10-11.

Hubbard, R. (2006) 'Abortion and disability', In L. Davis (ed.) *The Disability Studies Reader.* London: RoutledgeFalmer. (pp. 93-104)

Hudson, D. (1992) 'The Botanic Centre Middlesbrough', *Camphill Correspondence* (July/August).

Hughes, B. (1995) 'Why do managers need myths?', *Executive Development,* 8(7): 8-10.

Hughes, B. & Paterson, K. (1997) 'The social model of disability and the disappearing body: Towards a sociology of impairment', *Disability and Society,* 12(3): 325-340.

Hughson, A. & Uditsky, B. (2007) *Inclusive post-secondary (tertiary) education for adults with Down's syndrome and other developmental disabilities: A promising path to an inclusive life.* Southsea: The Down Syndrome Educational Trust.

Humphrey, J. (2003) 'New Labour and the regulatory reform of social care', *Critical Social Policy,* 23(1): 5-24.

Hunt, M. (ed.) (2001) *Shining Lights: Celebrating forty years of community in Camphill Village.* Copake, N.Y.: Camphill Village USA.

IARD. (2001) *Study on the State of Young People and Youth Policy in Europe: Final Report* http://ec.europa.eu/youth/archive/doc/studies/iard/summaries_en.pdf

Imegwu, R. (2002) Interview by author. Camphill Village, Copake, New York, 8 August.

Jackson, H. & Svensson, K. (eds.) (2002) *Ecovillage Living: Restoring the earth and her people.* Totnes, Devon: Gaia Trust & Green Books.

Jackson, N. & Carter, P. (1984) 'The attenuating function of myth in human understanding', *Human Relations,* 37(7): 515-533.

Jackson, R. (ed.) (2006) *Holistic Special Education: Camphill principles and practice.* Edinburgh: Floris Books.

— (2008) 'The Camphill Movement: The Moravian Dimension', *Journal of Moravian History,* 5: 89-100.

— (2011) 'The origin of Camphill and the social pedagogic impulse', *Educational Review,* 63 (1): 95-104.

Jackson, R. & Monteux, A. (2003) 'Promoting the spiritual well-being of children and young people', *Scottish Journal of Residential Childcare,* 2(1): 52-54.

James, A. & James, A. (2001) 'Tightening the net: children, community and control', *British Journal of Sociology,* 52(2): 211-228.

Janicki, M. & Ansello, E. (eds.) (2000) *Community Support for Ageing Adults with Lifelong Disabilities.* Baltimore: Brookes.

Jenkins, R. (2004) *Social Identity.* London: Routledge.

Jenks, C. (2005) *Childhood.* (Second Edition) London: Routledge.

Jokinen, N. & Brown, R. (2005) 'Family quality of life from the perspective of older parents', *Journal of Intellectual Disability Research,* 49(10): 789-793.

Journal of Policy and Practice in Intellectual Disabilities. (2006) *Special Issue on Family Quality of Life Research.* 3(40): 209-270.

Julius, F. (1949) Newssheet of the Anthroposophical Society in Holland. (March)

Karl König Archive. Minutes of School Community Meeting, 15 February 1952. Karl König Archive, Aberdeen

Kavanagh, B. (2005) Letter to author, 7 February.

Kehily, M. (ed.) (2004) *An Introduction to Childhood Studies.* London: Oxford University Press.

Kelly, G. (1998) 'The influence of research on childcare policy and practice: the case of 'children who wait' and the development of the permanence movement in the United Kingdom', In D. Iwaniec & J. Pinkerton, (eds.) *Making Research Work: Promoting childcare policy and practice.* Chichester: Wiley.

Kilbrandon, C J D Shaw, Lord, 1964, *Report of the Committee on Children and Young Persons, Scotland.* Edinburgh: HMSO.

König, K. (1942) 'Integration in medicine', *The Coracle* (Iona Community). January. (pp. 19-31)

— (1952) 'Study-Week on Curative Education', Camphill-Rudolf Steiner Schools, 10-17 August 1952. Aberdeen: Karl König Archive.

— (1954) *The Handicapped Child: Letters to parents.* London: New Knowledge Press.

— (1954) *First Memorandum to the Camphill community.* Quoted by R. Poole in 'Agricultural impulse or Corpus Christi?' *Camphill Correspondence* (May/June 2004), 1.

— (1956) Address entitled 'The Three Great Errors' given on the 27 May 1956 and quoted in H. Müller-Wiedemann (1996) *Karl König: a Central-European Biography of the Twentieth Century.* Botton: Camphill Books.

—. (1960) *The Camphill Movement.* Botton: Camphill Books.

— (1964) Address to the Lake Constance Group of farmers and gardeners given at Brachenreuthe on the 4 September 1964 and quoted in H. Müller-Wiedemann (1996) *Karl König: a Central-European Biography of the Twentieth Century.* Botton: Camphill Books.

— (1989) *Being Human: Diagnosis in curative education.* (C. Creeger trans.) Herndon VA: Anthroposophic Press/Camphill Press.

— (1990) *Man as a Social Being.* Botton: Camphill Press.

— (1993) *The Camphill Movement.* (Second edition) Botton: Camphill Books.

— (2009) *The Child with Special Needs – Letters and Essays on Curative Education.* Edinburgh: Floris Books.

Kornbeck, J. (2002) 'Reflections on the exportability of social pedagogy and its possible limits', *Social Work in Europe*, 9(2): 37–49.

Kosek, J. (2009) *Acts of Conscience: Christian nonviolence and modern American democracy.* New York: Columbia University Press.

Lakin, C. (2001) 'Challenge to Camphill from the perspective of a public policy advocate', Paper given at the Camphill Association of North America Symposium, Triform Camphill community, 3-4 April 2001.

LeBar, F. (2002) Interview by author. Camphill Village, Copake, New York, 7 August.

Lorenz, W. (1994) *Social Work in a Changing Europe.* London: Routledge.

— (2008) 'Paradigms and politics: Understanding methods paradigms in an historical context: The case of social pedagogy', *British Journal of Social Work*, 38(4): 625-644.

Luxford, M. (1994) *Children with Special Needs.* Edinburgh: Floris Books.

Luxford, M. & Luxford, J. (2003) *A Sense for Community: A five steps research paper.* Whitby: Camphill Books.

Lydon, P. (1999) 'Working in Partnership', *Camphill Correspondence* (November/December), 2-5.

— (2005) 'Renewable energy conference in Clanabogan', *Camphill Correspondence* (July/August), 6.

Madsen, P. (2002) Interview by author. Camphill Village, Copake, New York, 6 August.

Martin, F. & Murray, K. (eds.) (1976) *Children's Hearings.* Edinburgh: Scottish Academic Press.

— (eds.) (1982) *The Scottish Juvenile Justice System,* Edinburgh: Scottish Academic Press.

MacCulloch, D. (2009) *A History of Christianity.* London: Allen Lane.

Mason, J. (2002) *Researching your own Practice: The discipline of noticing.* London: RoutledgeFalmer.

McAdams, P. D. (1993) *The Stories we live by: Personal myths and the making of the self.* London: Guilford Press.

McKanan, D. (2007) *Touching the World: Christian communities transforming society.* Collegeville, Minnesota: Liturgical Press.

— (2008) *The Catholic Worker after Dorothy: Practicing the works of mercy in a new generation.* Collegeville, Minnesota: Liturgical Press.

McKenna, K. (1988) Interview with Rosalie Troester.

McWhinney, W. & Battista, J. (1988) 'How remythologising can revitalise organisations', *Organisational Dynamics,* (August), 46-58.

Meagher, G. & Parton N. (2004) 'Modernising social work and the ethics of care', *Social Work and Society,* 2(1): 10-27.

Messenger, S. (undated) *Lucifer and Ahriman under the bed.* (Accessed January 2007) www.isleofavalon.co.uk.GlastonburyArchive/ messenger/sm-lucifer.html

Meyer, A. (2007) 'The moral rhetoric of childhood', *Childhood,* 14(1): 85-104.

Milligan, I. (2009) *Introducing Social Pedagogy into Scottish*

Residential Childcare: An evaluation of the Sycamore Services social pedagogy training programme. Glasgow: Scottish Institute for Residential Childcare.

Milligan, I. & Stevens, I. (2006) 'Balancing rights and risks: the impact of health and safety regulations on the lives of children in residential care', *Journal of Social Work*, 6(3): 239-54.

Molloy, H. & Vasil, L. (2002) 'The social construction of Asperger Syndrome: The pathologising of difference?' *Disability and Society*, 17(6): 659-669.

Monteux, A. (2006) 'History and philosophy', In R. Jackson (ed.) *Holistic Special Education: Camphill principles and practice*. Edinburgh: Floris Books. (pp.17-36)

Morgan, A. (1942) *The Small Community, Foundation of Democratic Life: What It Is and How to Achieve It*. New York: Harper & Brothers.

— (1944) 'Hatching the egg of a good society', *motive* 5: 5-6.

Morgan, G. (2006) *Images of Organisation*. London: Sage Publications Ltd.

Moss, P., Petrie, P. & Poland, G. (1999) *Rethinking School: Some international perspectives*. York: Joseph Rowntree Foundation.

Movva, R. (2004) 'Myths as a vehicle for transforming organisations', *Leadership & Organisational Development Journal*, 25(1): 41-57.

Müller-Wiedemann, H. (1963) 'The training course in South Africa', *The Cresset*, 9 (3). Aberdeen: Camphill Rudolf Steiner Schools.

— (1996) *Karl König: A Central-European Biography of the Twentieth Century*. Botton: Camphill Books.

Murray, H. (1990) *Do Not Neglect Hospitality: The Catholic Worker and the Homeless*. Philadelphia: Temple University Press.

Nauk, E. (ed.) (2009) *We Came...: Biographic Sketches of the Twenty-Five Participants of the First Camphill Seminar in Curative Education: 1949-1951*. Aberdeen: Private Publication.

OECD. (2004) *Country Note: Early Childhood Education and Care Policy in the Federal Republic of Germany*. http://www.oecd.org/dataoecd/42/1/33978768.pdf

Office of the Deputy Prime Minister. (2005) *The Deputy Prime*

Minister's Award for Sustainable Communities 2005. London: ODPM.

Oliver, M. (1990) *The Politics of Disablement.* Basingstoke: Macmillan.

Owen, H. (1987) *Spirit Transformation and Development in Organisations.* Maryland: Abbott Publishing.

Paget, B., Eagle, G. & Citarella, V. (2007) *Social Pedagogy and the Young People's Workforce: A report for the Department for Children, Schools and Families.* http://www.gbyoc.org.uk/docs/social_pedagogy_and_young_people.pdf

Paterson, L. (2000) 'Civil society and democratic renewal', In S. Baron, J. Field & T. Schuller (eds.) *Social Capital: Critical perspectives.* Oxford: Oxford University Press.

Pax, T. (2000) Interview by author. Camphill Village Minnesota, Sauk Centre, Minnesota, 22 July.

Peabody, E. (1841) 'A glimpse of Christ's idea of society', *The Dial*, 2: 499 (October)

Pestalozzi, J. (1894) in L. Holland & F. Turner, (eds.) *How Gertrude teaches her Children.* London: Swan Sonnenschein.

Petrie, P. (2001) 'The potential of pedagogy/education for work in the children's sector in the UK', *Social Work in Europe*, 8(3): 23-26.

Petrie, P., Boddy, J., Cameron, C., Wigfall, V. & Simon, A. (2006) *Working with Children in Care: European Perspectives.*, Buckingham: Open University Press.

Petrie, P. & Cameron, C. (2009) Importing Social Pedagogy? In J. Kornbeck & N. Rosendal Jensen (eds.) *The Diversity of Social Pedagogy in Europe.* Bremen: Europaeischer Hochschulverlag.

Phethean, R. (1998) Reflections on the Easter Symposium 1998. *Camphill Correspondence* (September/October), 4-5.

Piehl, M. (1982) *Breaking Bread: The Catholic Worker and the origin of Catholic radicalism in America.* Philadelphia: Temple University Press.

Pietzner, C. (1986) *Village Life: the Camphill communities.* Boston: Neugebauer Press.

— (ed.) (1990) *Candle on the Hill: Images of Camphill life.* Edinburgh: Floris Books.

Pietzner, U. (2005) Interview by author. Camphill Special School, Beaver Run, Pennsylvania, 3 May.

Pirrie, A. & Head, G. (2007) 'Martians in the playground: researching special educational needs', *Oxford Review of Education*, 33(1): 19-31.

Pitzer, D. (ed.) (1997) *America's Communal Utopias*. Chapel Hill: University of North Carolina Press.

Plant, A. (2009) 'Community development and identity', *Camphill Correspondence* (July/August), 1-3.

Plato (1941) *The Republic,* Oxford: Clarendon.

Potter, N. (2000) Interview by author. Camphill Village Minnesota, Sauk Centre, Minnesota, 27 July.

Poulton, S. (2005) 'Organisational storytelling, ethics and morality: how stories frame limits of behaviour in organisations', *Electronic Journal of Business Ethics & Organisation Studies,* 10(2): 4-9.

Renwick, R., Brown, I. & Nagler, M. (1996) *Quality of Life in Health Promotion and Rehabilitation: Concepts, approaches, issues, and applications.* Thousand Oaks, CA: Sage.

Rigby, A. (1974) *Communes in Britain.* London: Routledge Kegan and Paul.

Robertson, F. (1949) 'A school where love is a cure', *Picture Post* (30 April 1949)

Rowe, J. & Lambert, L. (1973) *Children who wait: a study of children needing substitute families.* London: Association of British Adoption Agencies.

Russell, S. (2002) Interview by author. Community Homestead, Osceola, Wisconsin, 17 March.

Sabra, M. (2005) Interview by author. Camphill Special School, Beaver Run, Pennsylvania, 3 May.

Saunders, N. (1975) *Alternative England and Wales.* Private publication.

Schalock, R., Brown, I., Brown, R., Cummins, R., Felce, D., Matikka, L., et al. (2002) 'Conceptualization, measurement, and application of quality of life for persons with intellectual disabilities: Report of an international panel of experts', *Mental Retardation,* 40(6): 457-470.

Schalock, R. & Felce, D. (2004) Quality of life and subjective well-being: conceptual and measurement issues. In E. Emerson, C. Hatton, T. Thompson, & T. Parmenter (eds.) *International Handbook of Applied Research in Intellectual Disabilities.* London: John Wiley and Sons. (pp. 261-279)

Schippers, A. & van Boheemen, M. (2009) 'Family quality of life empowered by family-oriented support', *Journal of Policy and Practice in Intellectual Disabilities*, 6(1), 19-24.

Scotland, J. (1969) *The History of Scottish Education.* (Volume 2) London: University of London Press.

Scottish Christian Council for Refugees. (1941) 'The Christian refugee in Scotland' (December).

Scottish Government. (2001) *The Same as You: A review of services for people with learning disabilities.* (http://www.scotland.gov.uk/ Resource/Doc/1095/0001661.pdf)

Scourfield, P. (2007) 'Are there reasons to be worried about the 'cartelisation' of residential care?', *Critical Social Policy*, 27(2): 155-81.

Seed, P. (1973) 'Should any child be placed in care? The forgotten great debate, 1841-74', *British Journal of Social Work*, 3(3): 321-30.

Selg, A. (2008a) *Karl König: My task.* Edinburgh: Floris Books.

— (2008b) *Karl König's Path into Anthroposophy: Reflections from his Diaries.* (I. Czech trans) Edinburgh: Floris Books.

— (2008c) *Ita Wegman and Karl König: Letters and Documents.* Edinburgh: Floris Books.

Senge, M. (1990) *The Fifth Discipline: The art and practice of the learning organisation* , London: Random House Business Books.

Sersch, M. (2005) Letter to author, February.

Shakespeare, T. (2006) *Disability Rights and Wrongs.* London: Routledge.

Shilling, C. (1993) *The Body and Social Theory.* London: Sage.

Sievers, B. (1986) 'Beyond the surrogate of motivation', *Organisation Studies*, 7(4): 196-220.

Skinner, A. (1992) *Another Kind of Home: A review of residential childcare.* Edinburgh: HMSO.

Smith, H. & Smith, M. (2008) *The Art of Helping Others: Being around, being there, being wise.* London: Jessica Kingsley Publishers.

Smith, L. (2002) Interview by author. Camphill Village Minnesota, Sauk Centre, Minnesota, 4 June.

— (2005) Letter to author, February.

— (2009) *Rethinking Residential Childcare.* Bristol: Policy Press.

— (2010) 'A brief history of (residential childcare) ethics', *Scottish Journal of Residential Child Care,* 9 (2): 2–10.

Smith, M. (2005) 'Dare to be different', *The International Child and Youth Care Network.* Issue 77, (June). www.cyc-net.org/cyc-online/cycol-0605-smith.html

Smith, M. & Whyte, B. (2008) 'Social education and social pedagogy: reclaiming a Scottish tradition in social work', *European Journal of Social Work,* 11 (1): 15-28.

Sproll, C. (2005) Interview by author. Camphill Special School, Beaver Run, Pennsylvania, 4 May.

Steiner, R. (1998) *Education for Special Needs: The curative education course.* (Third edition) London: Rudolf Steiner Press.

— (2008) *Educating Children Today.* Forest Row: Rudolf Steiner Press.

Steinrueck, M. (2002) Interview by author. Community Homestead, Osceola, Wisconsin, 16 March.

Stolz, R. (2002) Interview by author. Camphill Village, Copake, New York, 7 August.

Struthers, A. (1945) 'Juvenile delinquency in Scotland', *American Sociological Review,* 10 (5): 658-662.

Surkamp, J. (ed.) (2007) *The Lives of Camphill: An anthology of the pioneers.* Edinburgh: Floris Books.

Swinton, J. & Powrie, E. (2004) *Why Are We Here: Understanding the spiritual lives of people with learning disabilities.* London: Mental Health Foundation.

Taylor, B. (1959) 'Making a future for the handicapped: they came to a village', *The Observer* (9 November).

Taylor, S. (1994) 'In support of research on quality of life, but again QOL', In D. Goode (ed.) *Quality of Life for Persons with Disabilities: International perspectives and issues.* Cambridge, MA: Brookline. (pp. 260-265)

The Teachers. (1978) *Directory of Alternative Communities in the British Isles.* Bangor: The Teachers.

— (1983) *Directory of Alternative Communities in the British Isles.* Bangor: The Teachers.

Thempra. (2009) 'The diamond model: social pedagogy theory meets practice'. (Accessed 23 June 2010) http://www.socialpedagogy.co.uk/concepts_diamond.htm

Thomas, G. & Loxley, A. (2007) *Deconstructing Special Education and Constructing Inclusion.* (Second edition) London: Open University Press/McGraw Hill Education.

Thorn, W., Runkel, P. & Mountin, S. (eds.) (2001) *Dorothy Day and the Catholic Worker Movement: Centenary Essays.* Milwaukee: Marquette University Press.

Troester, R. (1993) *Voices from the Catholic Worker.* Philadelphia: Temple University Press.

Turnbull, A., Brown, I. & Turnbull, R. (eds.) (2004) *Families and People with Mental Retardation and Quality of Life: International perspectives.* Washington, DC: American Association on Mental Retardation.

von Jeetze, H. (2002) 'The land and associative community building', *Camphill Correspondence* (November/December), 5-6.

Walker, A. (2008) Personal interview. 13 June.

Walsh, B. (2000) Interview by author. Viva House Catholic Worker, Baltimore, Maryland, 25 May.

Wege Zur Qualitaet, (Accessed 23 June 2010), www.wegezurqualitaet.info

Weihs, A. (1975) *Fragments from the Story of Camphill 1939-1940.* Aberdeen: Internal Camphill Paper.

Weihs, T. (1962) *The Camphill Rudolf Steiner Schools for Children in Need of Special Care.* Report 1955-1962. Camphill Rudolf Steiner School: Internal Publication.

— (1987) *Children in Need of Special Care.* Revised by A. Hailey, M. Hailey & N. Blitz. London: Souvenir Press.

Wessels, F. (1989) 'How can Camphill respond to the needs of our time?', *Camphill Correspondence* (November/December), 4.

Winkler, M. (1988) *Eine Theorie de Sozialpädagogik.* Stuttgart, Klett-Cotta (T. Gabriel trans. 2000).

Wolf, B. (2005) Interview by author. Camphill Special School, Beaver Run, Pennsylvania, 4 May.

Wolfensberger, W. (1972) *The Principle of Normalisation in Human Services.* Ontario: National Institute on Mental Retardation.

Wooldridge, A. (1994) *Measuring the Mind.* Cambridge: Cambridge University Press.

Yelloly, M. (1980) *Social Work Theory and Psychoanalysis*. New York: Van Nostrand Reinhold.

Zipperlen, H. (2005) Interview by author. Camphill Village Kimberton Hills, Pennsylvania, 6 May.

Zipperlen, H. & O'Brien, J. (1993) Cultivating Thinking Hearts: Letters from the lifesharing safeguards project. http://thechp.syr.edu/ThinkHrts.pdf.

Zuna, N., Turnbull, A. & Summers, J. (2009) 'Family quality of life: Moving from measurement to application', *Journal of Policy and Practice in Intellectual Disabilities*, 6(1): 24–31.

Zuzalek, J. (2002) Interview by author. Camphill Village Minnesota, Sauk Centre, Minnesota, 20 May.

Acknowledgments

This book would not have been possible without the enthusiastic response given by all the contributors to the challenge that was presented to them. I hope that they will feel that the end product justifies the time and effort so generously devoted by them to this project. I am particularly grateful to Sally Polson, Chani McBain, Helena Waldron and Christian Maclean of Floris Books for their ongoing encouragement, help and guidance throughout the production process. Finally, I would like to thank all those Camphillers who over the past ten years have so kindly allowed me to share in the unique, innovative and inspirational character of Camphill life and work. To them I shall always be thankful and to them and those in their care, this book is appreciatively dedicated.

Index